SNORKELING GUIDE TO MICHIGAN INLAND LAKES

By Nancy S. Washburne

Nanmar International, Inc.
East Lansing, Michigan

Snorkeling Guide to Michigan Inland Lakes
by Nancy S. Washburne
Published by: Nanmar International, Inc.
320 Whitehills, Drive
East Lansing, MI 48823
Fax: (517) 336-6751

First Edition 1997

- Book layout and text design by Martin Ruiz
- Back cover design by Martin Ruiz
- Back cover picture by Martin Ruiz
- Cover photo: Spawning male pumpkinseed
- Aquatic plant drawings courtesy of Maureen Houghton

Printed in the United States of America

A special request to our readers:

Public access sites may change, as well as road names, landmarks and signs. If you find that such changes have occurred near lakes described in this book, please let the author know, so that corrections can be made in future editions. Other comments and suggestions are also welcome. Address all correspondence to:

Nancy Washburne
Nanmar International, Inc.
320 Whitehills, Dr.
East Lansing, MI 48823

To Martin... My life partner and best friend

TABLE OF CONTENTS

UPPER PENINSULA

SCHOOLCRAFT COUNTY

NORTHERN LOWER PENINSULA

OGEMAW COUNTY... continues

OSCODA COUNTY

OTSEGO COUNTY

CENTRAL LOWER PENINSULA

SOUTHERN LOWER PENINSULA

BRANCH COUNTY

CALHOUN COUNTY

CASS COUNTY

SHIAWASSEE COUNTY

ST. JOSEPH COUNTY

VAN BUREN COUNTY

WASHTENAW COUNTY

SNORKELING GUIDE TO MICHIGAN INLAND LAKES

ACKNOWLEDGMENTS

Although I have worldwide diving experience I was a novice in Michigan's inland lakes, and in this area, I am much indebted to a number of people who advised and encouraged me throughout this project. I owe a debt of gratitude to both Dr. Wally Fusilier and his gracious wife, Bene, who enlightened me on the subject of limnology (the science that deals with the physical, chemical and biological properties and features of fresh waters, especially lakes and ponds), and to the renowned Dr. Clifford Humphrys, a giant in the Michigan lake research field as well as Professor Emeritus of the Fisheries and Wildlife Department of Michigan State University, who lent me his wise counsel, insight and unparalleled knowledge of Michigan's inland lakes.

For help with aquatic vegetation identification as well as moral support, I am grateful to Dr. Bruce Manny of the U. S. Geological Survey in Ann Arbor. The renowned botanist, Dr. Ed Voss, of the Herbarium at the University of Michigan, was invaluable in identifying the vegetation in my underwater videos. Dr. Tom Smith, Chief Naturalist, Huron, Clinton Metropolitan Authority of the DNR, his wife Lynne and his parents Lyle and Vivian Smith were unwavering in their belief in the value of the project. I cannot forget the support and enthusiasm of my family, Tom and Betty Washburne, Jean Hay, and my son, Martin, whose desire to go camping was the impetus for the research.

In a more peripheral but equally important way, I could not have enjoyed the project nearly as much as I did, without the network of the DNR throughout the State and the quality work they do. I cannot say enough for their maintenance of the lake areas, which they were constantly monitoring and keeping clean, as well as the helpful staff who everywhere cheerfully answered my questions, offered me tips and generally speeded me on my way with quality information. I found them to be uniformly a remarkable group of dedicated people who are to be highly commended for their efforts.

Most of all, I owe a huge debt to my husband Martin, who introduced me to the sport of diving. I was not a natural in the water, and the book could never have been written without the incredible patience he showed in those early years when I was a beginner. He instilled in me a love for the underwater world which has given me so many years of pleasure.

He also patiently viewed over 70 hours of my underwater video taken in the last 2 years. He has generously given so many hours of his time formatting the book at the computer and creating the text design. In addition, his moral support was pivotal in keeping my spirits up when the project sometimes seemed overwhelming.

INTRODUCTION

When I embarked on my snorkeling adventure in Michigan's inland lakes in the summer of 1991, I had no idea of the wonders that lay ahead. I thought I was just heading out on my first camping trip with my twelve year old son. He had a sudden urge to buy a tent and try his hand at a camp stove, and since his father was not that eager to mix with the ants or to spend nights in the wilderness, I agreed to accompany him. I had never camped out and wasn't at all sure I was going to like it. I was used to deluxe hotels and gourmet food, and though I had once briefly rafted the Colorado River and had spent some nights in deluxe tents in Mongolia, Afghanistan and East Africa, the tents had been fancy ones for tourists, and someone had always taken care of me. This would be the first time setting out on my own, and I knew my wilderness skills didn't amount to more than the little I had learned in my Girl Scout Days.

As it turned out, I had absolutely nothing to worry about, since the Michigan park system is so organized and easy to use. My only big question was: could we camp by clear lakes so I could use my snorkel and mask and experience even a tiny bit of the thrill I had felt in the Pacific, the Red Sea, Mexico and the Caribbean? I dialed Michigan State University's Fisheries and Wildlife Department looking for answers. I was surprised when the voice that answered said that information was not available---that neither they nor the DNR nor the National Biological Survey nor any of the regional fish biologists knew which lakes were clear and might provide a quality snorkeling experience. Since Michigan is a well-known water wonderland with over 11,000 inland lakes, I found the lack of knowledge amazing, but calls to fish biologists around the State proved that indeed the information was not available. I pondered on how this could be, and I could only conclude that when people thought of snorkeling, they thought only of Florida or the Caribbean. It apparently didn't occur to them that there was anything exciting right out their own back door. Since I had not yet done any investigating, I thought perhaps there really wasn't anything out there worth discovering. Still, I couldn't be sure, so thus the quest began.

The first 8 or 10 lakes were murky and lacking in interest, but then I got on a roll, and the next group amazed me to the point that I felt that there was an incredible treasure beneath the waters of our inland lakes. I immediately started keeping a diary of my findings, and I was struck by how unique each lake was. Each lake that made the list was absolutely different from the others, either in the depth or shape, or vegetation or fish life. Each lake had its own character and was as different from the others as Paris is from Rome. I was struck by the infinite variety that nature provides, as well as the impossibility of ever truly adequately conveying that beauty to anyone. It would be like trying to describe a sunset—you would have to see it and experience it for yourself.

THE BOOK FORMAT

Each time I snorkeled a lake I immediately wrote a diary entry with my strongest impressions of that lake--therefore, you will find the descriptions in a DIARY FORM rather than in a standard literary form with complete sentences. These are basically a series of first impressions, and I felt the recording of these observations would be the most accurate representation of that particular lake. The ACREAGE is also given, because by knowing the size of the lake, you can ascertain in advance the type of experience you are likely to have, i.e. a very small lake is unlikely to sustain heavy boat traffic, whereas a large lake will have all of the commercial aspects which will provide a totally different kind of experience.

The PAGE OF THE DELORME ATLAS is given to save you having to repeatedly thumb through page after page looking for the lake you are seeking. It is tough enough to find them, even when you have the exact page!

Lastly, the LOCATION of the lake is given so that I may save you all the hassle I had to go through to find not only the lakes, but to find the PUBLIC ACCESSES of those lakes. Your frustration level can really rise when you circle and circle, driving up one street and down another in search of that precious entry point. I have given very specific directions to make this process as easy as possible.

CRITERIA

In culling these lakes from the hundreds of Michigan's public access lakes I have based my choices on the following criteria:

VISIBILITY: This is obviously a vital factor, but it is very important not to judge a lake's visibility too quickly. I have snorkeled some lakes that initially seemed dark, only to gradually acclimate myself to the available light and to then find the lake among my most worthwhile experiences. It is very similar to entering a low lit or candle lit restaurant. At first, coming from the bright outdoors, you are straining to see, but as your eyes get used to the light, suddenly you are seeing everything and seeing it very clearly.   Crooked Lake in the Pinckney Recreation Area comes to mind. This lake looks almost black, even forbidding, but after just a minute or two in the water, the dark dramatic landscape suddenly becomes vividly clear, and now I can hardly wait to go back and cover the entire lake. Because you are always snorkeling and not diving, you will be at the surface, and because of that limitation, you will want to stay in the shallower areas to increase your visibility. This is actually a great advantage, because if you go way out in the lake you have a much greater chance of having interference from watercraft, whereas along the shoreline you are much less likely to face that hazard.

FISH VARIETY: And what will you see in these shallow areas? A great variety of fish, such as largemouth bass, the occasional smallmouth, suckers, bowfin, pickerel, pike, muskies, bowfin, shadow bass, rock bass, bullheads, pumpkinseeds, catfish, perch, walleye, bluegills, shad, darters, many varieties of minnows, the occasional salamander, even muskrat, and a wide variety of turtles. I am not going to tell you where to find golf balls or old tennis shoes or tin cans though I recognize that there are a number of people, especially teens, who love to find these objects.   I actually did see quite a number of golf balls, even though there wasn't a golf course or driving range for miles. So it is a mystery as to how these errant balls made their way into the lake! When locals tell me of an underwater object such as the ice shanty in Gun Lake or the airplane in Sunrise Lake, I do mention that, even though you would have to dive to see it.

The shallows offer amazing variety and the warmer termperatures found here attract a great many species. This is also where the spawning takes place in early and late spring, even as late as July when you head north. The spawning is a thrill to see---the underwater landscape suddenly becomes Grand Central Station when the various species engage in their spawning activities, and you can get quite close without disturbing them. It is at this time, and only at this time that you will, for example, see the large breeding male bluegills come in from the deep to prepare the nest for the females to lay their eggs. The females leave immediately after spawning, and it is then the males who stay and guard the eggs until they hatch, all the while fanning their tails over the nest to keep the silt from settling and to aerate the eggs. It's a great sight and very accessible to the snorkeler, since so much of it takes place in shallow water. You can spend hours watching these mating rituals, and they are endlessly fascinating, as the fish fight off the invasions of rivals and engage in some unique behavior.

Don't forget to appreciate the small critters. The minnows, darters, small snails and clams all have their uniqueness that makes them worthy of examination. I remember the first day of an underwater photography course I took in Grand Cayman. We were assigned to photograph only creatures that were 2-3 inches in size and to ignore all big fish. It wasn't an easy task to skip photographing a big grouper and instead take pictures of a tiny shrimp, but the lesson was learned. I was made aware that many good things come in small packages, and if you don't pay attention, you can easily overlook something that turns out to be fascinating. I found this out when I photographed my first jellyfish in our lakes, jellyfish that were about the size of a dime. By giving the little creatures a chance, you get a whole new perspective on your environment, your awareness is heightened and enriched and your appreciation is enhanced.

In my lake descriptions, just because I name the types of fish that I saw does not mean that you will not see other different fish or that you will necessarily see the same ones that I saw. The fish dynamics obviously can and do change, and what might have been a low key experience for me might be a fast action one for you or vice versa. What is stated in the lake descriptions is only what I happened to see on one or more occasions--had I stayed in longer and roamed further, I might have seen additional varieties of fish and vegetation. With approximately 800 public access lakes to survey, it obviously wasn't possible to spend nearly as long as I would have liked in each lake.

A SCENIC OR INTERESTING ENVIRONMENT: This is a necessary element both from an esthetic standpoint and from the standpoint of seeing fish. Habitat is essential for fish—they love to find a place to hide. For example, an experiment was done in which fish were put in a pool with no habitat whatsoever, but at one end of the pool a black line was painted. In no time, all the fish had congregated by the black line, feeling protected even by a dark line of paint. Thus I have tried to choose lakes where some kind of habitat is present. It could be fallen logs or branches or organic material, or it could be a great variety of weed beds. I have even found it an enormously pleasurable experience to float among scenic weedbeds where there were little or no fish present. I have been mesmerized by the scenic vegetation, and where I can name that vegetation , I have included it in the lake descriptions. I think most people like to put a name to things, and I think you will be just as amazed at the beauty of the vegetation as you are at the colors and variety of the fish. A number of lakes are flooded former forests, and the entire lake consists of hundreds of cut off trees, with fish swimming around them, an eerie and unusual sight. So environment plays a big part in your enjoyment, and many a crystal clear lake has not been included if it does not provide an esthetic surrounding. Great visibility over a layer of muck does not add up to a pleasant experience.

When snorkelers visit the Caribbean, they often see fish circulating among coral formations that are a major part of the ocean environment. Plastic cards may be purchased that picture and name the different types of coral, such as brain coral, staghorn, elkhorn, sheet, pillar, leaf coral, etc. It is just as satisfying to be able to name the types of coral as it is to identify the fish.

In the freshwater environment, the various types of vegetation provide habitat and background for the fish, just as the coral does in the ocean, and I want you to have that same opportunity to recognize the types of vegetation you are seeing. Therefore, just before the lake listings, I have provided a series of drawings of the common Michigan aquatic plants, to aid you in identifying the ones mentioned in my lake descriptions. This knowledge will I hope add substantially to your enjoyment of the snorkeling experience.

DECENT ACCESS: Note I did not say EASY access. I have not included any lakes where the access is too difficult, but there are many worthwhile lakes which do not necessarily have docks, ramps and a big wide access.

I do require that the ground be solid where you enter. If in doubt, you should always test with one foot on shore to be certain you're not stepping into muck, but I have eliminated those in which footing was not solid.

SHAPE: I have not eliminated any lakes on the basis of shape, but there is no doubt that a bowl shape makes for better snorkeling. When you enter the water, you don't want an immediate deep drop, as with depth you may not have the visibility. On the other hand, even if a lake is crystal clear, if it is only a few inches deep near shore and you have to go out very far before you get into comfortable snorkeling depth (Black Lake in Cheboygan County comes to mind), then you expend the time and effort going way out in the lake and, in addition, if the lake is a halfway busy one, you are in the line of fire of speedboats, jet skis and the like. And if something does come along, there just is not the time to get out of the way. I have nevertheless included lakes that are flat for some distance from shore because:

- if you have friends who have cottages, or if you ask friendly cottagers to let you enter at an area OTHER than the public access, the shape and depth near shore can be totally different, thus offering you a different snorkeling experience and

- you may have access to a boat, in which case you can wander all over the lake until you find the depth and structure to your liking.

Though all snorkeling experiences and all lakes are not created equal, and though some lakes for me offered more than others, I purposely did not make this a handbook of the 50 or 100 best snorkeling lakes in Michigan because:

- A small number of lakes would be overrun with people, and the resulting congestion would make for a lower quality (or diminished) experience for all, and

- By highlighting lakes all over both the Upper and Lower Peninsulas, the chances of a lake being near the reader is greatly increased.

Because of the nature of snorkeling, no two experiences, even in the same lake, are ever the same. So if the clarity and structure are there, even though one day produces little underwater activity, the next time out might be dynamite. And that's what makes it so much fun. I only hope this research which has produced so much revelation, fun and excitement for me, will also open YOUR eyes to the underwater wonder of Michigan's inland lakes.

It is important to note that the Delorme Atlas does not indicate every public access lake, and though I have covered every lake which has a public access of which I am aware, there are those that have a city or township public access not shown on the map, and some of these lakes may have been inadvertently overlooked. I am continuing to check these out, and this book will be revised and updated as needed.

In addition, there are many lakes in national forests that do not show a public access but indeed are open to the public. A good example of this is the Pigeon River National Forest. There are many lakes scattered throughout the forest but the roads are not marked, and it's a real labyrinth in there. If ever you felt like a rat in a maze, it's in the Pigeon River Forest, and if you go in, I wish you luck in getting out. A cell phone would certainly be handy in there and places similar to it. I intend this summer to delve further into some of these areas to snorkel the lakes, and I will then add to the book those lakes that qualify.

In addition, if there are any I have overlooked that you feel should be included, please feel free to fax me at 517 336-6751, and I will hasten to check out your recommendations.

WHY SNORKEL?

There is no question that encounters with nature can help people to combat stress and promote inner peace. Pulitzer-prize-winning Harvard University biologist Edward O. Wilson believes it is critical for humans to interact with plant and animal life to foster well being. "When we tune in to nature, we're engaging in behavior that makes us feel peaceful, healthy and safe," he writes. Some psychologists say contact with nature is as important to our health as personal relationships.

I have certainly found that to be true. After a hectic day, I love to put on my bathing suit, grab my snorkel, drive for an hour to a good lake, and within seconds of parking the car and entering the lake, I can literally feel the tension oozing out through my fingertips. It's a little bit like downhill skiing. While you're lying face down in the water, it's practically impossible to focus on anything but the strange and ever-changing underwater world before you.

In addition, snorkeling can be a great spiritual experience. For me it *always* is. The peace, the tranquility and feeling of inner harmony it provides just naturally leads one to thoughts of the Being that created this incredible universe. One can come out of the water in a state of spiritual and mental healing. There's no question, it can be that kind of powerful experience if you are open to it.

In looking over some of the lake descriptions, you may be struck by a certain sameness, either in the vegetation or the type of fish that are present. Don't be fooled by that. The variety is absolutely infinite. I am reminded of a similar situation I have had on African safaris. Many people think that once they have seen an elephant or a giraffe or a lion or whatever, that the trip is complete, and that there is no need to see them again and again. The fact of the matter is that no matter how many times you see them, the setting is always different, so it is a perpetually new experience.

The array and setting of the plant life, the movement of the fish, the lighting all combine to make each experience a new one. You will never repeat yourself, even in the same lake!

SOME IMPORTANT DO'S AND DON'TS

DO stay in the water long enough to give the lake a good chance. You may get action right away, but I found that many times it wasn't until after the first 15 minutes that I became acclimated to my surroundings, and things started to happen. If I had written off a lake based on the first 5 or 10 minutes I would have made a huge mistake and would have crossed off what proved to be unusually rewarding lakes. A perfect example is Littlefield Lake in Isabella County. Upon first entering the water, though the clarity was excellent, and the surroundings were interesting, there was absolutely no activity—not even a minnow—the lake appeared absolutely dead. I floated at the surface, cruising around for a good 20 minutes when I spotted something that is actually and fortunately a rarity—cigarette butts. There were a number of them, and I was thinking what a pity it was that such carelessness existed when an amazing thing happened. No sooner had my thought formed than there appeared on my left 2 large white suckers, each a good 2 feet long. Instantly one of the suckers, while the other hovered above, vacuumed up all the cigarette butts in sight with a swiftness I would not have believed possible. Behind them trailed a very large largemouth bass. This remarkable sight took only a few seconds, but had I not been patient I would have missed the whole show. With many lakes, it is very worthwhile to spend an entire day exploring, because there is so much variety, and the conditions are so conducive to a long stay. There is no question that there is a richer reward and an enhanced experience in more thoroughly examining one diverse lake than in jumping from lake to lake, spending only a half hour in each. You just can't jump to conclusions about a lake from a cursory look. This is wildlife, this is nature, and just as you must be patient when you go into the wilderness on land before you hit activity, the same is true underwater. I will say that you can almost always hit a "hot spot" underwater much more quickly than you can on land.

DON'T wear fins and **DON'T** stand up unless absolutely necessary. Rubber or aquatic shoes are fine, if you want to cover your feet, but absolutely no fins. Very often you are in shallow water, and fins only get in the way, scare off the fish, stir up sediment and make it difficult to see.

Because your snorkel allows easy and unlimited breathing, there should be no reason to have to stand up, and doing so will greatly diminish your experience, as you will then have to wait some time before visibility is restored. Sometimes you can lightly rest on vegetation below you if there is no silt or muck around you, and such a situation would only minimally affect visibility, but it would be hoped that even that could be avoided.

DON'T feel that it's only worth snorkeling if the day is sunny. In truth, midday in the bright sun does not necessarily provide the best visibility. The bright light of midday often produces moving patterns underwater that can be distracting and confusing, making some of the smaller fish harder to see and disturbing your focus and concentration. If a day is sunny without clouds, the ideal time to go out would be before 11AM and after 3PM. Of course if the day is overcast and cloudy, then any time of day is fine, but be sure not to rule out a snorkeling experience just because it isn't sunny. A cloudy bright day can provide an outstanding experience, and there is no question, if the day is sunny, that you would want to avoid the hours of 10-11AM to 2-3PM if you are doing any photography (see section on photography).

DO avoid strong windy days. If you were diving, a wind would not matter, since you would be well below the surface, but since you are floating on the surface, a strong wind will buffet you and give you less control, since you have nothing on which to anchor yourself, and choppy water and waves could conceivably bring water into your snorkel, a definite annoyance. It's almost impossible to focus and concentrate on what you are seeing when you are being thrown around by the wind.

DO get out of the water immediately on hearing any thunder. I have snorkeled many lakes when it is raining , and I've hardly been aware of it, but if there is an electrical storm, the last place you want to be is in the water, so leave immediately and don't take any chances, no matter what good things you are seeing below the surface.

DO move slowly. There is very little reason to use your legs more than minimally unless you decide to go a considerable distance. I use a slow turtle-like motion with my arms to propel myself forward, but more often, especially if I have just entered the lake, I don't move at all. It's as if there is a fish grapevine, as by lying completely still, very often fish will come right up to you.

As some come around, the word seems to spread, until before long, a whole crowd is gathered. They are often very curious—remember, they've never seen anything like you before, and it's natural to want to study this strange new creature. If I lie in an area for 8-10 minutes and there is no activity then I will gradually move to another area, using only my hands to push myself forward. There must be no quick motions or you will defeat your purpose.

DO look carefully at where you entered the lake. Of course, if there is a wide entrance and dock, as well as a big boat launch, you will have no trouble knowing where to get out, but in some of the most interesting lakes the entrance is made through a group of trees, and it is then important to pick out a landmark clump of trees or some sight you will remember, in order not to have to get out of the lake and walk back and forth looking for the entrance. Indeed, in some lakes there aren't necessarily that many spots to walk along the edge of the lake, so it is much better to visualize your entrance before you leave it. Later, if you haven't taken note of where you've entered, those trees can all look alike!

DO proceed very slowly when leaving a lake. Psychologically, it is natural, once you've decided you are through snorkeling a lake, to want to barrel toward shore. **DON'T.** Proceed slowly, as you head toward the entrance, as I've seen tiny colorful darters motionless at the shore, which I would have entirely missed. At the opposite end of the spectrum, I have actually stumbled over carp in only a foot of water as I'm getting out of a lake. After coming in from snorkeling in 5-8 feet of water and seeing only small pan fish, I have headed to shore only to find shallow reedy areas thick with good-sized suckers and largemouth bass.

DON'T always look down. When you're facing down it's only natural to look in that direction, and that's fine, but don't forget to periodically lift your head and look ahead closer to the surface. There are many, many fish, both large and small, that will swim near the surface, and many's the interesting fish that swam away because I looked too late and scared it off.

DON'T be afraid of anything bothering you or hurting you. There is nothing aggressive in there—even the big pike beat a hasty retreat if they see you coming, and this is also true of both big and small turtles. The big snapping turtles can't get away fast enough. If you're lucky and you see them before they see you, you can stop still and observe them—sometimes for as long as you want to. Of course any sudden movement will send them scurrying.

Obviously, you will **NEVER** try to restrain a turtle or fish or interfere with underwater life in any way. Snapping turtles will not bother you if you do not bother or attempt to restrain THEM.

DON'T feed the fish. They have their own natural food, and if you make a habit of feeding them, they learn to expect it, and twice I got a tiny nip from bluegills, in their eagerness to get fed.

DO protect against sunburn. The arms, shoulders and back of your legs are particularly vulnerable. I solved the problem by wearing a skin that zipped up the front and covered my whole body (see section under "clothing and equipment.") You can also wear a big shirt and long loose pants.

DO watch for dark spots in the weedbeds. This is where big bowfin like to settle, and initially I dismissed these big spots as just natural depressions, not realizing that they were actually bowfins resting. They were so still that it was not until I was close that I actually saw them.

DO remember that the lakes that I have listed in the guide, and which were clear when I snorkeled them, can occasionally have an algae blooom, where the visibility is affected. Usually if I would come back in a few days, visibility would be restored. Visibility can also be less after a heavy rain, so if this appears to be the case, come back at another time and give the lake another try.

DON'T be surprised if the fish you see look different than those in your fish guides. The colors you see underwater are often more intense than the drawings in the fish books, and I usually found the reality far surpassed any pictures for sheer unparalleled beauty. No drawing or photo can capture the colors that nature has created, and that color and detail is certainly a big part of the thrill and satisfaction of snorkeling.

DON'T expect a bluegill or a sucker or a bass or any other fish to look the same in one lake as they do in another. The variation is enormous, and some fish look dramatically different from lake to lake.

Sometimes even fish in the same lake can look quite different on different days, due to stress, climate and other environmental factors. In addition, if a lake is dark, the fish will be darker in order to blend in. If a lake is bright, with lots of white sand, the fish will be much lighter.

In one lake, I saw a small pike, a fish that is normally always brown, swimming over white sand, and he was absolutely white. This is one of the real surprises of the sport and part of what makes snorkeling Michigan's inland lakes so fascinating.

DO carry a red snorkel flag (obtainable at a local dive shop or by catalog). (See Equipment section) Get the smallest and lightest one you can get, so as to protect yourself and let others know where you are yet without dragging too much weight around.

DO carry good maps. I personally prefer the DeLorme Michigan Atlas, obtainable at most grocery stores, sporting goods stores and bookstores. It is essential that you have this detailed an atlas, as the standard maps do not begin to show all of the county roads you will need to take, in order to find the lakes. I found the DeLorme (about $15) the easiest to read. The Michigan County Map Guide is also very well done and contains much useful information.

DO carry binoculars so you can take full advantage of all the great wildlife viewing opportunities you will have as you drive betweeen the lakes. I saw countless deer, the spectacular blue heron, many of them perched on the edges of lakes I was snorkeling, all sorts of bird life from owls, hawks, merlins, bald eagles and bitterns to pheasants, and numerous wild turkeys, many times forcing you to come to a stop while the mother escorts her brood across the road. The roads and lakefronts are populated with a wide variety of butterflies from the yellow cabbage butterfly to the stately monarch. It's all yours and it's all free—part of Michigan's and nature's bounty.

DO plan to visit the local diners and bed and breakfasts (if you're spending the night) and make them part of your snorkeling experience. They're a far cry from the fast food fare that is becoming the unfortunate norm. They each have their specialties from the succulent sloppy Joe's at the 1907 Inverness Inn outside Chelsea on N. Territorial to Sally's in White Cloud, where her fresh whitefish dinners followed by home made strawberry shortcake for under $10 are as good a meal as any I've eaten.

These special treats are all over the state in our picturesque towns that still preserve their sense of community and which exhibit their own unique charm. You'll feel like you're wandering Charles Kuralt's America, and you will make your own discoveries. They add immeasurably to the overall experience.

DO enter the lake carefully, watching out for all watercraft and making sure to stay a safe distance and to keep near shore if there are skis or fast moving boats around. As mentioned earlier, sound travels quickly underwater, and you can hear a boat on the opposite side of the lake very clearly. Still, make it a habit to glance up periodically to assess your position and that of others around you. I have never even come close to having an accident.

DO take advantage, if possible, of the often superior snorkeling conditions during the week, as opposed to snorkeling on the busier weekends. Fortunately, many of the lakes I list don't get much traffic at any time, but at the larger, busier lakes, weekends can be more hectic.

DO take advantage of any little bay-like areas that a lake possesses. Boats and jet skis tend to stay away from these smaller areas, and they make ideal protected spots for snorkeling. I have tried in my lake descriptions to point out most of these, where they exist.

DO stay away from private lakes. Cottagers have paid good money to be there, and they do not appreciate trespassers, so go only if you are invited.

A Word About Michigan's Roads

I know that the many potholes on Michigan roads are a big source of complaint, but I must confess, I saw a completely opposite side of the picture. Once you get out of the urban areas, the roads are just one beautiful ribbon after another. I swear many of them looked like they had *never* been driven on, so smooth and unmarked were they. There were many stretches of road where I drove for miles without seeing a car and where I could have easily balanced a glass of water with nary a spill. In the Upper Peninsula, those roads designated as Forest Highways definitely belong in the picture books. I am told that back in the early thirties when FDR wanted to create jobs, he sent young men to the Upper Peninsula and set them to work building these roads. The roads were not actually needed from a high traffic demand point of view, but it was a way of creating jobs, and thus the roads were built. They are now a proud legacy, and in my travels throughout the world, these roads are unequalled. Try them--it's a treat you won't forget.

PHOTOGRAPHY

THE CAMERA

The sights and colors of the underwater beg to be photographed, and if you're used to enjoying photography on land, I think it won't be long before you're itching to try your hand below the surface. I found it difficult to produce good results with my still cameras, a Minolta sport model and the more sophisticated Nikonos. Both had either built-in flash or powerful flash attachments, but photography while snorkeling is quite different than photography while diving. In the diving situation you are able to control your depth through your buoyancy compensator, and you are also able to anchor yourself by kneeling on the bottom. In snorkeling, you are bobbing at the surface with nothing to hang onto, and you are also at the mercy of any wind that might be blowing. In addition, you are limited in your ability to get close to your fish or turtle subjects. If they swim up past your camera, you can grab a quick shot, but it is a very iffy proposition. When you are diving, you can move in on your subject no matter what the depth. While snorkeling, you may see a great pike several feet away and you can't get closer, and the result is a totally unsatisfactory picture. Telephoto lenses also do not do the trick, as any movement at all results in a blurred or less than sharp picture, and it is practically impossible to avoid movement when you are floating at the surface rather than anchored underneath.

So what is the best solution? I found it to be in video, which, besides producing high quality pictures, also captures the excitement of movement.

Once you've seen the fish and turtles cavorting and being themselves, I think you'll be sold on video. There is also considerable variety and sometimes spectacular color in the vegetation. Just the variations in the palette of greens is like seeing a Monet painting. The artistry of nature below will amaze and confound you, and it is a big thrill to share this with your family and friends. I found myself frustrated trying to explain to others the fascination and beauty that our inland lakes offer, and I don't think anyone was totally convinced until I could prove it with video.

Everyone knows the beauty found in our oceans and seas—you don't have to have pictures to convince your friends that the Cayman Islands underwater are a visual delight or that there are colorful wonders in the Red Sea or the Great Barrier Reef—many have already seen this on television, so they are presold. But what you can't see on television is the beauty beneath our inland lakes. When you watch underwater video on TV, you invariably are looking at fish swimming among the coral formations. The coral provides a picturesque backdrop, but in my opinion it is no more pleasing to the eye than lime green fields of chara, tall curly tape grass, coontail and the myriad other forms of vegetation that delight the eye in the inland lakes. They are absolutely worthy rivals of the ocean coral, and you can have the fun of showing footage to your friends that they cannot see anywhere else. You are literally charting new territory, and there is an exciting sense of discovery on every snorkeling venture.

Since there is no waterproof camcorder, you have two choices—either to buy a protective plastic covering (Ewa has a good one for about $200) that will allow you to enclose your camera while still having access to the controls, or to buy an outer housing built for your camcorder. The more professional results by far occur with a housing built specifically for your camcorder. Only the palm sized camcorders will fit into these housings for the amateur, but there are some satisfactory ones out there, Sony, Quest, Light and Motion and Bentley being among them. Pick up a copy of "Videomaker" or "Camcorder" magazines, and you will see many advertisements for the equipment at big discounts. Firms I have had success with include Berger Brothers and Genesis, but there are many more who are also reliable. It is of course vital to pay by credit card, as in case there are problems you have recourse to dispute the charges. You can choose from 8 millimeter, Hi -8, VHS or the high quality S-VHS.

The advantage of the S-VHS is that you can buy a device to fit your small tape in so that it will play in a standard VCR. With 8 mm and Hi-8 mm, the difference is not obvious until you start copying tapes, which is when the superiority of the Hi-8 becomes evident. Prices have come down significantly on this equipment making it still an investment but much more affordable. I found a video rewinder to be a valuable accessory, as it saves wear and tear on your camcorder.

The biggest difficulty I had in getting adjusted to taking underwater video was getting used to the tiny viewfinder at the back of the outer housing. At first it feels like you're looking through a pinhole and it seems impossible to see your subject. I can only say, don't give up, as you do gradually get used to the small size, but you will never see your subject through the viewfinder in anywhere near the detail that you will with the naked eye. Forget all those popout large viewing screens that they're offering on so many of the new camcorders. There isn't room in the housing for those screens, so you have to make do with your small viewfinder, or there are some expensive ($1000) attachments you can buy that will enlarge your viewfinder to 3 inches. It is in using your viewfinder that you appreciate a cloudy day. When you are at the surface, which of course you always are when snorkeling, the bright sun in the middle of the day practically eliminates the possibility of finding your subject in the viewfinder, though up until 10AM or after 3PM on sunny days, you will see very well through your viewfinder, as the sun is no longer shining directly on it.

The next decision you have to make is how to set your distance. One thing you cannot do is set your camera on autofocus, as when you are underwater, the camera on automatic becomes completely confused, and with fish swimming back and forth in big areas of blue water, the camera does not know what to focus on and therefore does not focus at all, leaving you with a tape full of blurred footage. The best solution is to preset your camera before entering the water, by choosing a distance where you are most likely to be taking your video. And how to choose that distance? I would experiment by setting your camcorder at varying distances, look at the results and decide which distance produces the sharpest footage. I would practice in my room by choosing a distance of a foot or so away and set the camera for that distance.

It is necessary to take a tape measure and measure the distance from the end of the lens to what you're focusing on in the room, so when you take the camera underwater you'll know which distance gave you the results you wanted. I put a tiny piece of scotch tape just above the lens so that I would know exactly where I wanted to keep it set in case the lens focuser would get moved around. Once I've chosen my set point for distance, I pretty much leave it there and then just move in on my subject. That's actually easier than you might think, as if you are *slow, deliberate,* and *patient,* fish and turtles will let you move in very close.

It is important to choose a camera with an image stabilizer, a feature common on all of the better camcorders, as the stabilizer practically eliminates camera shake, a problem that is very real when you are snorkeling.

You may be disappointed to find that using your camera zoom feature for closeups underwater doesn't produce good results, since you have to change your focus distance at the same time, and it can be difficult underwater to accurately measure the distance. If you miscalculate you have blurred footage and end up disappointed. With so much going on all around you it is impossible to keep jumping back and forth attempting to continually recalculate distance, and the result is NO result. It is best to just fix the focus, which then frees you up to concentrate on your surroundings, searching for good subjects and then moving in closer.

The best results are achieved by keeping the camera permanently set at wide angle for the greatest depth of field and just ignoring the zoom feature. If you keep the camera set at its widest angle and set your distance at about a foot, everything from a few inches from the lens up to 2 feet will be in sharp focus, and even several feet beyond will still be very acceptable. Though some of the more sophisticated housings do have focusing capability underwater, the reality of it is that with so much going on all around you, no sooner do you expend time and energy focusing on a distant spot than the subject suddenly moves up closer, or something else you want to photograph suddenly appears at a totally different distance. One just has to accept that you will not be able to take some of the distance shots, but what you do shoot will be in focus and will make for very acceptable viewing.

TAPES, BATTERIES AND EDITING

Most 8 or Hi-8 tapes are 2 hours in length, which gives you plenty of time and a good bit of freedom to experiment. The only thing you have to watch is your battery life. The best batteries will give you about an hour and a half of actual shooting underwater. This may seem like a long time, but if you hit a good bit of action, and I would plan on that, then you may need 2 or even 3 charged batteries. Just like film, tape is the cheapest part of the process, so shoot away, as you never know what nugget you may end up with.

To avoid having to go back to the car to change batteries, I keep my charged-up extra batteries in a plastic bag secured by a towel onshore. It is of course vital to wipe your hands, face and arms thoroughly before changing the battery to avoid any harmful droplets on the camera equipment. Buy batteries that have no memory, so in the event that there is still some charge left in the battery when you are through, you are not risking shortening the life of the battery, and there will be no "memory effect." As a precaution against this, I still like to use up the charge on the battery by using the camcorder without a tape, and then recharging the battery afterwards.

So what do you do with those hours of video once they're on tape? My first summer I ended up with 59 hours of tape, only 5% of which were really see-worthy. And of course even the best of friends are not likely to want to sit through more than an hour at the most. Agony! Editing is an absolute must, and you can either farm it out by writing down the exact segments that you wish to have included, or you can take matters into your own hands and do your own editing. This is what I did, and if I can do it, anyone can. I would not say that I was a computer illiterate, as I had used airline computers for many years, but this new project was a very different story. I was talking to my software help desk a good bit for a couple of months, but I was not even familiar with Windows, so it was pretty much starting from scratch, and I think my help desk was wondering if I would ever make it. I didn't even *own* a computer until I started editing. However, once I learned the process, it was magical, and I was able to take 30 different tapes, log all my segments by typing them into the computer, drag and drop, press the "make tape" button, and voilà!--there was a finished tape. The process seemed really miraculous, and I was so thrilled with the result I added titles, narration and music.

The following summer when I took about 20 videotapes, I was again faced with the editing process, but this time it was like riding a bicycle. In spite of many months away from editing, everything came back immediately, and in only a few hours I had logged and made another tape suitable for viewing. Here is where the Hi-8 mm. format instead of the 8mm really makes the difference. For preservation and safety purposes, you will want to use your original tapes as little as possible, so from your originals you will edit down to a work tape. This means that your work tape will be a generation away from the original. If you add music and/or narration, your final tape will be at least a third generation tape, depending on the type of equipment you have.

A third generation Hi-8 tape is going to retain almost all of the detail of the original if your camera and tapes are both Hi-8 (Hi-8 tapes will not record or play in an 8mm camcorder). There's no doubt that adding photography to your snorkeling will add much enjoyment to the experience. There is also no doubt that a degree of frustration goes along with photography until you get used to the equipment and the editing process (if you choose to do your own editing). There is also no doubt that there is a great freedom in just floating and absorbing the incredible satisfying underwater experience without feeling you have to record it. To some, a camera is a burden; to others it's essential. I love it either way, and it was only my eagerness to share it that nudged me toward photography.

EQUIPMENT

- snorkel and mask
- mask cleaner
- Swim Ear
- snorkel flag
- towels
- bathing hat, if desired
- first aid kit
- belt with plastic holder for car keys and mask cleaner
- Delorme County Atlas
- water resistant watch

You can either buy your snorkel and mask as part of a kit at a discount store, or, far more satisfactory, if you think you'll snorkel on a regular basis, get it at a dive shop. The established best way to assure a good fit is to try different shapes until one feels comfortable, then hold it in position against your face and then breathe in or suck in and hold your breath. If the mask stays in place without your touching it, that is an indication of a good fit. Feel around the sides for any gaps where water might seep in. It should be tight all the way around.

The best snorkels are those that have the widest barrels, and my favorite model, which is more expensive (at this writing it sells for about $50) is one that is closed at the top where air can get in but no water comes in, even if you should take it underwater.

These snorkels really relax you and leave you even freer to concentrate on the experience. There's no doubt that the proper mask and snorkel can make a big difference, and a bad fit can leave you frustrated, always stopping to clear your mask.

Swim Ear or a similar product also is very important, as a couple of drops in each ear *every* time you are through snorkeling, will prevent water clogging the ear with the chance of bacteria developing into an infection.

There is a common tendency of masks to cloud up, which can cause annoying stops and starts, even requiring you to stand up to clean your mask. Just a drop of mask cleaner on the outside and one drop each on the inside of the mask can totally prevent this. Rub the drops around the glass, then dip it into the lake to rinse, put it on and you're set. If you leave your mask on, you won't have to use the drops again—if you take your mask on and off several times, you may have to repeat the process. I found a brand called Sea Drops at my dive store that totally prevents fogging up, but there is more than one brand out there.

You can always hide your car keys somewhere under your car or on the wheels, but I prefer to keep them with me, as well as keep my Sea Drops handy, so I wear a belt with a plastic box attached which holds these items.

I mentioned the snorkel flag earlier. This is a safety precaution and is required to alert boaters and other craft that you are in the area. Get the lightest weight one you can find. There's no need to drag a big heavy flag.

WHAT TO WEAR

Wearing the right clothing is absolutely critical to enjoying the experience. Failure to protect your body from the sun can result in a bad burn that will keep you out of the water for days, not to mention the discomfort you will feel.

On the other hand, not dressing warmly enough in cool waters will have you shivering and will limit the time you can remain in the water, cutting short an experience that might have been an exciting one.

There is absolutely nothing to say that you *have* to have anything but a bathing suit, but wearing only a swim suit will not allow you to stay as long in the water if it is chilly, and on a sunny day it would be absolutely necessary to cover yourself with a tee shirt or a long sleeved shirt plus loose elastic waist pants to keep the back of your legs from geting scorched. My guess is that if you fall in love with the sport like I did, you will want to make an investment in clothing that will assure your comfort under all conditions. And with that thought in mind, I make the following recommendations:

- HOT WEATHER WETSUITS: one should be a thin Lycra skin, for the hot days, but one that is a full suit to prevent sunburn. These unisex Lycra skins come in different colors, zip up the front and are available through catalogs or on sale at your local dive shop.

- A COLDER WEATHER WETSUIT for the chillier days and for the days when you might be in for several hours. This would again be a full zip-up-the-front suit of 3mm neoprene that provides warmth without bulk. These are also available through catalogs or on sale at your local dive shop.

- LIGHTWEIGHT TROPICAL GLOVES 2 mm neoprene for warm to cool water, available through catalogs or dive shops.

- THERMO GLOVES 3 mm neoprene for colder water.

- AQUATIC SHOES available at sporting good stores, for warm water.

- TALLER SPORT BOOT 6 mm neoprene that zips up the side for use in cooler water.

The two different suits should pretty much cover all but the most extreme conditions. A full suit, either light or heavier, gives you protection against sunburn and protects you against all the elements, as well as against anything you might brush up against in the water. You can be assured of not contracting any rashes or itches by being fully covered, and I find many people, my teenage son included, much more eager to participate when they feel their body so protected. As to which suit to wear when, you will have to make your own judgment calls based on the air and water temperatures, whether it is sunny or cloudy and how long you want to stay in the water. If you want to stay in for several hours you will probably want the heavier suit, except in very warm water on very hot days.

If you go snorkeling in May or October, women at least, would want a 6 mm neoprene jacket and farmer john, which is a bigger investment, approximately $250. The advantages of snorkeling in spring or fall are the lack of crowds, fewer watercraft, and the fact that the students have gone back to school, giving you more of the lake to yourself. In addition, May to mid-June snorkeling can produce some spectacular spawning viewing, especially of catfish, largemouth bass and carp.

I cannot emphasize strongly enough the importance of gloves. You would be surprised at how quickly your hands get chilled, and physical discomfort of any kind cuts into your enjoyment and makes you want to cut your experience short.

The same importance applies to your feet—the longer you are in the water, the more protection you will need from chill. There is a psychological advantage to having your feet covered, in the event your feet would rub against scratchy vegetation or you are forced to stand up in weeds or hard bottoms covered with sticks and stones. The sense of protection your gloves and boots give you is a big plus.

ENTRANCE FEE

The only entrance cost is for a $20 car sticker, good for one year. This sticker goes on the inside lower left hand windshield of your car and can be purchased the first time you enter a lake where it is required.

Beyond that, snorkeling Michigan's inland lakes is absolutely free. And you enjoy one big advantage not available to your friends snorkeling in other exotic locales: you can stay in as long as you want and as long as you are comfortable, since you are snorkeling from shore. By contrast, if you snorkel the oceans or seas, you seldom have the opportunity to snorkel from shore. Invariably you are part of a group in a boat, and you are taken to the snorkeling spot, given a maximum of 45 minutes and are charged at least $35. It's a very frustrating experience for the avid snorkeler, and as you keep repeating this experience, the costs mount up.

So as you can see, snorkeling Michigan's inland lakes is one of the State's best vacation bargains. Inexpensive motels abound, in case you decide to spend the night. Meals are very reasonable as well, as you wisely patronize the many reasonably priced family style restaurants that are such a refreshing change from the homogenized fast food outlets.

CHILDREN

What an opportunity to get the kids away from the TV set and out into the world of nature! Let their senses be awakened to a world most people don't know exists. They will come back stimulated, full of life and full of questions. It is so important at an early age to nurture these young minds with rich experiences. At one lake I saw a father snorkeling with a 3 year old with a tiny snorkel and mask. He was holding the child in front of him, pushing him gently along, and the child was squealing with delight. Time magazine in their February 3, 1997 issue told of the importance of this kind of experience for a child's brain development. It's never too early—we had our child in the pool at 6 months, and he's been a water bug ever since.

However, it's not too late if they're in their teens—they will still soak up the new experience, learn and be that much better for it. As Nike says, JUST DO IT!

COMMON AQUATIC PLANTS OF MICHIGAN

Following is a description of some of the most commonly occurring aquatic plants in Michigan. Some, such as coontail, milfoil, and elodea, reproduce by fragmentation and can quickly reach nuisance density levels.

The pondweeds, genus *Potamogeton*, are highly variable in form and only a few representative types are described here.

If you have an aquatic plant not included here and have difficulty identifying it, refer to a professional consultant. You may also send a small sample in a plastic bag to:

INLAND LAKES MANAGEMENT UNIT
LAND AND WATER MANAGEMENT DIVISION
MICHIGAN DEPARTMENT OF NATURAL RESOURCES
PO BOX 30458
LANSING MI 48909-7958

cross-section

Chara spp.; **stonewart, muskgrass**

Chara is an advanced form of algae which resembles higher plants. It is easily identified by its musky odor and gritty texture due to mineral deposits on its surface. Chara rarely creates a nuisance as it usually grows in low, dense mats, or grows sparsely where nutrient levels are low. The water is clear where chara grows densely because, like other algae, it filters nutrients out of the water instead of the sediments. In this respect, chara is highly beneficial vegetation.

Lemna minor; **duckweed**

Duckweed is a floating plant so small that a teaspoon could hold a dozen or more plants. At a distance, a congregation of duckweed plants may resemble algae on the water surface. This plant is common in ponds and quiet water of lakes and streams.

5 x actual size

Myriophyllum spp.; water milfoil

Milfoil is a submerged plant, however, the flower stalk, when present, protrudes above the water surface. Leaves are arranged in whorls around stem. Leaflets are unforked and arranged in a feather-like pattern (see cross-section illustration). Spacing between whorls varies so that plants may appear long and sparse or bushy. Milfoil can quickly become a nuisance by forming dense mats to the surface of the water.

cross-section

Ceratophyllum demersum; coontail

Coontail is a submerged plant without roots. The leaves are arranged in whorls around the stem. Leaflets are forked, not feather-like as in milfoil (see cross-section illustration). Plants may be long and sparse, but are often bushy, especially toward the tips of branches, resembling a raccoon's tail, hence the common name "coontail".

cross-section

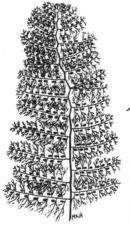

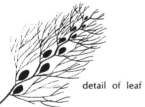

detail of leaf

Utricularia spp.; bladderwort

Although bladderwort is not as common as other aquatic plants presented in this booklet, it is sometimes confused with milfoil. A closer look reveals that the leaflets are branched, not feather-like as on milfoil (see detail illustration). The most distinguishing feature, however, is the presence of bladder-like structures which trap small aquatic invertebrates. The "bladders" may be large and dark in color or small and inconspicuous.

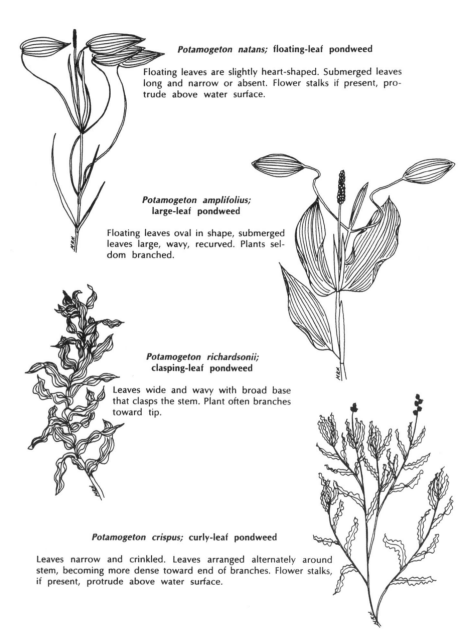

Potamogeton natans; floating-leaf pondweed

Floating leaves are slightly heart-shaped. Submerged leaves long and narrow or absent. Flower stalks if present, protrude above water surface.

Potamogeton amplifolius;
large-leaf pondweed

Floating leaves oval in shape, submerged leaves large, wavy, recurved. Plants seldom branched.

Potamogeton richardsonii;
clasping-leaf pondweed

Leaves wide and wavy with broad base that clasps the stem. Plant often branches toward tip.

Potamogeton crispus; curly-leaf pondweed

Leaves narrow and crinkled. Leaves arranged alternately around stem, becoming more dense toward end of branches. Flower stalks, if present, protrude above water surface.

Potamogeton pectinatus; sago pondweed

Leaves long and thread-like, arranged alternately on stem. Leaves form dense clumps on branches, providing a broom-like appearance. Flower stalks, if present, protrude above water surface.

Najas flexilis; common naiad

Nodes (swelling) present at base of leaf whorls. Leaves tapered to fine point with minute spines on margin of leaves in some species. Spacing between whorls of leaves highly variable.

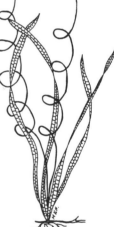

Vallisneria americana; wild celery

Roots buried in bottom material. Leaves long and grass-like. Horizontal stem system connects tufts of leaves. Flower stalks, if present, spiral toward surface of water.

Elodea canadensis; american elodea

Leaves oval shaped, arranged in whorls around stem. Whorls densely compacted at tips of branches. Commonly used as an aquarium plant.

POPULAR MICHIGAN SPORT FISH
IDENTIFICATION KEY

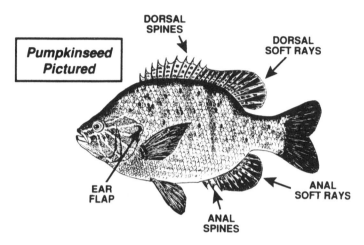

DORSAL SPINES

DORSAL SOFT RAYS

Pumpkinseed Pictured

EAR FLAP

ANAL SOFT RAYS

ANAL SPINES

SUNFISH FAMILY

General: In Michigan, the sunfish family contains two black basses, the largemouth and the smallmouth. These fish are much larger and their bodies longer and slimmer in relation to depth than the rest of the sunfish family.

Black Bass

Largemouth — Dorsal spiny and soft-rayed fins almost separated by deep cleft. Mouth large with upper lip extended beyond rear of eye. Greenish or blackish; belly whitish; sides marked with dark band running entire length.

Smallmouth — Dorsal spiny and soft rayed fins not separated. Mouth smaller with upper lip extending to middle or rear of eye. Brownish or bronze, belly whitish, sides marked with vertical bars.

The rest of the sunfishes have dish shaped bodies. Three species have 5 or more anal spines and the rest have only 3 anal spines.

Black Crappie — 5 or more anal spines, 7 spines in dorsal fin. Mouth large, body compressed and slab-sided. Silverish with dark mark over sides and fins.

White Crappie — 5 or more anal spines, 6 or less spines in dorsal fin. Mouth large, body compressed and slab-sided. Silverish with few to no dark markings.

Rock Bass — 5 or more anal spines, 10 spines in dorsal fin. Mouth large, eye reddish. Goldish with a pattern of dark spots, horizontal rows.

Warmouth — 3 anal spines. Mouth large, eye reddish. Sides a splattering of purple, yellows and browns; sides of head and cheeks dark horizontal bars.

Bluegill — 3 anal spines. Mouth small, body with vertical bars. Dark spot at rear of soft dorsal fin; ear flap large and black.

Pumpkinseed — 3 anal spines. Mouth small. Body gold and brown with dark vertical bars. Head, cheek and gill covers with turquoise stripes; ear flaps small with red dots; throat and stomach orange to red.

Longear — 3 anal spines; breeding males have orange fins. Mouth small. Seldom exceed 6"; body bluish with orange dots; head bluish with orange dashes along cheeks and gill covers; large ear flaps, black with white edging.

Green — 3 anal spines; soft dorsal, anal and tail fins trimmed in yellow. Mouth medium large. Chunky body with base color greenish; ear flap dark with orange trimming.

Redear — 3 anal spines. Mouth small. Body shaped like bluegill but no unusual markings; rear margin of ear flap bright red; large scales.

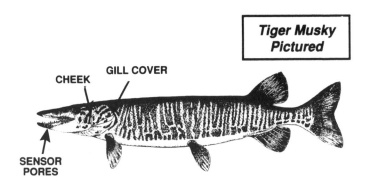

Tiger Musky Pictured

GILL COVER
CHEEK
SENSOR PORES

PIKE FAMILY

General: All members look basically alike having cylindrical shaped bodies, slim and tapered large jaws, sharp teeth, smooth scales with dorsal and anal fins set well back giving fish a slick torpedo look.

Great Lakes Muskellunge — Large sharp teeth; both gill covers and cheeks scaled only on top half; six or more sensory pores per side of bottom jaw. Body light with dark markings; body spotted like a dalmatian dog.

Northern Muskellunge — Large sharp teeth; both gill covers and cheeks scaled only on top half; six or more sensory pores per side of bottom jaw. Series of vertical bars (whole or broken) along entire length of body; bars may be dark or faintly visible.

Tiger Muskellunge — Hybrid of the northern muskellunge and the northern pike. Large sharp teeth; gill covers scaled only on upper half. Cheeks fully scaled; six to eight sensory pores per side of bottom jaw. Series of dark tiger-like stripes along entire body; tail and fins orange with worm-like markings.

Northern Pike — Large sharp teeth; cheek fully scaled; gill cover scaled only on top half; 5 or less sensory pores on each side of lower jaw. Body dark with pattern of light colored bean shaped markings running lengthwise. Tail, dorsal and anal fins orange with dark worm-like markings.

Grass Pickerel — Teeth large; both cheeks and gill covers fully scaled. Small, rarely exceeding 11-12" (Often mistaken as "baby northern pike"); body greenish, large vertical dark bar extending across eyes and jaw.

SPINY DORSAL

Walleye
Pictured

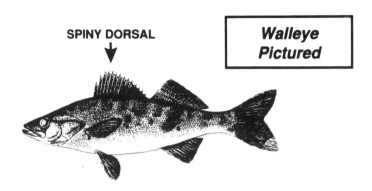

PERCH FAMILY

General: This family includes 3 popular sport fish, Perch, Walleye and Sauger, along with a number of small minnow-sized darters.

Yellow Perch — No large sharp teeth. Back olive to yellow; sides yellow with 6 to 8 dark vertical bands; belly white; lower fins may be orange tinged.

Walleye — Large sharp teeth. Body greenish or yellowish with 6 to 7 saddle like bands; lower lobe of tail white; large black botch at rear of spiny dorsal fin.

Sauger — Large sharp teeth. Body grey with 3 to 4 saddle like bands; lower lobe of tail has white strip along entire lower edge; membranes between spines in dorsal fin has vertical rows of spots.

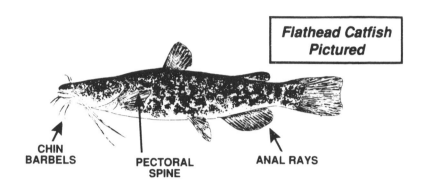

Flathead Catfish Pictured

CHIN
BARBELS   PECTORAL   ANAL RAYS
                       SPINE

CATFISH FAMILY

General: All members are scaleless with smooth slick skin; have 8 barbels (whiskers) on head; have sharp spine on dorsal and each pectoral fin; and have relatively small eyes.

Channel Catfish — 24-29 anal rays; anal fin is rounded. Tail deeply forked; snout narrow. Silverish-grey or bluish; young fish have pepper-like spots over body, tail and fins. Spots may be missing on large fish.

Flathead Catfish — 15-17 anal rays. Tail rounded; head flattened, shovel like and large; band of teeth in upper jaw extend across front and toward rear. Mottled yellowish brown or grey.

Black Bullhead — Grey or blackish chin barbels. Pectoral spines weakly barbed; tail round; band of teeth in upper jaw extends across front but not toward rear. Dark olive to black; belly white or yellowish; tail round;

Brown Bullhead — Grey or blackish chin barbels. Pectoral spines strongly barbed; tail round; band of teeth in upper jaw extends across front but not toward rear. Black to dark brown; belly grey to yellowish and often mottled.

Yellow Bullhead — Whitish chin barbels. Tail round; band of teeth in upper jaw extends across front but not toward rear. Entire fish yellow although entire fish may be various shades of black or brown.

Stoneroller — All barbels light colored. Spines are small and diminutive but sharp and slightly toxic. Tail rounded. Very small in size, body color light brownish to pink.

> **Pink Salmon Pictured**

ANAL RAYS

TROUT AND SALMON FAMILY

General: Salmon — Anal fin longer than it is deep, except Atlantic; Chinook lower jaw pointed, coho lower jaw is rounded. Trout — Anal fin deeper than it is long; Anal rays should be counted at base because the ends may split; Chinook and Atlantic — Have bony support at base of tail which allows the fish to be picked up ("tailed"). Look-a-likes — Steelhead Trout and Coho Salmon; Atlantic Salmon and Brown Trout, Splake and Lake Trout, Splake and Brook Trout.

Chinook Salmon — Large spots over entire tail. 15-17 anal rays. Mouth and gums dark or black. Dark tongue.

Coho Salmon — Small spots on upper half of tail. 13-15 anal rays. Mouth dark grey with light gums. No teeth on tongue.

Atlantic Salmon — Tail/fins dark; no spots on tail. 9 anal rays. White mouth. Weak teeth on tongue, tongue pointed.

Brown Trout — Tail square; no spots, tail and fins brown to tan (light colored). 9-10 anal rays. White mouth. Big teeth on tongue, tongue square.

Pink Salmon — Tail large with spots. Scales very small.

Steelhead (Rainbow) Trout — Spots over entire tail. 10-12 anal rays. White mouth. No teeth on tongue.

Lake Trout — Deeply forked tail; white leading edge on lower fins; no black stripe on lower fins. Whitish spots on body; teeth on entire shaft on roof of mouth.

Brook Trout — Square tail. White leading edge on lower fins; black stripe near leading edge of lower fins. Wormy marking on back; body often marked with white with red spots; teeth on front of shaft on roof of mouth.

Splake Trout (Lake Trout/Brook Trout Hybrid) —Slight forked tail; white leading edge on lower fins. Whitish spots on body often in combination with wormy markings on back; teeth in single row on shaft on roof of mouth. (May resemble either parent.)

UPPER PENINSULA

ACKERMAN LAKE   ALGER COUNTY

Acreage: 14.9 acres   **page 102 of the DeLorme Atlas**

Location: on the south side of 94 just west of H05, right next to the road. This is a very clear lake, offering great snorkeling and great visibility. Scattered pondweed, sparse vegetation, sloping walls, bowl shape, lots of underwater trees, logs, brush piles. Saw schools of perch and black striped minnows. Midweek and not a soul was there. Lake issurrounded by high trees. Organic material on a silty bottom. Attractive setting.

BEAVER LAKE   ALGER COUNTY

Acreage: 765 acres   **page 115 of the DeLorme Atlas**

Location: next to Little Beaver State Forest Campground, just off the coast of Lake Superior, at Pictured Rocks National Lakeshore. Take H15 north from Shingleton, then pick up H-58 which takes you directly there. Or as an alternative, go east out of Munising on H-58.

The good news here is that the lake is gin clear and everyone loves snorkeling it. The bad news is that you can't get there except by going into Little Beaver Lake at the public campsite and snorkeling over to Beaver from there. So it's a bit of a long haul but worth it. The last 8 miles of road coming in is like a washboard, so you have to take it slowly!

FISH LAKE   ALGER COUNTY

Acreage: approx. 75 acres   **page 102 of the DeLorme Atlas**

Location: Just west of H-13, off of Red Jack Lake Road, southwest of Moccasin Lake.

Great visibility, tons of vegetation—you have acres of it underneath you as you snorkel. Fields of elodea, chara, curly pondweed, yellow lilies, broad leafed pondweed, coontail, tall grasses. One side of the lake is lined with tall white birch trees. Very scenic. No cottages. The lake is part of the Hiawatha National Forest. Great public access. Lots of parking. Saw minnows, schools of perch, pumpkinseeds, rock bass, small largemouth bass. Quite shallow—you can go out quite far before it becomes deep.

GRAND SABLE LAKE   ALGER COUNTY

Acreage: 630 acres   **page 115 of the DeLorme Atlas**

Location: on H-58 just west of Grand Marais and just a few feet from Pictured Rocks National Lakeshore.

Good visibility, beautiful surroundings with the Pictured Rocks sand dunes to climb just across the street and Lake Superior beyond. Saw bluegills, largemouth bass, minnows, sunfish.

HOVEY LAKE   ALGER COUNTY

Acreage: 17.20 acres   **page 102 of the DeLorme Atlas**

Location: southwest of Munising, just south of H-94, on the west side of H-09 (Buckhorn Road).

The lake has excellent visibility but is shallow, only about 3 feet deep. Attractive underwater setting with the usual pan fish. It's a spring fed lake in a lovely setting on a bluff. There is a walk of 56 steps down to the lake. Stay at the Timber Lodge Motel.

IRWIN LAKE   ALGER COUNTY

Acreage: 10 acres   **page 102 of the DeLorme Atlas**

Location: on Red Jack Lake Road. Go south off 94 onto H-09 (Buckhorn Road), and take a right onto Red Jack Lake Road. Sign and map say "Wide Waters" but lake is actually called Irwin.

This is located on a Hiawatha National Forest Campground. It's a beautiful small lake surrounded by high pines and hardwoods. You feel like you are in the Pacific Northwest. The lake looks dark but there is decent visibility, though slightly red tinged. It gets deep very fast, so you need to snorkel always looking forward toward shore. There's fallen logs, tall grass, schools of minnows and other pan fish.

ISLAND LAKE   ALGER COUNTY

Acreage: 32.5 acres   **page 102 of the DeLorme Atlas**

Location: north on H-13 or south of 94 onto H-09 (Buckhorn Road) Island Lake is just a little west of H-09.

State Forest Campground. Park at the campground and walk down to the lake. It's a great scenic spring-fed lake. No cottages and on a Wednesday in July no one was on the lake except a handful of campers. The water is very clear with water lilies on both sides of the entrance. There's not a lot of vegetation on the bottom except a little chara and short grass. Saw large school of perch. Look up close to the surface and see big schools of bluegills going in and out of the lilies. Hard sandy bottom entrance—very easy to enter. Lake is surrounded by tall pines and hardwoods, typical Upper Peninsula Pacific Northwest feel. Best snorkeling is along the lilies—beyond that it gets too deep.

MOCCASIN LAKE   ALGER COUNTY

Acreage: 77 acre   **page 102 of the DeLorme Atlas**

Location: right on H-13 on the east side of the road.

Go down the wooden steps that lead from the road to the lake. It's a beautiful lake—super clear—rather shallow near the shore but venture out a ways and it's perfect snorkeling. Here, even when it gets deeper, you can still see very well. Very little vegetation—only some scattered pondweed. Go over to the right, and into the bulrushes. By some brushpiles are some big schools of rock bass, bluegills and largemouth bass. The fish were super friendly with one largemouth leaping all the way to the surface right in front of me—he repeated this 5 times—quite amazing, almost like he was showing off for me. Swarms of minnows here. No people—lake was empty.

OTTER LAKE   ALGER COUNTY

Acreage: 65 acres   **page 102 of the DeLorme Atlas**

Location: just a little south of H-94 on H-09 on the east side.

Very clear. Sandy beach. Peat bottom, campground, no cottages—the campground is on one side—the rest of the lake is surrounded by tall pines and hardwoods. Very scenic. Excellent for families—children's playground, volleyball. The only drawback is the shallowness of the lake—it takes more energy to snorkel a shallow lake, and you cannot stand up to rest because the bottom here is soft.

THORNTON LAKE   ALGER COUNTY

Acreage: 29 acres   **page 102 of the DeLorme Atlas**

Location: one half mile north of Moccasin Lake on H-13.

There is a little turnaround where you can park, right next to the road. A scenic lake with very clear water. Very little vegetation and only a few bulrushes. Unspoiled, no cottages, sandy beach, soft bottom so you can't stand up. Schools of perch and small panfish.

WIDE WATERS LAKE   ALGER COUNTY

Acreage: approx. 15 acres   page 102 of the DeLorme Atlas

Location: Go west of Manistique on U.S. 2 to Nahma Junction, then head north on H-13, another one of those gorgeous Forest Highway Roads til you hit Red Jack Lake Road--go left (northwest) on it and Wide Waters Lake will be on your right.

This is part of the Indian River, so there is a slight current. Great snorkeling and very clear water here. Gravel and peat bottom. Big clams, chara, coontail, curly pondweed, wild celery, tons of perch, black striped minnows, rock bass. The drive through the forest from Wading Waters to Fish Lake is breathtaking. No cottages.

BIG LAKE   BARAGA COUNTY

Acreage: 127 acres   page 110 in the DeLorme Atlas

Location: West of Marquette, take Highway 41/28 til it becomes 28 only, then take a right at Plains Road and another right at N. Big Lake Road.

A National Forest Campground, this has an idyllic setting. It's a clear lake with good but not exceptional visibility. Hundreds of small perch greeted me at the entrance. Also saw a number of largemouth bass. The bottom is hard sand covered with chara. Snorkel to the right along the lily pads. The lake is shallow at the entrance and a little ways out, but it's not too shallow to snorkel comfortably.   The lake is narrow enough to snorkel across, and there are some wonderful campsites next to the lake--#13 and #14 have especially attractive views.

ANDRUS LAKE   CHIPPEWA COUNTY

Acreage: 33 acres   page 117 of the DeLorme Atlas

Location: Take Highway 123 north of Tahquamenon Falls--then before reaching Whitefish Point, take a left at Vermillion Road--the lake is on the left side of the road.

The water has decent visibility and offers perch, largemouth bass and bluegills--otherwise not a particularly memorable lake, but it is well worth a stop if you are already in the area visiting Tahquamenon Falls--this makes a nice little sidetrip. The water has a slightly red tinge from the sap of the cedar trees, giving you the feeling of seeing the world through rose colored glasses.

CARIBOU LAKE   CHIPPEWA COUNTY

Acreage: 825 acres   page 107 of the DeLorme Atlas

Location: Take I-75 north of St. Ignace til you hit highway 134, take a right on 134 and a left on highway 48, then a right on N. Caribou Drive to the lake. (4.2 miles off M-48.)

Water is not super clear but definitely good enough to snorkel. Bottom is sandy with chara groundcover, logs, branches and organic material. At the end of the dock is a big log embedded in the bottom--lots of good-sized rock bass and crayfish at the entrance. The lake is scenic with a view across into a pine forest. You don't see the cottages as they are on the same side as you. It's easy to get sidetracked by the wildlife here--I saw many birds, deer, wild turkeys and hatching butterflies.

CLARK LAKE   CHIPPEWA COUNTY

Acreage: 145 acres   page 117 of the DeLorme Atlas

Location: Take I-75 North of St. Ignace, go west on 123, continuing west on 123 at the town of Paradise until arriving at Tahquamenon Falls State Park (Upper Falls). Walk along the path from the highway to Clark Lake.

This is an excellent clear lake with all the usual pan fish--good snorkeling but a little hard to get to--it's about a 3/4 mile walk from Highway 23 in the opposite direction of the Lower Tahquamenon Falls.

HIGHBANKS LAKE   CHIPPEWA COUNTY

Acreage: 18.7 acres   **page 106 of the DeLorme Atlas**

Location: Take I-75 to M-28, go left, pass by the town of Raco and Raco Field--watch for the sign on the right hand side--the lake is just a short distance north of M-28. Follow the dirt road til you get to the big yellow sign that says "Dead End". That is the public access--the lake will be on your left.

This is a clear, beautiful and remote lake with a sandy and grassy bottom. Snorkel along the shore to see bluegills and perch, minnows.

HULBERT LAKE   CHIPPEWA COUNTY

Acreage: approx. 600 acres   **page 105 of the DeLorme Atlas**

Location: Just a little south of M-28 just west of the juncture of M-28 and M-123.

This is a gorgeous lake, maybe the clearest in the U.P. There is a bit of a catch--the lake belongs to Marge's Hulbert Lodge, so I suspect that you would have a better chance of snorkeling it if you booked one of Marge's great dinners or lunches (the food is excellent). Accommodations are attractive and are at this writing $55 double without meals. Individual log cabins overlook the lake You snorkel right in front of the lodge. Head over to a small island of bushes just offshore. On the other side of this island is a dropoff with logs, branches, big largemouth bass--just great. Enter the lake by a lovely wooded entrance way.

It's a real fairyland. I only snorkeled a small part of the lake--I'm anxious to get back and spend at least a day there.

MONACLE LAKE   CHIPPEWA COUNTY

Acreage: 146 acres   page 106 of the DeLorme Atlas

Location: Take I-75 north, cross M-28, continue on, then take a left at 6 mile road which will take you into Brimley. Continue on this road along the shore of Lake Superior past Point Iroquois Lighthouse. The next left will take you to the lake.

This incredibly clear and beautiful lake is situated adjacent to a State Forest Campground in the Hiawatha National Forest, so there are *no* cottages. There were not even any boats on the lake when I was there on July 3. This is one of only a few places where I saw smallmouth bass in shallow water--they usually prefer the colder water. There were big ones here as were the pike. I saw rock bass guarding their eggs. The lake starts shallow, then gets deeper, then gets shallow again. Not a great deal of vegetation. Sandy and rocky bottom. Just great snorkeling. Also saw good sized suckers. Great beaches, a really pristine environment. There was so much here, I barely scratched the surface.

SOLDIER LAKE   CHIPPEWA COUNTY

Acreage: 18.8 acres   page 106 of the DeLorme Atlas

Location: just a little south of M-28, west of Raco and Raco Field, just across the highway from Highbanks Lake.

A tiny lake in a State Forest Campground in Hiawatha National Forest. This is a great lake for beginning snorkelers--visibility was good. Lake had a sandy bottom with grass and logs, perch, minnows, largemouth bass. Go to the water lilies on the left. Park in the last parking lot and walk down the small hill.

WALKER LAKE   CHIPPEWA COUNTY

Acreage: 15.6 acres   page 106 of the DeLorme Atlas

Location: just west of Highbanks and Soldier Lakes, off M-28. Heading west on M-28, take a left at Strongs Corner onto Strongs Road. Walker Lake is next to the road and on your left heading south.

State Forest Campground in Hiawatha National Forest. This is a very clear lake in a gorgeous setting. Few or no boats. Surrounded by pines and total wilderness. Almost no one was there the Fourth of July weekend. Saw thousands of newborn bullhead and hundreds of perch. Lake has a hard, sandy bottom with grass and scattered logs. Scattered short weed beds. Great for beginners, but excellent snorkeling for anyone. It would be logical to combine this lake with Solder, Highbanks and Monacle, due to their proximity. This would make for a great snorkeling weekend.

CAMP SEVEN LAKE   DELTA COUNTY

Acreage: 60 acres   **page 102 of the DeLorme Atlas**

Location: Go west of Manistique on U.S. 2, take a right at H-13, then another right at 442, which will take you to Camp Seven Lake on your left.

This is another outstanding lake, very clear, with a hard sandy and rock bottom, scattered pondweed, grasses, fallen branches and logs. Look for sunfish under the growth at the left hand shore (left side of the pier) There are many bluegill beds here--they were spawning when I was here, and it is quite a sight. Saw several largemouth bass. It's hard to beat these wilderness U.P. lakes.

CHICAGO LAKE   DELTA COUNTY

Acreage: 180 acres   **page 102 of the DeLorme Atlas**

Location: Go west of Manistique on U.S 2, take a right and go north on H-13, go 8 miles, take a right turn on blacktop (442), go 5 miles, take a left, then another immediate left and go 5/10 of a mile to the lake.

This is a very remote lake with no cottages and only a few campers. It's surrounded by high hardwoods in a very scenic setting. Visibility is good in the first 5 feet of water. Go left among the bulrushes and bushes--I saw lots of minnows, a small northern pike, good sized clams, small snails, crayfish. Hard sandy bottom, so you can stand up (always check first, in case conditions have changed).

NORWAY LAKE   DELTA COUNTY

Acreage: 53.4 acres   **page 102 of the DeLorme Atlas**

Location: go west of Manistique on U.S. 2, take a right on 437 (Cooks School Road), go north and take a left at 440, then a right at 2438, go one and a half miles and take a right at the bottom of the hill onto 2717. Then go half a mile to the lake which will be on your left. The lake is 1.8 miles from 440, which is a very scenic and nice-riding road.

This is a beautiful wilderness lake that feels totally untouched. No people were there. Drive to the top of the hill and then walk down. *Don't* drive down, as the turnaround is too difficult. Lake is very clear and spring fed but shallow. It's a spectacular setting, surrounded by many dead trees--no jet skis here! This is a lake where you need to be sure to watch where you came in, as the trees tend to look alike.

LAKE ANTOINE   DICKINSON COUNTY

Acreage: 748 acres   **page 87 of the DeLorme Atlas**

Location: Take U.S. 2 west of Escanaba to the town of Quinnesec, take a right at the road in the center of town, and just outside of town on the left hand side of the road is Lake Antoine.

The lake has excellent visibility with a rock and gravel bottom near shore, which gives way to a brown silt bottom as you go deeper. It's a sloping, bowl shape, fun to snorkel. Some grass, pondweed and watermilfoil, big crayfish, zillions of clams. It's fun to watch the crayfish move backwards. Saw small perch as well as the biggest perch I have ever seen outside of Nichols Lake. Unusual minnows here. Lake is just across the street from the entrance to the north side of big Fumee Lake.

EDEY LAKE

DICKINSON COUNTY

Acreage: 79 acres

Page 99 of the DeLorme Atlas

Location: Take 95 north from Iron Mountain, pass through the town of Channing, take first main road after Sawyer Lake, go left, take the second right which will take you to the lake.

This lake is definitely worth a look, with a beautiful wilderness setting and no cottages. It is a narrow lake with a very short distance across and perfect for snorkeling either around or across. Saw lots of bluegills and perch. Bottom is a combination of chara, big boulders, logs and underwater trees and branches where fish are found. Lake is surrounded by high hardwoods and pines. You can snorkel across to the point. Very scenic setting and a real postcard.

FUMEE LAKE

DICKINSON COUNTY

Acreage: approx 420 acres

page 88 of the DeLorme Atlas

Location: Take U.S. 2 west through Escanaba and on through the town of Norway. Take a right at 396 and follow the signs. The lake will be on your left. Park in the lot and walk to the lake, taking care to note how you came in. Little Fumee is the small lake to your right--big Fumee is the larger body of water to your left.

This lake, along with Little Fumee, has been called by the "Detroit Free Press" "the lake that time forgot." This lake is the only lake in the entire Midwest that has never been fished; therefore, the fish are allowed to grow to their natural size and die of old age. This makes for some pretty big specimens, and I have to say I saw a good number of monster largemouth bass in here. With several of them around me at once I felt slightly intimidated by their size, although they were of course very friendly and harmless. The water is very clear and the setting is beautiful--just lots of wilderness. The water is very shallow--at the deepest part of the lake it is only 15 feet deep--the south side where you enter is only about 3 feet deep. There are a very few tall bulrushes and fallen logs on the edges, and there are loads of smallmouth bass spawning beds. They spawn in early June, and the crowds come out from Norway to see them spawning, which you can easily do while you are standing on shore.

Generally, there are only a few hikers here, since fishermen are not allowed. Another option is to enter on the north side by driving back out to U.S. 2 and heading west through Quinnesec. Take the only right in the middle of town and drive just a short distance where you will see Lake Antoine on your left right next to the road (this is a great lake to snorkel, too!) Park at Lake Antoine and walk across the street (east) and follow the signs--there is an easy path (it goes right by the Indiana Mine on your right--good snorkeling there also) and it is about a half mile walk to get to the north entrance of Big Fumee Lake, which will be on your right. Enter at about the middle of the side of the lake and head straight out where you will find the deepest (15 feet) part of the lake. This is where the fish go in the winter time to survive when the shallow parts freeze over, and this is where you will find the majority of the smallmouth bass which this lake is famous for, although it is also famous for the size of its pumpkinseeds and bluegills as well. Be sure it isn't windy, as you just get thrown around and can't focus on anything. Not much vegetation that I could see--just a few scattered weedbeds over the silty bottom.

NOTE: I found the Hillcrest Motel in Quinnesec to be a good value--about $27-30 with a good family style restaurant, St. Arnauld's Holiday Kitchen across the road. Great barbecue rib sandwiches and big raspberry sundaes with extremely reasonable prices.

LITTLE FUMEE LAKE   DICKINSON COUNTY

Acreage: approx. 25 acres   page 88 of the DeLorme Atlas

Location: See Fumee Lake above

This is the first lake you come to after you leave the parking lot (see Fumee Lake for more arrival details.) This lake has all the vegetation that the big Fumee Lake does not have. It is small, intimate and very inviting. Visibility is excellent. Big rocks along the shore, white sand bottom, sometimes white silt. Big weed beds in the center with pondweed, watermilfoil, grass and coontail. Lots of spawning beds in the shallow areas. It takes about 2 hours to explore the entire lake.

Lots of pumpkinseeds, bluegills, smallmouth and largemouth bass. Center is divided into many pits, each black, each containing flat sticks, possibly spawning beds. When it is a windy, choppy day in Big Fumee, it is still tranquil in the more sheltered Little Fumee.

HAMILTON LAKE   DICKINSON COUNTY

Acreage: 75 acres   **page 88 of the DeLorme Atlas**

Location: Take U.S. 2 west of Escanaba through the town of Waucedah. Take the second left outside of Waucedah, which takes you to the lake.

A great variety of vegetation here, jungly in feeling. Go only to the left of the boat launch--to the right it gets too deep too fast. Big clumps of pondweed near shore on the right contain a variety of panfish, perch, largemouth bass, sunfish, bluegills. Excellent visibility.

HANBURY LAKE   DICKINSON COUNTY

Acreage: 89 acres   **page 88 of the DeLorme Atlas**

Location: Take U.S. 2 west of Escanaba and just west of the town of Vulcan on the left hand side is Hanbury Lake. (just east of Norway).

East entrance (though the map shows none). Tall northern watermilfoil, lilies, coontail, large beds of chara, tall tufts of grass, excellent visibility. Largemouth bass, perch, bluegill, school of long-ear sunfish greeted me. Excellent visibility once you get away from the launch ramp. Quite deep. Not sloping, but flat. Lots of scenery in the vegetation, made interesting by the variety as well as the varying heights. Lots of area to roam in. Very remote, no boats or cottages. Big expanses of white sand and gravel in the deeper areas. Two varieties of minnows. Lake does not look that inviting from the outside, but it is actually excellent.

INDIANA MINE   DICKINSON COUNTY

Acreage: approx 5 acres   **page 88 of the DeLorme Atlas**

Location: across the street from Lake Antoine, on the path to the north entrance of Big Fumee Lake. Along the path to big Fumee, the first body of water you will see is the Indiana Mine on your right.

It's a small but interesting area, an old abandoned mine--if you snorkel on the north side you will see the remains of the old mine shafts. Huge schools of black striped shiners, pumpkinseeds, bluegills, rock bass, a good sized pike went whipping past me. The mine is long and narrow, so it's easy to snorkel back and forth across it. Water is colder than expected, wonderful visibility, sides are quite steep and sloping with lovely weedbeds. North side has sheer rock slabs--south side contains sloping weed beds. East end contains many branches with hiding fish.

MARY LAKE   DICKINSON COUNTY

Acreage: 86 acres   **page 88 of the DeLorme Atlas**

Location: Take U.S. 2 west through Escanaba to the town of Loretto. Go south on the main road out of Loretto and the lake will be on your right.

This is a great lake in every way. Excellent visibility, very clean. Go to the left of the boat launch to get to the vast weed beds. Flat watermilfoil in big areas but also tall aquatic plants, coontail, water lilies, tall pondweed. Lots of largemouth bass, lovely schools of good sized perch, crayfish, snails, lots of clams, striped shiners.

SAWYER LAKE   DICKINSON COUNTY

Acreage: 241 acres   **page 99 of the DeLorme Atlas**

Location: Take 95 north out of Iron Mountain. Shortly after passing through the town of Channing, Sawyer Lake will be on your left.

This is a lake of good visibility, high weeds, very attractive vegetation. A large variety of panfish, including sunfish, bluegills, pumpkinseeds, as well as largemouth bass. Beach, cottages, dock, boat launch.

CLARK LAKE   GOGEBIC COUNTY

Acreage: 820 acres   **page 97 of the DeLorme Atlas**

Location: Take U.S. 2 west of Iron River. West of Watersmeet, take a left and go south on Thousand Island Road into the Sylvania Recreation Area to Clark Lake.

State Forest Campground in the Ottawa National Forest. It is run by the U.S. Department of Agriculture, and they do an outstanding job whenever they are in charge, as they are in the National Forests. Great roads, grounds all manicured and mowed. Big, tasteful easy-to-read signs. The lake is crystal clear and clean feeling. Popular with canoeists.

Come during the week if you can, as it is a busy popular lake. In the water, go either left or right--good snorkeling in either direction. The lake is bowl shaped and you can see well even in the deeper areas. Bottom is hard sand and boulders, with fallen limbs and logs. Black striped minnows, perch, bluegills.

CROOKED LAKE   GOGEBIC COUNTY

Acreage: 565.4 acres   **page 97 of the DeLorme Atlas**

Location: Take U.S.2 west of Iron River. West of Watersmeet, take a left and go south on Thousand Island Road. Crooked Lake will be on your left in the Sylvania Recreation Area.

A fabulous, clear lake with all kinds of vegetation, water lilies, pondweed, coontail, lots of fallen branches and logs, schools of perch, largemouth bass and loads of bluegills. Crooked is part of a series of connected lakes. Loon Lake and High Lakes are also super clear, but you have to walk to them. You can also snorkel over to High Lake from Crooked. This whole area is excellent, a great cluster of clear lakes offering an endless variety of scenic underwater views.

LAKE GOGEBIC   GOGEBIC COUNTY

Acreage: 12,800 acres   **page 96 of the DeLorme Atlas**

Location: Take U.S. 2 west of Watersmeet and go north on either 64 or 525 to go to the west or east sides of the lake.

This is a mammoth lake, cold and super clear, with several different entry points. I entered at Lake Gogebic State Park, an excellent area for families as there is a playground and park with something for everyone to do. As in all large lakes, it takes time to get out and find anything, because of the size, but the clarity and all the usual pan fish are here. To stay in any great length of time would mean wearing something heavier than a bathing suit (see "what to wear" section).

IMP LAKE   GOGEBIC COUNTY

Acreage: 84 acres   **page 97 of the DeLorme Atlas**

Location: Go west of Iron River on U.S.2 just after Forest Highway 109. Take the next left into Imp Lake.

This is an outstanding snorkeling lake--super clear in all directions. It's part of a State Forest Campground in the Ottawa National Forest. Hard, sandy bottom with stones, rocks, and grass. Not a lot of vegetation--mostly grass and chara. Go either left or right and snorkel among the logs and branches. Lots of perch, largemouth bass and bluegills in among the branches. Nice bowl shape. Picturesque small island a very short distance from shore that is easy to snorkel to. You can go all around the lake and spend endless pleasurable time here. Great therapy!

MARION LAKE   GOGEBIC COUNTY

Acreage: 318 acres   **page 97 of the DeLorme Atlas**

Location: Take U.S. 2 west of Iron River, and go north on Marion Lake Road (before Watersmeet). The lake will be on your right. Lake is 1.7 miles north of U. S. 2.

A State Forest Campground in the Ottawa National Forest. This is total wilderness! A pine and birch surrounded lake. You snorkel in one arm or inlet of the lake--it feels very private and secluded. The setting is really out of this world. Go left among the water lilies to see the perch and the gill beds. Visibility is average--good enough to see whatever is there. Lots of rocks and sand at the entrance--soft grassy bottom beyond. A few branches and logs. Fairly shallow but enough depth to snorkel comfortably.

MOON LAKE   GOGEBIC COUNTY

Acreage: 93 acres   **page 97 of the DeLorme Atlas**

Location: Go west on U.S. 2 and in Watersmeeet, take 45 south, go west on Moon Lake road and the lake is on your left 6 miles east of Watersmeet.

Moon Lake provides a great snorkeling experience. Snorkel in the little bay, then go on into the main part of the lake. It's very clean and perfect for beginners, as you can snorkel across the bay and see bottom all the way. It's very scenic, surrounded by pines and hardwoods, with a picnic table on top overlooking the lake. At the end of the ramp I counted 40 good sized largemouth and rock bass suspended there. You can also see good sized largemouth bass as well as juveniles scattered throughout the bay. The bottom is hard--grass, boulders and sunken logs. Water lilies to the left. Excellent and worth a full day of your time.

MOOSEHEAD LAKE   GOGEBIC COUNTY

Acreage: 54 acres   **page 96 of the DeLorme Atlas**

Location: Take U.S. 2 west of Watersmeet and go south on county road 527. Continue south on S. Thayer Road, then go west on Langford Lake Road, then go south on County Road 525 (Forest Highway 118--you won't believe how beautiful these forest highway roads are!) Pomeroy Lake Road will be on your right--go past that and your next left (south) will take you to the lake.

This looks more like a Lower Peninsula lake due to the greater amount of vegetation here.

The lake is not super clear but still has good visibility. It is a State Forest Campground in the Ottawa National Forest. There are lovely campsites up on the bluff overlooking the lake. Surrounded by hardwoods, the lake is long and narrow, so it is intimate to snorkel as you can cross it so easily. Go either left or right--the scenery is similar. Lots of chara, elodea, pondweed, water lilies, tall grasses. There's a fascinating little inlet to snorkel on the opposite side of the lake. Fish are here in quantity as soon as you enter the lake. Large bluegills and pumpkinseeds, rock bass, clams, black-striped minnows. The gill beds are near shore on either side. There is a dropoff at the end of the boat landing but you can still see well. Would have liked to have stayed much longer, as it was such an esthetically appealing underwater landscape.

SNAP JACK ALONG LAKE   GOGEBIC COUNTY

Acreage: 59 acres   **page 97 of the DeLorme Atlas**

.Location: Take U.S. 2 west of Watersmeet, go south on Thousand Island Road, pass Clark Lake on your left, and take a right before getting to Long Lake. This right turn will dead end into Snap Jack Along Lake. 4 miles south of U.S. 2.

Part of the Sylvania Recreation Area. A wilderness lake with no cottages, surrounded by pines and hardwoods. A popular hangout for loons. You start out in a neat little bay, then snorkel out to the main part of the lake. Good visibility, good bowl shape, sparse vegetation, grassy bottom, water lilies, tall grasses. Many deep gill spawning beds on the right. Saw schools of perch, bluegills on the left among the fallen branches.

THOUSAND ISLAND LAKE   GOGEBIC COUNTY

Acreage: 1020 acres   **page 97 of the DeLorme Atlas**

Location: Take U.S. 2 west of Watersmeet, go south on Thousand Island Road (County Road 535). Stay on this road all the way to the lake, which will be on your right.

Good visibility, a fairly busy lake--go either right or left of the dock and see fallen logs and branches; the scattered tree trunks combine to make an interesting underwater landscape. Saw crayfish and schools of gill and perch.

CLEAR LAKE   **HOUGHTON COUNTY**

Acreage: 24.8 acres   **page 110 of the DeLorme Atlas**

Location: Take M-38 west of Baraga to M-26, then head north--at the tiny town of Winona, head south--there will then be a right hand turn into Clear Lake. Located in the Copper Country State Forest.

And clear it is--super clear, a real fairyland, as good as its name. I have never been in a Clear Lake that wasn't. This has a picturesque, peaceful setting. Go left or right into a landscape of sunken logs and branches. Hundreds of fish were around me within a few minutes, pumpkinseeds, shad, large black-striped minnows, bluegills, on both sides. Don't forget to look in front of you close to the surface--in this lake there were a great many fish close to the surface. Because of the bowl shape, you can look along one side and see way down into the lake, at the same time looking the other way and seeing all the shore fish. The way the logs and branches are positioned in the water is very artistic and esthetically pleasing. Little or no vegetation here. Although this is not a heart pounding lake for excitement, it is incredibly therapeutic to snorkel through a paradise like this.

LAKE ROLAND   **HOUGHTON COUNTY**

Acreage: 292 acres   **page 110 of the DeLorme Atlas**

Location: Take M-38 west of Baraga to M-26, then head north to Twin Lakes State Park. Lake Roland will be on your right.

A lovely, clear lake. Somewhat busy in summer, but the boats stay out in the middle, and snorkeling closer to shore is not a problem. Sandy beach, hard sand bottom, tall weeds sparsely scattered among low grasses. Plenty of perch and bass and bluegills over their spawning beds (in season). In front of the brown A-frame house there are pilings and a sunken boat. Lots of logs and sunken concrete bricks.

CHICAGON LAKE   IRON COUNTY

Acreage: 1100 acres   **page 98 of the DeLorme Atlas**

Location: Take U.S. 2 north of Iron Mountain, go through Crystal Falls--then take 639 south and the lake will be on your right. The drive in is very scenic (it is even so marked)--5 picturesque miles through a canopy of birches to a dead end. Take a right to Pentoga Park and enter there.

This is a big commercial lake that has had big newspaper publicity because of all the big fish caught here. Thus it is very popular with fishermen as well as pleasure boaters, who like it for its large size. There is a pavilion for picnics, a huge grassy area, and picnic tables. There is an entrance fee of $2 per adult, $.50 for seniors. Best snorkeling is on either side of the swimming area. The water is very clear, and there are loads of fish, including largemouth bass, perch, bluegills, muskies, all the usual panfish, plus many tiny clams. The bottom is littered with dead and live crayfish, large ones. Keep near the shore among the branches and logs. You can also go to the public access site, just a little south. But it's shallow here, so you need to head out further. If you use this area, you should come during the week when it is not as crowded, since when you get out further, you run the risk of interference by boats.

LAKE ELLEN   IRON COUNTY

Acreage: 144 acres   **page 99 of the DeLorme Atlas**

Location: Take U.S. 2 west to Iron Mountain, then go north on 95 into the town of Channing. At Channing, take a left, and this road dead ends into Lake Ellen. The lake is 4.4 miles from M-95.

This is marked on the map as a State Forest Campground, but the campground is closed. This is an excellent lake with good visibility. It's a complete wilderness setting surrounded by thick hardwood trees, ferns and the occasional pine. This is a spring-fed lake with very clear water--90 feet deep in the parts with lake trout. I saw bluegills, largemouth bass and perch pretty much everywhere.

The lake slopes gently; you will snorkel over boulders, fallen white birches, big logs and branches, fields of chara and wild celery. The bottom is hard sand and gravel. It's a beautiful drive in through white birches.

FIRE LAKE   IRON COUNTY

Acreage:128 acres   **page 99 of the DeLorme Atlas**

Location: Take U.S. 2 to just west of Crystal Falls, then go north on 141, then head south on 643, taking your first left into Fire Lake.

Hallelujah--this lake does not allow jet skis or power boats. It is a slow, what is known as a no wake lake. It is a very clear lake, just the right depth and shape for good snorkeling. It has a hard rocky/sandy bottom sprinkled with big logs and branches. A gorgeous wilderness setting, intimate and secluded, surrounded by high hardwoods. Beautiful winding pines surround the entrance. Plenty of the usual pan fish. Only drawback is that the lake is cold, so dress accordingly.

FORTUNE LAKE   IRON COUNTY

Acreage: 199 acres   **page 99 of the DeLorme Atlas**

Location: Take U.S. 2 to Crystal Falls; the lake is just west of Crystal Falls on the left hand side of U.S. 2 in Bewabic State Park.

This is an attractive setting with picnic areas. A little busy so try to come during the week, if possible, as it is popular with jet skiers. The lake is clear--go to the right and snorkel near shore among the fallen logs and branches.The bottom is hard rock and sand. Lots of panfish among the pondweed, as well as crayfish.

GOLDEN LAKE   IRON COUNTY

Acreage: 285 acres   **page 98 of the DeLorme Atlas**

Location: Take U.S. 2 west of Iron River and go north on Forest Highway 16 after the town of Beechwood.

This is a State Forest Campground in the Ottawa National Forest. It's a long narrow lake surrounded by hardwoods and pines. A super clear lake in all directions, a place where it is worth spending a lot of time. The bottom is stony with big boulders, sunken logs and huge tree trunks. Saw a school of 11 good sized largemouth bass. There were many perch hanging out at the edge of the entry boat ramp. Not much vegetation--just scattered grass.

HAGERMAN LAKE   IRON COUNTY

Acreage: 584 acres   **page 98 of the DeLorme Atlas**

Location: Take U.S. 2 to Iron River, then south on 73--take a right turn and go past Little Hagerman Lake--the public access for Hagerman Lake will be on your right.

This is an excellent and super clear lake in the Ottawa National Forest. A vast expanse of stones, sand and crayfish in every direction. Look for the big bass at the end of the DNR ramp. Shallow until you get out a ways. Hard sandy bottom.

INDIAN LAKE   IRON COUNTY

Acreage: 85 acres   **page 99 of the DeLorme Atlas**

Location: Take U.S. 2 through Iron Mountain. At the town of Panola, south of Crystal Falls, go west on 424 through the town of Alpha, and the public access for Indian Lake will be on the right hand side of the road.

The lake has good visibility, not outstanding but as good as it needs to be. Sparse vegetation consisting mostly of pondweed and wild celery. Snorkel to the left where there is an underwater white pipe that extends out parallel to the end of the DNR dock--lots of fish gather around this area--lots of rock bass, largemouth bass and bluegills. Go right and there is a sizable weed bed off the end of the first dock--pondweed and coontail. Plenty of fish circulating there.

JAMES LAKE   IRON COUNTY

Acreage: 212 acres   **page 98 of the DeLorme Atlas**

Location: Take U.S. 2 west of Iron River, go north on Forest Highway 16 ; take the second left into James Lake.

A beautiful remote lake in a wilderness setting in the Ottawa National Forest. On a Sunday in July I was the only one there. Tens of thousands of frogs had just left the tadpole stage and were swarming through the water--frogs only a fraction of an inch long--an amazing sight. Sandy hard bottom with lots of small stones, logs and sunken trees. There's plenty to explore here. A fairly shallow lake--you can go out quite far before it gets deeper.

LONG LAKE   IRON COUNTY

Acreage: 60 acres   **page 99 of the DeLorme Atlas**

Location: Take U.S. 2 to Crystal Falls, --continue on past Bewabic State Park, take the next right (north) which will take you to Long Lake. 2 and a quarter miles north of U.S. 2.

A great slow "no wake" lake--a marvelous clear lake, bowl shaped in a beautiful wilderness setting surrounded by white birches. Few or no people, only a few cottages. Just the right depth to snorkel. Head right among the fallen birch trees, logs and birch trunks. I saw tons of rock bass here and lots of big bluegill, as well as schools of small perch. This is a great lake--I would like to have stayed much longer. It is especially distinguished by the white birches everywhere. It's a lovely drive in through a canopy of hardwoods.

NESBIT LAKE   IRON COUNTY

Acreage: 35 acres   **page 98 of the DeLorme Atlas**

Location: Take M-28 west of Marquette; in the little town of Sidnaw, head south on Sidnaw South Road, go left (east) on Norway Lake Road, which will take you to the lake.

An intimate little lake in the wilderness surrounded by high pines. Very secluded. Clear water, sandy beach and roped off swimming area. Both to the right and left of the swim area are many water lilies, sunken logs, many bluegill beds which on July 14 still had jumbo breeding males guarding their eggs. Snorkeling here is a beautiful wilderness tranquil experience. Wood cabins for rent overlooking the lake.

NORWAY LAKE   IRON COUNTY

Acreage: 53 acres   **page 98 of the DeLorme Atlas**

Location: Take M-28 west of Marquette; in the little town of Sidnaw, head south on Sidnaw South Road. Continue past Nesbit Lake to Norway Lake, only a quarter of a mile from Nesbit Lake.

A State Forest National Campground in the Ottawa National Forest. A beautiful paved road through the wilderness leads you there. A secluded, intimate and inviting lake surrounded by high pines. This is a very clear lake with a hard grassy bottom--you feel like you are snorkeling over a sunken golf course. On both sides are water lilies, bulrushes and largemouth bass, perch and bluegills. This is the perfect wilderness lake, both above and below, a lake that is worth spending a day in.

LAKE OTTAWA   IRON COUNTY

Acreage: 551 acres   **page 98 of the DeLorme Atlas**

Location: Take U.S. 2 west to Iron River. Just west of Iron River, go south on 73 and take the first right (west) on Forest Highway 101. Go 4 miles and Lake Ottawa will be on your right hand side.

A drop-dead drive through the Ottawa National Forest takes you to Lake Ottawa. This is a wilderness lake surrounded by towering white birch and other hardwoods. The lake is very remote feeling and there are no cottages. There's a great hiking trail from the boat landing. This is a fabulously clear lake--you can see well in all directions. Stony and sandy hard bottom. The crayfish were everywhere you look with their bright blue and orange colors. Come on a sunny day if possible, as the crayfish will then go under the logs.

SUNSET LAKE   IRON COUNTY

Acreage: 545 acres   **page 98 of the DeLorme Atlas**

Location: Take U.S. 2 west of Crystal Falls. After the town of Mapleton and before reaching Iron River, go north on 651 which will take you directly to the lake.

It's a gorgeous drive in to the lake, with tall, slender birches forming a canopy overhead. Visibility is very good. Hard sandy bottom with some organic matter. Lots of snorkeling area here--you can go way out, as it's only a few feet deep for a long way. Lots of perch, bluegills and black striped minnows. Big clams, loads of huge crayfish. Saw several big ones climbing up the bulrushes on the left side of the entrance--a real sight to see. The Bates Campground is on a bluff overlooking the lake.

SWAN LAKE   IRON COUNTY

Acreage: 165 acres   **page 99 of the DeLorme Atlas**

Location: Take U.S. 2 to Crystal Falls, then go north on 141--watch the signs and take a left (south) --lake is very close to 141.

A slow "no wake" lake--no jet skis or power boats. Great wide access, very picturesque setting, a wonderful wilderness feeling--only a few barely seen cottages. A very clear lake with a rocky bottom, branches and organic matter. Go either right or left--on the right is a sunken pine tree with fish and crayfish scurrying around. You can go way out and still see bottom clearly. Lots to explore here. Lake is famous for its walleyes.

TEPEE LAKE   IRON COUNTY

Acreage: 115 acres   **page 98 of the DeLorme Atlas**

Location: Take U.S. 2 past Iron River. After the town of Beechwood, go north on Forest Highway 16 then go east on Highway 143--the lake will be on your right.

A State Forest Campground in the Ottawa National Forest.

The road in is a beautiful paved highway lined with thousands of white daisies. Clarity of the lake is good and the bottom is rocks and sand. Saw little vegetation, mostly grass, lilies on both right and left hand side. Big boulders, fallen logs, largemouth bass and panfish. Lake is a little colder than others.

BASS LAKE   **LUCE COUNTY**

Acreage: 145 acres   page 104 of the DeLorme Atlas

Location: Take M-28 west to McMillan--go north out of McMillan on 415, then west on 421 which will place Bass Lake on your left. It's 9 miles from M-28 to the lake.

State Forest Campground in Lake Superior State Forest. This is simply awesome--a snorkeler's paradise. Crystal clear water, and no matter how far out you go, it seems like you can always see bottom. I saw big largemouth bass, schools of black striped minnows, bluegills, perch, pumpkinseeds. Saw a turtle sunning himself on a log in the water. Snorkel along the shore which is loaded with tree stumps, logs, branches. I could have stayed at least a day here. At first it looks rather empty--you have to stick around for awhile before the action starts.The lake is not deep and has a hard sandy bottom. No cottages as the land is part of the State Forest. It's complete wilderness--no power boaters here--just fishermen and canoeists. It's really hard to leave. The drive in is of incredible beauty.

BODI LAKE   **LUCE COUNTY**

Acreage: 306 acres   page 117 in the DeLorme Atlas

Location: Take I-75 north, then west on M-28, then at Eckerman Corner go north on 123, then when 123 turns east, take 500 north , pass Culhane Lake on the right, then take 437 east to Bodi Lake.

This is a clear lake with lots of clams, schools of panfish in the bulrushes to the right. A lovely setting. Hard sandy bottom with scattered rocks.

CULHANE LAKE   LUCE COUNTY

Acreage: 97.5 acres   **page 117 in the DeLorme Atlas**

Location: Take I-75 north, then west on M-28, then at Eckerman Corner go north on 123, then when 123 turns east, take 500 north and Culhane Lake will be on your right.

Lake is part of State Campgrounds. Clear lake with a slightly red tint. Picturesque surroundings. The lake is flat in the snorkeling area, with a hard sandy bottom. Minnows, clams, and the usual pan fish.

OLD HEADQUARTERS LAKE   LUCE COUNTY

Acreage: 9.3 acres   **page 116 of the DeLorme Atlas**

Location: Take M-28 west to Roberts Corners, then north on 123 to Newberry, west at Fourmile Corner onto H-37--the lake is on the left hand side just before Perch Lake.

This is a clear lake with bluegills, the usual panfish, but unfortunately a somewhat difficult entry. Not a place to spend a lot of time, but if you're on your way to Perch Lake, this is worth a short stop.

HOLLAND LAKE   LUCE COUNTY

Acreage: 5.19 acres   **page 116 of the DeLorme Atlas**

Location: Take M-28 west to Roberts Corners, then north on 123 to Newberry, west at Fourmile Corner onto H-37, then west at 416--Holland Lake will come up on your right.

This is a lake known for its trophy brook trout, though special bait rules apply. Enter from the parking lot. A bowl shaped lake with a hard sandy bottom, sparse weed beds. It's July 5 and I'm the only one here. Sand darters, minnows, the usual pan fish. A tiny, picturesque lake--feels like your own private one.

LITTLE LAKE   LUCE COUNTY

Acreage: approx. 78 acres   page 117 of the DeLorme Atlas

Location: Take I-75 north, then go west on M-28, then at Eckerman Corner turn north on 123, then when 123 turns east, take 500 north and Little Lake will be on your left. It is 12 miles from the time you get on 500 til you arrive at the lake.

County road 500 is a good wide scenic road. Little Lake runs into Lake Superior, so it was not surprising that it was just about as cold. It's a "safe harbor" where Great Lakes boaters can gas up and take safe haven from storms. Here I saw two "necturus maculosus" also called mud puppies, which look like large salamander. Though the lake is very clear, it is very cold and deep, so I suggest coming in August when it has warmed up. The place was deserted the Fourth of July weekend. Bottom is hard and sandy, with vegetation consisting mostly of elodea and curly pondweed. Well worth a visit.

PERCH LAKE   LUCE COUNTY

Acreage: 125.7 acres   page 116 of the DeLorme Atlas

Location: Take M-28 west to Roberts Corners, then north on 123 to Newberry, then west at Fourmile Corner on H-37--pass Old Headquarters Lake on your left, and Perch Lake will be up the road on the right hand side.

State Forest Campground in Lake Superior State Forest. A great lake for snorkeling--good visibility. Lake is flat by the shore with a sandy hard bottom. Must have seen at least 200 perch by the campground lake entrance, slightly to the left of shore. Also rock bass and pumpkinseeds, and by the boat entrance pike and splake. Then head to the right, down to the branches lying above the water, and some below--here I saw dozens more of rock bass and pumpkinseeds. Also here are pondweed, bulrushes and gill spawning beds to the right of the campground beach entrance. I saw striped darters by the boat landing, as well as many large clams.

PIKE LAKE   LUCE COUNTY

Acreage 292 acres   **page 117 of the DeLorme Atlas**

Location: Take M-28 west to Roberts Corners, then north on 123 to Newberry, then when 123 heads east, go north on 500, watching for the Pike Lake sign, at which point you will turn left (west), and this road will take you to the lake.

It's a beautiful drive in to this State Forest Campground in Lake Superior State Forest. It's a clear flat lake with a sandy bottom. There were perch, panfish and minnows, and pike. Watermilfoil was flattened on the bottom, along with logs and branches.

PRETTY LAKE   LUCE COUNTY

Acreage: 47 acres   **page 116 of the DeLorme Atlas**

Location: Take M-28 west to Roberts Corner, then go north on 123 to Newberry, then at Fourmile Corner, take H-37 north to 416. Here you take a left (west) and watch for the sign for Pretty Lake, which will be on your left.

This is just what it says, a pretty lake and crystal clear--you can see a dime 20 feet down. It is what is known as an oligotrophic lake, that is one that is very clear with little or no vegetation, much like Clear Lake and Avalon Lake in Montmorency County. Go in at the attractive picnic area. Lovely sandy beach. Hard sandy bottom, bowl shaped, many schools of perch, many tadpoles. Very little structure here. Delightful snorkeling experience.

ROUND LAKE   LUCE COUNTY
(also known as N. Manistique)

Acreage: 1722 acres   **page 104 of the DeLorme Atlas**

Location: Take U.S. 2 from St.Ignace through Naubinway, then go north on H-33. Round Lake or N. Manistique Lake will be on your left on County Road 417. It is also 11 miles east of Germfask.

Located in Luce County Park, this is a big commercial lake--there's a big area to snorkel in protected by buoys. Clear water, sandy bottom, scattered cottages. Shallow water, without structure near the shore, so not too many fish for snorkelers to see. You have to be willing to commit some time here to be rewarded.

TWIN LAKES   **LUCE COUNTY**

Acreage: 103 acres   **page 104 of the DeLorme Atlas**

Location: Take M-28 west to Roberts Corner, and instead of going north to Newberry, keep going on U.S. 2 and on the left hand side of the road is Twin Lakes.

This is a great lake with good visibility--go either left or right into schools of shad and perch, big pumpkinseeds and bluegills--other visitors here spoke of trout and splake. Two snorkelers near me had just seen pike. Vegetation consisted mostly of chara, pondweed, grasses and lilies.

BAY CITY LAKE   **MACKINAC COUNTY**

Acreage: 24.8 acres   **page 107 of the DeLorme Atlas**

Location: Go north on I-75 from St. Ignace, then east on 134, in Hessel, go north on 3 mile road, then west on Bay City Lake Road. This is a stony road with no marker--it is the first road after the Hessel Airport--the lake is about one mile in.

This is a small lake in complete wilderness--there wasn't a soul when I was there on a hot sunny July day. The lake is as crystal as the water in Cayman--fabulous clarity. Hundreds of baby tadpoles were swimming near shore. The lake is shallow for quite a ways out, perfect for snorkeling or swimming, with a sandy beach. Bluegill beds are to the left in among the cattails and pondweed. There is also a sunken boat to the right in about 12 feet of water. The lake felt so clean, and the bottom was carpeted with chara. The lake has a beautiful setting among lovely wildflowers. Daisies and Indian Paintbrush were on both sides of the entryway and two blue heron, as well as a variety of big butterflies greeted me on my arrival. Traveling along 134 offered breathtaking views of Lake Huron--it's a beautiful paved wilderness road.

S. MANISTIQUE LAKE   MACKINAC COUNTY

Acreage: 4001 acres   **page 104 of the DeLorme Atlas**

Location: Take U.S. 2 heading west, then north on H-33 will take you right into the attractive town of Curtis , with some interesting sporting goods stores and attractive local shops. The lake is right in the middle of town.

There are 3 places to enter the lake, plus the one at the campground. I felt this lake was very worthwhile if you have the time. Because of its size, you will need to stay in a while and roam around before you start seeing much. I entered into the lake in town, just west of the Shipwreck Bar. There is good clarity, a sandy beach, and if you stay in long enough, you will see the usual panfish, and maybe some surprises—as there are almost always surprises if you stay in long enough!

NOTE: Be sure while you are in Curtis, to go over to the Whitetail's restaurant--behind the restaurant about 200 yards is a bald eagle's nest. There are or were 2 adults and a baby there and they are easy to see, but do take binoculars for a better look.

MILAKOKIA LAKE   MACKINAC COUNTY

Acreage: 1956 acres   **page 104 of the DeLorme Atlas**

Location: Take U.S. 2 from St. Ignace, and Milakokia Lake is on the south side of the road right after you pass the intersection of H-33.

Good wide public access. Much like Lake McDonald in shoreline and sand and gravel bottom. Only a few cottages. Lake is quite shallow--I went out very far but it never got deep, so there's lots of room to roam. A clean and flat lake--no sloping sides.

MILLECOQUINS LAKE

MACKINAC COUNTY

Acreage: 1062 acres   **page 104 of the DeLorme Atlas**

Location: Take U.S. 2 from St. Ignace to Naubinway; in Naubinway, head north on Naubinway Road, then go west on Hiawatha Trail –Millecoquins Lake will be on the immediate right hand side of the road.

This is a clear lake--the visibility is excellent. Bottom is lovely sand, and it is solid--no muck. Saw crayfish, walleye, perch and people were catching pike. Bottom is littered with clams, some very large. Also saw large crayfish. The only disadvantage of this lake is that there is no weed structure near shore, so you have to go out quite far to get to the weed beds, which are then very thick and interesting. By the time you are out that far, you could have boat traffic, depending on how busy it is. So your enjoyment may well depend on how much traffic there is. Of course go during the week if possible.

BASS LAKE

MARQUETTE COUNTY

Acreage: 217 acres   **page 101 of the DeLorme Atlas**

Location: Take U.S. 2 to Rapid River, then go north on 41, with a left at 428 which becomes 35 heading north. After the town of Little Lake, there will be a propane gas tank on the north side of the road. Turn south on the road opposite the propane tank, and that road will take you to Bass Lake. Follow the signs.

This is a very secluded lake with easy access, plenty of parking, just a few cottages. There is a beautiful wilderness road leading in surrounded by tall hardwoods. Good visibility. This is well worth a look if you're in the area visiting Johnson Lake. Go straight out and slightly to the right of the boat ramp. Just off the ramp is a weed bed of brown curly pondweed containing many good sized perch. Fun and attractive to see. The lake stays shallow quite a ways out--locals say there are big muskies in here. Fallen logs and brush, hard sandy bottom. A little island in the middle of the lake that is fun to snorkel to.

BASS LAKE   MARQUETTE COUNTY

Acreage: 77 acres   **page 100 of the DeLorme Atlas**

Location: Take U.S. 2 west from Manistique to Rapid River, go north on 41, then west on 428 which becomes 35 heading north. Keep on 35 through the town of Gwinn. Outside of Gwinn, when 35 turns straight north, take Charlie Lakes Road south. Take the first road left, which will take you first to Pike Lake, followed by Bass Lake. It's a great paved road and is 2 miles beyond Pike Lake.

State Forest Campground in the Escanaba River State Forest. I was here on a dark, rainy day and underwater I could still see perfectly. At first it didn't look like it was going to be that clear but after about a minute my eyes adjusted and everything was not only clear it was actually bright. The bottom consists of sand and organic matter, fallen leaves, etc. Not much vegetation--just scattered chara and pondweed. There are two boat entrances--snorkel between the two as there is some weed structure there--saw good sized perch and largemouth bass. Then go to the right fairly near shore where there are many fallen logs and branches that contain hundreds of bluegills, schools of shad and perch. Excellent experience.

BIG TROUT LAKE   MARQUETTE COUNTY

Acreage: 26.7 acres   **page 101 of the DeLorme Atlas**

Location: Take U.S. 2 west through Gladstone, then north on 41, then west on 460. You will go south (a left hand turn and the first dirt road--there's no sign-- east of Sawyer Air Force Base) to Big Trout Lake.

Lots of parking and a few cottages, but it's still very unspoiled. The clarity is excellent. It's like snorkeling through a ghost forest--tons of brushpiles, big trees sprawled in every direction. Bottom is hard so you can stand up. When you snorkel into the deeper areas you can still easily see bottom. Very interesting.

HORSESHOE LAKE   MARQUETTE COUNTY

Acreage: 123 acres   **page 99 of the DeLorme Atlas**

Location: Go west on U.S. 2 to Iron Mountain, then north on 95, then go west on the road just before Witch Lake. Hoeseshoe Lake will be on your right. There's a good paved road to the entrance-- then a good dirt road beyond which will take you to the lake.

State Forest Campground in the Copper Country State Forest. Lake is surrounded by tall hardwoods in a great wilderness setting. Beautiful campsites on a bluff overlooking the water. Bottom is organic, lots of leaves, fallen logs, trees and branches. Sloping sides, so it is easy to snorkel. Rocks and gravel at the entrance. Average visibility, but more than worth a look if you are in the area visiting Squaw and Twin Lakes. Crayfish, schools of small and larger perch, schools of bluegills, largemouth bass.

ISLAND LAKE   MARQUETTE COUNTY

Acreage: 45.5 acres   **page 99 of the DeLorme Atlas**

Location: Take U.S. 2 west to Iron Mountain, then north on 95 just before Witch Lake. Take a left (west) and Island Lake will be on your left.

This does not have a regular public access, but there is a place for 3 or 4 cars to pull off to the side of the road and enter the lake from the side of the road. This lake is worth a look while you are in the area visiting Squaw and Twin Lakes, although it is not quite as clear as the others. Still very acceptable, with many fallen trees, logs, pondweed, clams, crayfish and good sized perch. Daisies and irises were blooming at the entrance to this attractive lake.

JOHNSON LAKE   MARQUETTE COUNTY

Acreage: 78 acres   **page 101 of the DeLorme Atlas**

Location: Take U.S. 2 to Rapid River, then north on 41, taking the next left on 428 which becomes 35 heading north into the town of New Swanzy; then take 553 south and the second right hand turn will take you to Johnson Lake.

There is marvelous clarity here, and the lake has gently sloping sides, perfect for snorkeling. The bottom is an attractive array of pondweed, chara and wild celery on an organic bottom. Lots of branches, logs and pine needles. I was in the water only a short time when I saw a snapping turtle, big enough to ride on, coming up for air. Almost immediately after, just to the left of the DNR dock, I saw a large pike--he looked for all the world like an alligator, stretched out on the bottom. I visited the lake several times at different hours of the day, and the pike was always there, moving only slightly, stationed right in front of a row of weeds. Good sized largemouth bass. I didn't begin to scratch the surface of what was here. There are a few cottages, but it is not busy--instead very tranquil. There's easy access and plenty of parking.

LITTLE LAKE   MARQUETTE COUNTY

Acreage: 448 acres   **page 101 of the DeLorme Atlas**

Location: Take U.S. 2 west to Rapid River, then north on 41, west on 428 which becomes 35 heading north. Go into the town of Little Lake and, heading east, take a right after the American Legion Building to the lake.

State Forest Campground in the Escanaba River State Forest. There's a nice little island to snorkel to, quite near shore. I was there in the pouring rain, and even under those conditions the lake was very clear. There is no structure near shore, so you need to spend a little more time here to cover more territory. Bottom is sometimes sandy, sometimes mucky, so check with your hand before standing up.

PERCH LAKE   MARQUETTE COUNTY

Acreage: 46.5 acres   **page 100 of the DeLorme Atlas**

Location: Go west on 28 from Ishpeming, going south on 95 to the town of Republic. Just east of town, the lake will be on your left hand side.

This is a big yes. Float over an underwater forest in Perch Lake. Very wide entrance in a picturesque setting with no cottages. This is a long narrow lake surrounded by tall hardwoods--totally isolated. Very good clarity. The bottom is gravel with huge boulders, rocks and organic material. Both right and left are many fallen trees, logs, branches in many twisted shapes--just a fascinating landscape. Several largemouth bass and perch greeted me at the entrance. Snorkel along the rocky slope for best results. Large spawning area here.

BIG SHAG LAKE   MARQUETTE COUNTY

Acreage: 194 acres   **page 100 of the DeLorme Atlas**

Location: Go east from Ishpeming to Negaunee, then south to the town of Palmer where you pick up 35 south to 557, then west to Big Shag Lake.

I could have snorkeled here all day. Great entrance, wide and easy, very picturesque, tall hardwoods and pines around the lake and entrance. Great visibility. Bottom consists of pondweed, chara and organic material. Very attractive weed structure and the depth is just right for snorkeling--about 5-8 feet deep. A few cottages but still uncommercial. Go straight out to the right or left--the weed structure is everywhere. Brown pondweed and coontail flourish here--also a green, cactus-like elodea. Swarms of pumpkinseeds at the entrance--also good sized perch and bluegill--go right and see big largemouth bass under the logs, along with black-striped minnows. It's just a great experience--it should not be hurried as there is so much to see. Fresh water weed structure is like coral in the ocean--it can have great eye appeal and gives perspective and dimension to the whole experience, not to mention that it usually harbors lots of fish.

LITTLE SHAG LAKE   MARQUETTE COUNTY

Acreage: 103 acres   **page 101 of the DeLorme Atlas**

Location: Either go south from Negaunee as if going to Big Shag Lake (see above) or go west on U.S. 2 to Rapid River, then north on 41 to 428, where you go west. 428 becomes 35 north which you take through the town of Gwinn. Little Shag Lake will be on your left.

This is just a great lake with outstanding visibility. A wonderful sloping bowl shape--very comfortable and effortless snorkeling. Organic matter, branches and logs on the bottom. Saw no vegetation but grass, but there might well have been weed beds if I had gone further. Hundreds of fish will come if you lie still by the rocky entrance. Hundreds of sunfish, black striped minnow and a few tiny spotted darters. These darters are not that common and it's fun to watch them move in their unique jumpy fashion. Lots of sunfish also under the docks.

SPORLEY LAKE   MARQUETTE COUNTY

Acreage: 76.5 acres   **page 101 of the DeLorme Atlas**

Location: Go south from Marquette on 41 and go west (right) on 460, then go south past Big Trout Lake. Sporley Lake will be on your left.

A good road in, and wide lake entrance. Lake is surrounded by high pines, very scenic with only a few cottages. Good visibility, nice bowl shape with gently sloping sides--I cannot emphasize strongly enough how much the bowl shape contributes to the pleasure of snorkeling--sort of like diving the Wall in Grand Cayman, in that you can see life at several levels. Silty bottom, loads of logs and branches--lots of black striped minnows.

SQUAW LAKE   MARQUETTE COUNTY

Acreage: 221 acres   **page 99 of the DeLorme Atlas**

Location: Take U.S. 2 to Iron Mountain, then north on 95. Just before reaching Witch Lake, go west and take the first right (north) after Horseshoe and follow the signs to Squaw Lake.

Squaw Lake is just down the road from Twin, Horseshoe and Island Lake, so there's a chance to sample several worthwhile lakes close together. This is a very clear lake with good sized largemouth bass and rock bass.

Bottom consists of huge boulders scattered around, as well as many fallen trees, broadleaf pondweed, clams, chara, elodea, lilies. A very nice experience. There's lots to explore here. A beautiful drive in through a winding fern forest.

TWIN LAKES   MARQUETTE COUNTY

Acreage: 21.52 acres   **page 99 of the DeLorme Atlas**

Location: Take U.S. 2 to Iron Mountain, north on 95 and just before Witch Lake, go west and Twin Lakes will be immediately on your left (south side).

State Forest Campground in the Escanaba River State Forest. An underwater forest! Very clear. Snorkel along the rocky slope and see schools of bluegill among the branches. An awesome sight as trees are so tall and so visible. Big chunks of vegetation clinging to the tree trunks. Lots of fun. Bottom is full of rocks and organic material. Lake has a wide entrance and is very remote with no cottages and surrounded by high hardwoods. Lots of water lilies. Beautiful winding road entrance through the woods.

LITTLE BASS LAKE   SCHOOLCRAFT COUNTY

Acreage: 160 acres   **page 103 of the DeLorme Atlas**

Location: Take U.S. 2 west to Manistique, then north on 94 to 437; go west on 437 and south on Bass Lake Road. Little Bass Lake will be on your right, two and a half miles south of Steuben.

State Forest Campground in the Hiawatha National Forest. Entry is up on a bluff with a fabulous view of the wilderness lake below. No cottages, very little activity. Excellent visibility in every direction--fairly shallow everywhere I went. Snorkelers are free to roam all over. Lake is surrounded by tall pines and hardwoods. Saw big clams, small snails, crayfish, perch, schools of shad. Small fish beds were on both sides of the entrance. Hard sand/silt bottom. You can stand up in many spots. All types of vegetation--tall bulrushes, pondweed. Bass Lake Road going in is very scenic and lined with birches.

CANOE LAKE   SCHOOLCRAFT COUNTY

Acreage: 34.5 acres   **page 103 of the DeLorme Atlas**

Location: Take M-28 west of McMillan and after the town of
Creighton, head north on 454, then east on 450, then right on Wolf
Lake Road--Canoe Lake will be on your left.

A great State Campground in Lake Superior State Forest. I saw
only 4 campsites--it's like your own private lake. Outrageously
beautiful scenery. This lake is only for the diehard snorkeler.
Some visibility near shore--lots of fallen logs, clams but the tannic
acid gives it a reddish tinge. It's a storybook entrance down a
narrow winding road. I cannot emphasize strongly enough how
spectacular Lake Superior State Forest is--truly breathtaking.

COLWELL LAKE   SCHOOLCRAFT COUNTY

Acreage: 148 acres   **page 103 of the DeLorme Atlas**

Location: Take U.S. 2 to Manistique, then north on 94. Colwell
Lake is right next to the road on the right hand side. Take Clear
Lake Road heading east to get to the lake.

A State Forest Campground in the Lake Superior State Forest.
Beautiful wooded entrance, no cottages.   This is a scenic,
uncommercial, fabulous lake. Very clear--go to the right, fairly
near shore, and you'll see hundreds of bluegill beds and hundreds
of gills--the water was thick with them, as well as large rock bass,
pumpkinseeds and many big largemouth bass hiding under the
various logs lying on the bottom--an impressive sight. I got great
photos here. Big clams. Saw one huge perch. Bet there were a
thousand bluegills--many spawning. Pondweed, chara and a little
coontail. Visibility was outstanding.

CORNER LAKE   SCHOOLCRAFT COUNTY

Acreage: 144 acres   **page 102 of the DeLorme Atlas**

Location: Take H-13 straight south of Munising and go east on
440--lake will be on your left hand side.

Or go west out of Manistique on U.S. 2 and north at Nahma Junction on H-13, go east on 440 and the lake will be on your left hand side.

State Forest Campground in the Hiawatha National Forest. A nice setting with a few cottages and extremely clear water--you could easily see objects on the bottom 10-15 feet away. There was no suspended sediment. Scattered pondweed, chara, lots of big clams, small snails, crayfish, fallen branches and logs. Straight out and to the left, I saw schools of perch, black striped minnows. Largemouth bass were just beyond the edge of the ramp. But they were the color of the water and well camouflaged so you have to be alert to see them. Hard sandy bottom.

CRANBERRY LAKE   **SCHOOLCRAFT COUNTY**

Acreage: 11 acres   **page 103 of the DeLorme Atlas**

Location: Take 450 northwest out of Seney . Just before you get to Wardies Landing Field, stay on 450 and go south. Cranberry Lake will be on your right.

Park by the side of the road and walk in from there. A very tiny lake, and chances are good that you will have it all to yourself. Complete isolation. Surrounded by tall pines. Very clear with fallen branches and logs. Tadpoles were there by the thousands in July.

CUSINO LAKE   **SCHOOLCRAFT COUNTY**

Acreage: 140 acres   **page 103 of the DeLorme Atlas**

Location: see directions for Cranberry Lake, and continue on after Cranberry, and Cusino Lake will be on your right.

State Forest Campground in Lake Superior State Forest. Very scenic campsites. Enter from one of the unoccupied campsites. These are some of the choicest campsites I have ever seen. Very tranquil here; I saw no boats, no people on a July weekend. Big fallen tree visible in the water had bluegills around it.

The lake is flat, hard sand and gravel bottom, sparse vegetation. You can go out quite far and still stand up. Then the lake slopes gently down. Clear and clean.

DODGE LAKE   SCHOOLCRAFT COUNTY

Acreage: 87.5 acres   **page 103 of the DeLorme Atlas**

Location: go west on U.S. 2 to Manistique, then north on 94, take the first road out of town that goes west, pass Jack Lake on your left and Dodge Lake will be on your right.

This is a lovely scenic lake in the Lake Superior State Forest with very few cottages and easy access. Here I saw my first 2 snorkelers. The bottom is hard and grassy with wild celery, pondweed, lots of fallen branches and big logs. Go to the right fairly near shore to see schools of rock bass, isolated largemouth bass, large pumpkinseeds gathered in groups, bluegills and crayfish. There's a nice dropoff to snorkel and visibility is good.

DUTCH FRED LAKE   SCHOOLCRAFT COUNTY

Acreage: 27.5 acres   **page 104 of the DeLorme Atlas**

Location: Go straight north out of Seney on 77, take your first left and follow the signs--Dutch Fred will be on your left. It's kind of a rugged trip in--not a bad road--it just seems quite a while before you get there, but it's worth it, so hang in.

There are places to camp here, though it's not an official campground. This is truly the middle of nowhere. The lake is a trophy brook trout lake and a lake with outstanding visibility. Bowl shaped, it is excellent for snorkeling. Don't neglect the shallow areas to the right of the entrance. I found a whole group of fathead minnows in their spawning colors, each male guarding his eggs next to his small rock or piece of wood. It was truly fascinating to watch, and they allow you to get extremely close--I got outstanding video. There were also a couple of small salamanders and various other small critters I hadn't seen before or since.

SOUTH GEMINI LAKE   SCHOOLCRAFT COUNTY

Acreage: 120 acres   page 103 of the DeLorme Atlas

Location: Take M-28 west of Seney to the town of Creighton, then head north on 454; after the town of Cusino take a right at 450, cross Wolf Lake Road, and South Gemini Lake will be on your left.

Snorkel in scenic splendor in this gorgeous lake in Lake Superior State Forest. A State Forest campground. The campsites here are outstanding. The water is very clear. Bottom is a combination of sand and silt. Saw map turtle, minnows, lots of chara and wild celery as well as cactus type plants, lots of fallen logs, water lilies. This is as scenic as it gets—really the forest primeval! An August weekend and no boats or people on the lake. The lake is surrounded by a variety of pines and hardwoods.

GULLIVER LAKE   SCHOOLCRAFT COUNTY

Acreage: 836.5 acres   page 91 of the DeLorme Atlas

Location: Go west from Naubinway on U.S. 2 and before you get to Manistique, Gulliver will be right on U. S. 2 on the left hand side of the road.

A large lake with excellent public access and good visibility. Shore is sandy beach, stones and rocks. To the left of the ramp is about a 6 foot wide strip of weed bed stretching out into the lake, beds consisting of pondweed, coontail and wild celery. Some clams were settled on the bottom. Further out in the lake is a big concrete bowl. This is interesting but not as esthetically attractive as some of the other lakes. Worth stopping at for its convenient location, and because on any given day you never know what surprises are in store.

KITCHI-ITI-KIPI SPRING*   SCHOOLCRAFT COUNTY

page 103 of the DeLorme Atlas

Location: in Palms Book State Park just north of Manistique.

I include this not because you can snorkel it but because if you are snorkeling lakes in this area you really should not miss an opportunity to absorb this unique experience.

Park your car and walk over to the raft which leaves whenever there are a few people, and enjoy the opportunity to pole yourself across this scenic deep natural spring which has been planted with many lake trout which you can see very clearly as you pole back and forth. Unique. Don't miss it. Like snorkeling without actually being in the water.

MCDONALD LAKE   SCHOOLCRAFT COUNTY

Acreage: 1600 acres   **page 92 of the DeLorme Atlas**

Location: Take U.S. 2 to the town of Gulliver, then go southeast on 432; McDonald Lake will be on your left.

This is a big lake surrounded by lovely scenery--it's really spectacular in the fall with fantastic color. The lake is shallow for quite a ways out; the bottom and shore have lovely medium brown powdery sand with small white stones. A great variety of aquatic plant life is here; endlessly fascinating weedbeds, and I was puzzled at the lack of fish--I'm going back to spend more time, as conditions here were conducive to lots of excitement and I felt more time spent here would have yielded that. A fascinating experience even if you don't see that many fish.

PETE'S LAKE   SCHOOLCRAFT COUNTY

Acreage: 194 acres   **page 102 of the DeLorme Atlas**

Location: Take U.S. 2 west of Manistique, the north on H-13. Just before Moccasin Lake (on your left) go east and Pete's Lake will be on your right.

State Forest Campground in the Hiawatha National Forest. Entry is via a beautiful paved road through the woods. An extremely clear lake with a peat/sand/marl hard bottom. Lots of brush piles. On the right are fallen logs containing thousands of large black striped gold minnows, scattered chara--otherwise vegetation is sparse. You can snorkel out into the deep and still see bottom perfectly. Attractive tall water lilies.

ROSS LAKE   SCHOOLCRAFT COUNTY

Acreage: 196 acres   **page 103 of the DeLorme Atlas**

Location: Take M-28 west of Seney to Creighton, then go north on 454, east on 450, take Crooked Lake Road to the north which will put Ross Lake on your right.

State Forest Campground in Lake Superior State Forest. This is a popular lake with local snorkelers. Saw a large painted turtle here, as well as big clams and the usual pan fish. Lots of lilies, coontail and chara. Scenic with no power boats or jet skis. Very deserted. This area contains some of the most beautiful wooded drives with huge overhanging trees--it rivals any scenery in the state or beyond.

SNYDER LAKE   SCHOOLCRAFT COUNTY

Acreage: 80 acres   **page 104 of the DeLorme Atlas**

Location: Take 77 north of Seney, go for 12 miles--a great paved scenic road. Snyder Lake will be on your left. It's a half mile west of 77.

This is just a spectacular lake. No cottages, no power boats, complete wilderness. The water is extremely clear--the instant you go under you are into great snorkeling territory. Fields of the most beautiful lime green chara, elodea, curly pondweed, schools of minnows, perch, pumpkinseeds. The lake is known for its perch and pike. There are just tons of perch everywhere. Big patches of sand and a hard sand bottom. You can stand up almost anywhere. A varied and very pleasing underwater landscape.

SWAN LAKE   SCHOOLCRAFT COUNTY

Acreage: 46 acres   **page 102 of the DeLorme Atlas**

Location: Go west of Manistique on U.S. 2, then at Nahma Junction, go north on H-13, take 440 east past Corner Lake, then your next left followed by almost an immediate right will bring up Swan Lake on your left.

It's an excellent road coming in, and the lake offers easy access. (except the last .8 of a mile has some potholes you have to drive around) This is a super clear lake, small, no cottages, offering a small campground. The lake has a hard sandy bottom. It's shallow, so swim straight out to the deeper area since you will probably find it like your own private lake. It's a vivid dark blue with a sandy beach and that perfect snorkeling bowl shape. Big mature bass shot out of the shallows and I followed them into the deep where they were joined by more. The lake seems devoid of vegetation and you think there's not much happening til these big bass come up to startle you and set your heart pounding with their size. Snorkel right over to the big fallen tree with all its branches including the pine cones still attached. Great place for fish to hide. There's a big spawning box next to the tree. Saw good sized clams.

THUNDER LAKE   SCHOOLCRAFT COUNTY

Acreage: 340 acres   **page 103 of the DeLorme Atlas**

Location: Take U.S. 2 west of Manistique and west of Thompson and go north on 437 (Cooks School Road). Follow the signs and Thunder Lake will be on your left. Take the entrance left of the Thunder Lake Lodge. The Thunder Lake Lodge is a lovely resort with beautiful modern cabins on the lake and open year round. If heading east, take a left at Ramsdam Road. County Road 437 is another great wilderness "natural beauty" road.

The lake is shallow with a sandy bottom and sandy beach. It's very picturesque surrounded by white birch, very tranquil and placid with only a few fishermen. Lots of chara, clams and small snails. My snorkeling was unfortunately cut short by a thunderstorm.

NORTHERN LOWER PENINSULA

HORSESHOE LAKE
ALCONA COUNTY

Acreage: 15.6   **page 78 of the DeLorme Atlas**

Location: Take 72 east out of Grayling or Mio--turn south on 65, then take the first right after Sunny Lake Road. Go one mile and this road will dead end into Horseshoe Lake.

State Forest Campground in the Huron National Forest. This lake is very worthwhile, with beautiful clumps of green vegetation, a small lake in a jewel-like setting. A very clear and shallow lake with the usual pan fish and a silt bottom.

HUBBARD LAKE
ALCONA COUNTY

Acreage: 8850 acres   **page 79 of the DeLorme Atlas**

Location: Take 72 east from Grayling--then north on Hubbard Lake Road which dead ends into Swede Road. Hubbard Lake is on your left.

This is a huge crystal clear lake, 8 miles long. Best to enter here in the Bay Area, which is calmer than other entry points. Fish shelters have been put in here by the Sportsmen Association. Rocks and boulders on the bottom. This is one of those very large lakes that is best seen by boat, so you can seek out your own snorkeling area.

JEWELL LAKE
ALCONA COUNTY

Acreage: 193.1 acres   **page 79 of the DeLorme Atlas**

Location: Take 72 west of Grayling or Mio and north on Sanborn Road--go west on Trask Lake Road and Jewell Lake will be on your left.

State Forest Campground in the Huron National Forest. A beautiful, serene, scenic setting. A narrow lake surrounded by white birch and other hardwoods. A good sandy beach for campers. Lake has a sandy bottom which turns to silt when you go out a ways. Scattered patches of chara and pondweed. A few big clams. This lake should definitely be explored, as the clarity and attractive snorkeling conditions are there. I snorkeled here in the fall, and looking up through the fall color was truly spectacular. This lake has been leased by the U.S. Department of Agriculture to a concessionaire who exacts a fee of $3. I had a great picnic at a table next to the launch site. M-72 east of 65 and Sanborn Road may be one of the most beautiful roads in Michigan--smooth as glass and very scenic.

LONG LAKE   **ALPENA COUNTY**

Acreage: 5652 acres   **page 85 of the DeLorme Atlas**

Location: Take 32 east of Hillman into Alpena, then north on U.S. 23--the lake is on your left just before reaching Rayburn Highway.

Enter in Alpena County Park--there is a $2 fee for day use. The lake is quite clear--a bottom of big boulders--another large lake where it would really be handy to have a boat to get around and choose your spot. Worthwhile if you can choose your area.

ROCKPORT PUBLIC ACCESS*   **ALPENA COUNTY**

Lake Huron   **page 85 of the DeLorme Atlas**

Location: Take U.S. 23 north of Alpena, go east on Rockport Road--follow this road north to Rockport--the public access will be on your right.

Strictly speaking, this doesn't belong in this guide, but locals convinced me to include it since they raved about its clarity, its walleye and brown trout. I can certainly verify the truth of the great clarity--it's just fabulous, but it's very very cold--a heavy wetsuit is a must here. Big boulders everywhere--visibility is tops.

LAKE BELLAIRE   ANTRIM COUNTY

Acreage: 1775 acres   **page 75 of the DeLorme Atlas**

Location: Take M-88 west of Mancelona--lake will be on your left.

A very clear lake with a hard sandy bottom. Like all very large lakes, the best results are obtained when you have a boat to seek out your snorkeling spot. The clarity is definitely here, so it is worth making the effort.

ELLSWORTH LAKE   ANTRIM COUNTY

Acreage: 120 acres   **page 81 of the DeLorme Atlas**

Location: Take C-48 west of East Jordan into the town of Ellsworth; just south of town is the public access for the lake.

This is an opportunity to dine at one of Michigan's finest restaurants--the renowned Tapawingo. The food is outstanding and expensive.

The lake is located in Ellsworth Park. It's a narrow lake with some current in parts, but you can always stand up in the shallow area. The largest spotted darters I have ever seen were here. Lots of bluegills, largemouth bass, pumpkinseeds, big perch as well as schools of smaller perch circulating over beds of chara and wild celery, with lilies on either side. The fish surround you almost immediately on entering. The bottom is sandy, and though the water is slightly cloudy, the fish and vegetation are clearly seen.

GREEN LAKE   ANTRIM COUNTY

Acreage: 40 acres   **page 75 of the DeLorme Atlas**

Location: just off 131 west of Mancelona. Take 131 south of Mancelona and go west on Elder Road. Cross Bailey Road and take your first road south (left) which will take you directly to Green Lake. It's 2.3 miles from 131 to the DNR sign, then another half mile to the lake.

This is a small wilderness lake with no cottages. Very scenic, a real gem. Crystal clear water over low soft green chara beds--go either left or right--bulrushes on both sides contain hundreds of rock bass and bluegills. Just a gorgeous setting--looks like the proverbial old swimming hole. Very clean. The lake is surrounded by hardwoods,. with lots of white birch both above and under the water. Scattered logs and branches underwater. An exceptional snorkeling experience. Fairly shallow--snorkel along the edge of the dropoff. This is a great lake for beginning snorkelers because of the great quantities of fish. Sometimes young people get intimidated by vegetation, but there's nothing here to frighten a youngster. Come and spend a long and happy time.

INTERMEDIATE LAKE   ANTRIM COUNTY

Acreage: 1520 acres   **page 81 of the DeLorme Atlas**

Location: Take 88 west out of Mancelona and it will turn north and take you right alongside both of the public accesses for Intermediate Lake, which will be on your right.

This is a great snorkeling lake, crystal clear with a bottom of marl and sand, with some scattered chara. It's a flat, shallow lake--you can walk halfway across it before it gets deep. Vegetation is sparse; snorkel to the right where there are perch and bluegills--I saw the big breeding males here in August. Tiny snails. A very pleasurable experience.

LAKE OF THE WOODS   ANTRIM COUNTY

Acreage: 141 acres   **page 75 of the DeLorme Atlas**

Location: go west on M-88 out of Mancelona. Go south on Lake of the Woods Road, for one mile and the lake will be on your right.

A beautiful scenic wilderness lake surrounded by high hardwoods and with no visible cottages. Good but not great clarity. Shallow lake, only 5-10 feet deep with a maximum depth of 14 feet. Low beds of chara.

The bulrushes on the left side of the entrance are filled with bluegills, rock bass and swarms of black striped minnows. Also you can go straight out to the bulrushes in the middle for lots of small panfish.

TORCH LAKE   ANTRIM COUNTY

Acreage: 18,770 acres   **page 81 of the DeLorme Atlas**

Location: Take 131 to Kalkaska, and go west on 72 to 31, then going north on 31 will take you to the public access for Torch Lake, with the lake on your right.

Torch Lake is renowned for top clarity, and it definitely lives up to its reputation. It also has a reputation for being very cold, and it also lives up to that. So go prepared and dress comfortably if you want to stay in for any length of time. The bottom is sandy, and I did not see weed beds in the public access area. You can walk out quite far before it is over your head. I didn't even need a mask for this lake--it was that clear! It's a totally gorgeous lake to swim, snorkel--whatever! As is the case with any lake as large as this, having a boat is a tremendous advantage, as you can go where the weed beds are and if it's fish you're after, you'll have a much better chance of seeing them.

LAKE ANN   BENZIE COUNTY

Acreage: 527 acres   **page 74 of the DeLorme Atlas**

Location: Go west out of Traverse City on 72, then south on 651 (Goodrick Road), west on Cedar Run Road , then south on 665 (Lake Ann Road) to a dead end at 610 (Almira Road). Go east on Almira and you will see the lake on your left. Don't enter at the Campground entrance--go to the next entrance which is the boat launch entrance.

State Forest Campground in the Pere Marquette State Forest. The water was quite clear but there was a bit of an algae bloom when I was there which will hopefully be cleared up when you are there. You are in lovely bay-like surroundings with white birch background.

Go left for the bluegill beds--there's good weed structure of chara, watermilfoil, various kinds of pondweed, elodea and coontail, big clams, rock bass, largemouth bass, schools of shad, perch, black striped minnows. Worthwhile.

BETSIE LAKE   BENZIE COUNTY

Acreage: approx. 200 acres   page 73 of the DeLorme Atlas

Location: in downtown Frankfort. Entrance is off 9th Street.

Good but not great visibility. Snorkel along the docks among the big boulders. I saw big schools of the black striped minnows, and this was one of the few lakes where I saw a good number of smallmouth bass.

BROOKS LAKE   BENZIE COUNTY

Acreage: 21 acres   page 73 of the DeLorme Atlas

Location: Take 72 west from Traverse City, south on 669, then west on County Line Road. The first road south will lead you to Brooks Lake. Or, coming from the south on U.S. 31, heading north on 669, west on County Line Road, the first road south leads you to Brooks Lake.

This is a small, secluded wilderness lake where the fish I saw were small but in an attractive environment. There was a big stand of tape grass at the entrance with a combination of chara, curly pondweed and wild celery, along with bluegills, pumpkinseeds, largemouth bass, rock bass and black striped minnows. Nothing startling but still worthwhile.

CRYSTAL LAKE   BENZIE COUNTY

Acreage: 9711 acres   **page 73 of the DeLorme Atlas**

Location: Take U.S.31 southwest of Traverse City, and the lake
will be on your right. Or come up from the south on U.S. 31 and
the lake will be on your left.

This is an extremely clear lake--very much like Higgins
Lake--almost unlimited visibility in every direction--just great for
beginning snorkelers or young people who might not like
vegetation. Stone and sand bottom, almost no vegetation, and
small schools of panfish. Long sandy beach with many cottages
for rent at very reasonable prices. We paid $50 a night for a
2-bedroom cottage with kitchenette and living room, beautifully
decorated.

GRASS LAKE   BENZIE COUNTY

Acreage: approx. 140 acres   **page 74 of the DeLorme Atlas**

Location: Go southwest out of Traverse City on U.S. 31, then south
on Reynolds Road, west on 608 (Cinder Road), then take the first
left (south), go 3 miles and turn left (east) which will take you to
the lake.

Or come north on U.S.31, go south on Reynolds Road, west on 608
(Cinder Road),then take the first left (south), go 3 miles and turn
left (east) which will take you to Grass Lake.

State Forest Campground in the Pere Marquette State Forest. This
is a super clear lake which is actually part of the Betsie River.
There is therefore a mild current, making it a different snorkeling
experience. Worthwhile.

HERENDEENE LAKE   BENZIE COUNTY

Acreage: 36 acres   **page 74 of the DeLorme Atlas**

Location: Take 72 west of Traverse City, go south on 667
(Reynolds Road), cross Fowler Road, and Herendeene Lake will be
on your right.

Or come north on U.S. 31, take a left (north) on 669 , go east on 72, south on 667 (Reynolds Road), cross Fowler Road and Herendeene Lake will be on your right.

This is excellent snorkeling. The water is not super clear but it's good enough. To the left, there's lots of tree stumps. Go to the right for the bluegill beds; lots of fallen logs and branches loaded with pumpkinseeds, bluegills, largemouth bass, both adults and juveniles. Pleasing fields of chara and pondweed, some watermilfoil. The lake is in a lovely wilderness-like setting, very scenic. Only a couple of fishing boats when I was there in high season. I saw no cottages.

LOWER HERRING LAKE   **BENZIE COUNTY**

Acreage: 450 acres   **page 73 of the DeLorme Atlas**

Location: Take U.S.31 north, go west on 604, pass Upper Herring Lake, go south on Fort and west on Buena, and Lower Herring will be on your left.

This is a very clear lake, clearer then Upper Herring, but cottagers keep the vegetation cleared out so there is not as much to see near the public access (which has parking for only 2 or 3 cars). Beautiful beach, great for kids to swim and do beginning snorkeling, but you'd have to bring your own objects to look at or get a boat and take off for a weedier area. Along the end of the dock there were baby largemouth bass and gold striped minnows.

UPPER HERRING LAKE   **BENZIE COUNTY**

Acreage: 540 acres   **page 73 of the DeLorme Atlas**

Location: Take U.S. 31 north, go west on 604 and Upper Herring Lake will be on your left.

This is not as clear as I would like but there's still about 5 feet of visibility. Snorkel down a pathway with thick bulrushes on either side. Go to the right where there's a dropoff with lots of fish. Sandy bottom with chara vegetation, coontail, fallen branches.

LITTLE PLATTE LAKE   BENZIE COUNTY

Acreage: 805 acres   **page 73 of the DeLorme Atlas**

Location: Take U.S. 31 north to Benzonia, continue to the town of Honor, then go northwest on 708, north at Indian Hill Road, west at Martin Road to a dead end, then west on Northland Highway. Little Platte Lake is immediately on your left.

The lake is very clear. The usual pan fish were here as well as good sized brown bullhead. Vegetation consisted of chara and pondweed with a sandy bottom.

TURTLE LAKE   BENZIE COUNTY

Acreage: 38 acres   **page 73 of the DeLorme Atlas**

Location: Take 31 west of Traverse City, south on 669 (Thompsonville Highway), east on 608 (Cinder Road), pass N. Carmean Road, and Turtle Lake will be on your right.

There are a few cottages here, but it feels very isolated. The maximum depth is 22 feet, so the lake is quite warm. There's a nice wide entrance with a gravel bottom--it's soft when you go out, so don't stand up (never a good idea anyway). Go out through the shallow area about 30 yards to chara and pondweed beds. This is the dropoff and a comfortable depth to snorkel in. There are two sunken posts with a couple of hundred fish around them--then off to the left near the docks is the remains of a sunken boat. A few small snails. Lots of perch and black and gold striped minnows. A few stumps over near the lilies on the left side.

ADAMS LAKE   CHARLEVOIX COUNTY

Acreage: 48 acres   **page 81 of the DeLorme Atlas**

Location: Take U.S. 31 north to Charlevoix, then southeast on 66, south on Loeb Road, east on Novotny, and Adams Lake will be on your right.

This is wilderness--one house high on the hill, otherwise no cottages. This is a fascinating lake, worth a good deal of time.

Spring fed and very clear. Sandy bottom just littered with big clams. Go a short distance straight out and there are *great* weedbeds with hundreds of rock bass, schools of largemouth bass, perch, schools of black striped minnows, red eared sunfish. Varied vegetation of different heights makes for a very scenic landscape. There's coontail, bladderwort, chara, curly pondweed, tall grass, small snails. A wide ring of sand in the shallows abruptly ends the tall vegetation with patches of sand. It's a great depth for comfortable snorkeling. Teeming with hundreds of fish. Sand darters in the shallows. Snorkel along the edges of the weedbeds. The deepest part of the lake is only 15 feet, and most of the lake is only 5-10 feet deep, so you can cover the whole lake and always see bottom. The bluegill beds are straight out.

LAKE CHARLEVOIX   CHARLEVOIX COUNTY

Acreage: 17,260 acres   **page 81 of the DeLorme Atlas**

Location: Take U.S. 31 north to Charlevoix, then go southeast on 66, the south arm entrance of Lake Charlevoix will be on your left. Or you can go on to Boyne City and enter there. You can also enter in downtown Charlevoix, one of the most attractive towns in Michigan or the Midwest. Endlessly fascinating boutiques and upscale restaurants here, as well as great inexpensive sandwich shops with huge portions on homemade bread.

The clarity in Lake Charlevoix is outstanding. In Charlevoix, park by the brick building that houses the public restrooms. The vegetation is sparse, but there's plenty of fish--bluegills, sunfish, perch. The bottom is silt, stones and large boulders.

DEER LAKE   CHARLEVOIX COUNTY

Acreage: 443 acres   **page 82 of the DeLorme Atlas**

Location: Head north on U.S. 131 toward Petoskey, go west on 75 (Boyne City Road), south on Deer Lake Road, and Deer Lake will be on your left.

This is a very clear lake--go either right or left and snorkel among the bulrushes for best results.

Besides the usual panfish, there's tons of clams, snails. The bottom is hard sand with mostly chara for vegetation.

HEART LAKE   CHARLEVOIX COUNTY

Acreage: 9.9 acres   **page 82 of the DeLorme Atlas**

Location: Take U.S. 131 north heading towards Petoskey, go east on 32, north on Camp Ten Road--pass Reynolds Road and Heart Lake will be on your left.

This is a very tiny lake with plenty of shallow area near shore to snorkel. Lily pads at the entrance. Bottom is muddy, with bluegills, sunfish and bullheads, which are always fun to look at as they can be quite friendly. It's kind of a mucky entrance, but don't be deterred by that. Can be easily combined with a visit to Hoffman Lake.

HOFFMAN LAKE   CHARLEVOIX COUNTY

Acreage: 120 acres   **page 82 of the DeLorme Atlas**

Location: Take U.S. 131 north heading towards Petoskey, go east on 32, north on Camp Ten Road, northeast on Bingham Road, then east on Huffman Road. Hoffman Lake will be on your left.

A tranquil peaceful uncommercial lake. On a Saturday in August I was the only one there. The bottom is silt and there are weedbeds of chara and pondweed, but vegetation is generally rather sparse. There is a strange ghostly grey hue to the lake. Plenty of crayfish, tons of clams, logs, branches, detritus.

NOWLAND LAKE   CHARLEVOIX COUNTY

Acreage: 126 acres   **page 81 of the DeLorme Atlas**

Location: go north on U.S. 31 to Charlevoix, then southeast on 66, south on Wickersham which dead ends into Nowland (sometimes spelled Knowland) Lake. Or take 66 northwest from East Jordan,

west on Ironton and south on Wickersham which dead ends into
Nowland Lake.

This is a beautiful and secluded lake, non commercial. No one
was there on a Sunday in August. Very tranquil without even a
boat. Some good weed beds of chara, curly pondweed, sand/silt
bottom with stones, logs, and boulders. Go just beyond the edge
of the dock into a weed bed where there are bluegills, big schools
of perch, some largemouth bass, a few clams.

SUSAN LAKE   **CHARLEVOIX COUNTY**

Acreage: 130 acres   **page 81 of the DeLorme Atlas**

Location: Take Boyne City Road northwest out of Boyne City.
After crossing Quarter Line Road, curve right on old 31 and Susan
Lake will be on your right.

A super clear lake in a beautiful wilderness setting. No visible
cottages. There is also access on the other side of the lake with a
little pull-off spot with limited parking. Snorkel there among the
lily pads all along the shore. Marl and peat bottom with some
hard sand. Fairly flat lake. Lots of sand darters, bluegill beds are
straight ahead in the bulrushes. Plenty of perch, pumpkinseeds,
largemouth bass, bluegills, sunfish. This is a lake worth spending
a good deal of time at. You cannot really see it quickly.

THUMB LAKE   **CHARLEVOIX COUNTY**

Acreage: 484.5 acres   **page 82 of the DeLorme Atlas**

Location: Take U.S. 131 heading toward Petoskey. At Boyne Falls,
go east on Thumb Lake Road and Thumb Lake will be on your left.

A fine lake with good visibility. Bowl shaped with lots of
vegetation, chara, pondweed, elodea, lots of sunken logs on the
right--full of rock bass, bluegills, largemouth bass, red eared
sunfish, some very big crayfish, big clams, small snails, baby
largemouth bass. Go either left or right but most of the logs and
branches are on the right.

WALLOON LAKE   CHARLEVOIX COUNTY

Acreage: 4,320 acres   **page 82 of the DeLorme Atlas**

Location: take U.S. 131 north towards Petoskey.   After passing Larson Road, Walloon Lake will be on your left.

Another very large lake that is best snorkeled if you have a boat and can therefore seek your spot. Visibility is a bit cloudy, but your eyes get used to it. Saw only small panfish, clams, snails, logs and tree limbs. Hard sandy bottom. Good depth for snorkeling.

BLACK LAKE   CHEBOYGAN COUNTY

Acreage: 10,130 acres   **page 83 of the DeLorme Atlas**

Location: Take I-75 north, then take 68 going east to the town of Onaway. Head north out of Onaway on 211 and continue around Doriva Beach Road, which runs along the north side of Black Lake.

State Forest Campground in the Mackinaw State Forest. The lake area around the campground is awesomely clear. Sandy bottom with some rocks. Unfortunately you have to go terribly far out to get to the dropoff, which can mean running into boat traffic. I had better luck on the south side by getting permission to go in at the Black Lake Hotel or Coleman's Cove--but you can't go without permission, so you must ask and hope to be lucky. There was a jungle of coontail, watermilfoil and pondweed where I saw largemouth bass, lots of rock bass and shiners. Because of its size, this is obviously another lake where having a boat would be a great advantage to the snorkeler.

BURT LAKE   CHEBOYGAN COUNTY

Acreage: 17,120 acres   **page 82 of the DeLorme Atlas**

Location: Take I-75 north and go west on 68--Burt Lake and its public accesses will be on your right.

I went in at Maple Bay public access. Burt Lake is a very busy, commercial lake with a huge park attached, as well as being part of a State Forest Campground in the Mackinaw State Forest.

Go to the bulrushes to the right of the campground---lots of sand darters, snails and clams.   Look closely as the darters are fascinating to watch but they're terribly well camouflaged. The lake has outstanding clarity and is another of those very large lakes that would be greatly enhanced for the snorkeler if a boat was available or rented.

COCHRAN LAKE   CHEBOYGAN COUNTY

Acreage: 27.5 acres   **page 83 of the DeLorme Atlas**

Location: Take I-75 north to the town of Indian River--at Indian River go east on Onaway Road.   Cochran Lake will be on your right.

This is a gorgeous super clear lake with no cottages.   The maximum depth is only 15 feet, so it's perfect for snorkeling. Hard sand bottom in some spots--soft silt in others.   Never stand up without checking the bottom first. The lake is flat and shallow but still a comfortable depth for snorkeling. The lake is very secluded and uncommercial.   Go straight out to the clumps of chara vegetation and wait for the fish to come. Largemouth bass should come, along with pan fish, and lots of black striped minnows.   A very delightful experience. I had a strange feeling in this lake, a feeling that I was swimming in a sea of unconditional love.   It sounds pretty corny, but snorkeling can do that to you--it really plays with your senses.

LANCASTER LAKE   CHEBOYGAN COUNTY

Acreage: 52 acres   **page 94 of the DeLorme Atlas**

Location: Take I-75 north and get off at C-66. Head west on C-66 (Levering Road). Go south on Koepke Road , and the lake is on the left hand side.

Due to the large amount of thick vegetation, this lake is recommended for advanced snorkelers only. The access sign is a little hidden. It's a picturesque setting and an uncommercial lake. Good but not great visibility. It feels like you're making your way through a labyrinth of vegetation and this might make some people nervous.

It's still very interesting, although slightly red tinged. You have to steer your way through coontail, watermilfoil, lilies, wild celery and pondweed, and you need to have the patience to stay in a while before you start seeing life. It's a cold spring-fed lake, so dress accordingly.

MULLETT LAKE   CHEBOYGAN COUNTY

Acreage: 17,360 acres   pages 82-83, 94-95 of the DeLorme Atlas

Location: Take I-75 north heading toward Cheboygan. Take the Topinabee Exit and drive along 27 until you see the public access on your right hand side.

This is a very busy and commercial lake and though I don't particularly want to, I feel I have to include it because of its clarity and because so many people are familiar with it and might want to try it. Again, as is the case with the larger lakes, a boat will open up so many more possibilities to you--a chance to get away from the jet skis and power boats and find your own secluded spot. Hard sand bottom. Almost no vegetation--saw only panfish and minnows, but a boat would no doubt have yielded much more.

MUNRO LAKE   CHEBOYGAN COUNTY

Acreage: 694 acres   page 94 of the DeLorme Atlas

Location: Take I-75 and get off going west on C66. Go south on Heilman Road, and west at the first left after Brandau--this road takes you directly to the lake.

This is an unimproved area, not even any toilets, but it is an absolutely OK entry. It's a flat lake with a hard sand bottom. Very clear with no vegetation that I could see except bulrushes. You can walk way out and still stand up. Plenty of scattered logs, branches, big clams, schools of black striped minnows.

SILVER LAKE   CHEBOYGAN COUNTY

Acreage: 74.5   **page 82 of the DeLorme Atlas**

Location: Take I-75 north to Wolverine, then west on Silver Lake Road. The lake will be on your left.

This is a clear, awesome, outstanding lake. Excellent for beginning snorkelers. Go to the right and hundreds of fish will surround you--red eared sunfish, bluegills, rock bass, fathead minnows and perch-- all along the shore. Marl and sand bottom. Leaves, logs and branches on the bottom as well as big beds of chara. You can go out quite deep and still see bottom. Top visibility.

TWIN LAKES   CHEBOYGAN COUNTY

Acreage: 210 acres   **page 95 of the DeLorme Atlas**

Location: Going south from Cheboygan, take 23 east, then go south on Black River Road to the four corners of Alverno. Keep heading south on Black River Road until it becomes Twin Lakes Road heading east. It will bring you out to the Chateau Lodge, which I thought was a fabulous spot for an overnight or two while you are discovering this fine chain of lakes. The Lodge is situated up on a bluff overlooking one of the lakes (the only one of the lakes in the chain that is not good for snorkeling). The lodge has a view that reminds me a good bit of some of the views in the Canadian Rockies--just spectacular, although of course the big mountains are not there. Nevertheless it is a jewel of a setting, the rates at the Lodge are reasonable, and the food was outstanding, both the buffet breakfasts and the whitefish dinners. Superlative, if the chef is as good as he was the last two years.

The public entry point is arrived at by taking a left off Twin Lakes Road onto S. Smith Road and taking it to a dead end.

There is a State Forest Campground here, and you can enter the lake here and snorkel to any of the others as they all connect, and they are all equally fascinating. The clarity is as good as it gets, and there's plenty of fish in all of the lakes. I was surprised by big bowfins, taking their ease on top of big soft clumps of grasses--one bowfin rose from below to display himself before me--quite an impressive sight.

Breeding Male Bluegill

Spawning Male Black Crappie (Top)
Spawning Female Black Crappie (Bottom)

Red Ear Sunfish

Spawning Male Green Sunfish

Largemouth Bass

Yellow Perch

Northern Brown Bullheads

Northern Pike

Many of the cottagers throw their Christmas trees off the end of their docks, so all through the lakes there are big largemouth and large rock bass by the dozens weaving in and out of these abandoned holiday trees. In some of the lakes, there is a carpet of chara, but there is not much heavy vegetation except the occasional bed here and there of watermilfoil and coontail. It would take 2-3 days to really begin to explore these lakes, but I feel the investment of time is worth it, and more than once when I was snorkeling, I had cottagers putt-putt by in their pontoon boats and ask me to board with offers to tote me around. The hospitality of the cottagers here is tremendous and a number of them invited me to come and snorkel whenever I wanted. Of course you have to have permission or be invited. And of course you can always go in at the public access on the campground with no one's permission. I found many largemouth bass in most of the lakes--at one point I had 9 big largemouths in a semicircle around me--all staring curiously as largemouth bass do--you feel an interaction with this particular fish--they seem to really relate to snorkelers, and the size of them here is impressive. One fisherman had pulled in a 3 foot muskie, and I was told there were plenty of them here. These are "no wake" lakes, so you don't have to worry about jet skis or power boaters, thank heavens.

WEBER LAKE   CHEBOYGAN COUNTY

Acreage: 28.5 acres   **page 82 of the DeLorme Atlas**

Location: Take I-75 north to Wolverine, then west on Silver Lake Road, then go north on Peters Road, west on Wolverine. Continue on this past Watson Road, and then take your next right after Watson. This will take you to Weber Lake. The map incorrectly places this lake and so is inaccurate.

This is a State Forest Campground and is a small delightful lake. It's spring-fed, very clear with a nice bowl shape--perfect for the beginning (or any) snorkeler. Very little vegetation--mostly sunken logs and branches. I was surrounded by a school of largemouth bass almost immediately. Go either left or right--you see well even when going into the deeper water. Bottom has both hard and soft sand.

BLUEGILL LAKE   CRAWFORD COUNTY

Acreage: 30 acres   **Page 76 of the DeLorme Atlas**

Location: Go north on I-75; get off at the town of Waters (just north of Grayling) go south on old U.S. 27, take your third left, pass Horseshoe Lake and Bluegill Lake will be on your right.

This is an outstanding lake--great visibility with a silty bottom which makes some of the vegetation look grey. Go left from the sandy beach entrance--then go just a short distance to the weed beds; there's lots of perch and largemouth bass. The shallow areas are swarming with bluegills and sunfish--I also saw one sucker. Lots of fallen logs and branches in the shallow area to attract fish. It's an excellent lake for beginners as there are no tall weeds. Elodea vegetation is all over the bottom.

HORSESHOE LAKE   CRAWFORD COUNTY

Acreage: 25.3 acres   **page 76 of the DeLorme Atlas**

Location: go north on I-75; get off at the town of Waters (just north of Grayling) go south on old U.S.27, take your third left and Horseshoe Lake will be on your right.

A small picturesque lake that is very clear. Only a few fishermen here--very uncommercial--even Labor Day weekend there were few people here. Perfect for beginning snorkelers as there are no tall weeds, just a few lilypads and elodea all over the bottom. Mostly small pan fish and rock bass. The water is so clear that as you get into the deeper area, the bottom is still very clear 15-20 feet deep. A big weed bed straight out from the middle of the entrance just before you get to the lily pads is a good attractor of fish. Combining Horseshoe, Bluegill and Big Bradford, since they are so near to each other, makes a logical and pleasant snorkeling experience.

JONES LAKE   CRAWFORD COUNTY

Acreage: 42.5 acres   **Page 76 of the DeLorme Atlas**

Location: go north on I-75, go east onto 612 and after crossing White Road, Jones Lake will be on your right.

This is a State Forest Campground in the Camp Grayling Military Reservation. There are no visible cottages on this small remote lake, which is clear though not crystal clear. Go left to the bulrushes and among the bulrushes I saw plenty of bluegills, sunfish, tons of crayfish, snails, big clams and medium sized largemouth bass. There is a sand/silt bottom, swamp grass--no other weed structure that I saw.

KP LAKE   CRAWFORD COUNTY

Acreage: 110 acres   **page 77 of the DeLorme Atlas**

Location: go north on I-75, go east onto 612 and after passing Jones Lake, KP Lake will be on your right.

Hallelujah! no power boats allowed on this lake. This is a clear, clean and incredibly scenic lake. Go straight out from the public access and slightly to the right, not far from shore is a string of pondweed beds loaded with largemouth bass and perch. Within 10 seconds I had a dozen good sized largemouth bass swimming around me. I strongly recommend this lake, and it's convenient to quite a few others mentioned in this guide, so you can get some great variety in this area.

LAKE MARGRETHE   CRAWFORD COUNTY

Acreage: 1720 acres   **page 76 of the DeLorme Atlas**

Location: go north on I-75, then west on 72 and the lake will be on your left, right next to the road.   The public access is on the opposite side of the lake, so take a left (south) before getting to Eagle Point, and follow this all around the lake and the public access will be on your right. Or you can continue driving til you get to the State Forest Campground which will also be on your right.

This is a good sized lake with very clear water that provides some excellent snorkeling. I just snorkeled up and down in front of the docks and saw the biggest rock bass I have seen anywhere. Besides rock bass, there were great quantities of bluegills, largemouth bass and big pumpkinseeds. I was able to actually reach over and pet a big black bluegill here. I don't know the reason for his unusual color. I obtained the best results by going in at the Campground entrance rather than the public launch site.

SECTION ONE LAKE   CRAWFORD COUNTY

Acreage: 56 acres   **page 76 of the DeLorme Atlas**

Location: go north on I-75 and north of Grayling, get off at Marlette Road heading east, then go south on Sherman Road, west on Kenney Road and north on Fascination Drive. Section One Lake will then be on your right hand side.

Crystal clear! Deserted except for a couple of fishing boats on the Labor Day Holiday weekend. A great lake for beginning snorkelers, as the weeds are low and flat. Attractive elodea on the bottom and a few lily pads—otherwise not much vegetation. Bottom is peat/marl and organic. Lots of great fish hiding places. Go to the right of the boat entrance for big clams and good sized largemouth bass. Plenty of minnows for the fish to feed on.

SHUPAC LAKE   CRAWFORD COUNTY

Acreage: 107 acres   **page 77 of the DeLorme Atlas**

Location: Go north on I-75 north of Grayling and go east on 612 to the town of Lovells, then head north on Shannons Drive, and Shupac Lake will be on your right.

A State Forest Campground in the Au Sable State Forest. This is an awesome scenic lake, a long narrow lake that is gin clear. This is as good as it gets in clarity. There's a small beach area and a small boat launch. Because the lake is narrow, you can snorkel across.

There's a nice shallow area near the entry, then straight out it becomes deep--go to the right which is the shallower part of the lake--there's lots of sunken logs there to create cover for the fish. Hard sand and marl bottom; as it gets deeper there are chara beds and pondweed. Don't forget to enjoy the hundreds of bluegill nearer to shore. Scattered clams, snails and crayfish. A few cottages on the opposite side of the lake nestled among the hardwoods. Peaceful and picturesque, snorkeling here is a very therapeutic experience.

CROOKED LAKE   EMMET COUNTY

Acreage: 2300 acres   **page 82 of the DeLorme Atlas**

Location: Take I-75 north to the town of Indian River, then go west on 68 and before entering the town of Bayview, go east on Pickerel Lake Road which becomes Channel Road. Crooked Lake will be on your right.

This is a very clear lake with a hard sandy bottom--shallow for quite a ways out. In among the bulrushes are loads of big crayfish, snails, many large clams, minnows and darters. There are many spots around the lake in which to pull off the road and snorkel.

ARBUTUS LAKE   GRAND TRAVERSE COUNTY

Acreage: 395 acres   **page 74 of the DeLorme Atlas**

Location; Take Garfield Road out of Traverse City heading south--just before Arbutus Lake there will be a fork in the road--take the left side of the fork and it will lead to the DNR public access. There is also a State Forest Campground access just off of N. Arbutus Road.

Go to the right along the shore--I saw good sized largemouth bass and loads of big sunfish, basking bass, perch, bluegills. The fields of chara were especially beautiful here. Lily pads on both sides of the entrance, loads of pan fish under the dock. Black striped minnows near shore. Lots of dead trees present stark contrast to the high pines and hardwoods.

East Bay Township Park is on the other side, and I also entered there where I found interesting snorkeling among the rocks and vegetation. Underwater landscape is actually more interesting on this side. Go over sand, rocks and pondweed to fields of soft green chara, good sized perch, largemouth bass, red eared sunfish, bluegills--tall celery-like weeds in a lovely setting.

BROWN BRIDGE POND   GRAND TRAVERSE COUNTY

Acreage: 180 acres   **page 74 of the DeLorme Atlas**

Location: Take 611 south of Traverse City--go east on Brown Bridge Road and Brown Bridge Pond will be on your immediate left.

Located in the Pere Marquette State Forest, this is a lake with good clarity which I had the misfortune to snorkel on a cold rainy day. This is a cold lake, known for its northern pike. The bottom is gravel, rocks and sand with wild celery-like weeds widely scattered. I was not dressed warmly enough, a cardinal mistake for you *not* to make.

CEDAR LAKE   GRAND TRAVERSE COUNTY

Acreage: 50 acres   **page 74 of the DeLorme Atlas**

Location: Take 72 west out of Traverse City, go south on Lake Ann Road (Bright Road in some parts) , go east on Richardson Road. When Richardson curves right, you go left to Cedar Lake DNR access. The sign is on the left side right at the entrance and a little hard to see.

This lake is a real winner. Come and make a day of it. Clear water and great to snorkel because of its bowl shape--it's a bowl full of chara, pondweed, fallen branches and logs. The lake drops off almost immediately, so it's fun to snorkel the sides. There's big perch, largemouth bass, hundreds of bluegills, and near shore, black striped minnows. The chara here is a heavenly green color, and you feel like you are floating through a wonderland.

The entrance is fairly small, so it resembles the old swimming hole. Only a cottage or two barely visible. Feels very much like total wilderness.

CEDAR HEDGE LAKE   GRAND TRAVERSE COUNTY

Acreage: 195 acres   **page 74 of the DeLorme Atlas**

Location: Take 31 south of Traverse City, go north on Wildwood, and take your first right into the DNR access. Just one mile north of 31.

This is a good clear lake with a few cottages and lots of white birch. Bottom is gravel and marl with acres of chara beds and scattered pondweed. Along the shore are sunken logs with largemouth bass, minnows, bluegills and rock bass. There are loads of hiding places for fish near the shore. The lake is shallow for some distance out--you have to go out about 25 yards before it starts to get deeper.

LAKE DUBONNET   GRAND TRAVERSE COUNTY

Acreage: approx. 200 acres   **page 74 of the DeLorme Atlas**

Location: Take 31 southwest of Traverse City, go north on Wildwood Road which will dead end into the State Forest Campground.

This is a State Forest Campground in the Pere Marquette State Forest. There are beautiful campsites up on the bluff overlooking the lake. Find a parking spot and take a pathway down to the water. I went in down the concrete walkway. There is no boat launch here. Hard sand bottom--gets deep fairly quickly, but it's a good snorkeling depth, 10-12 feet. Perch, largemouth bass, bluegills, red eared sunfish. A very scenic and uncommercial lake. Good visibility. Lots of attractive watermilfoil, chara, coontail, elodea, pondweed and clams.

DUCK LAKE   GRAND TRAVERSE COUNTY

Acreage: 1930 acres   **page 74 of the DeLorme Atlas**

Location: Take 31 south out of Traverse City, then 137 south into
Interlochen State Park. The lake will be on your left.

This is a big and busy lake that is enhanced enormously by having
a boat, so you can get away from the crowds and seek your own
snorkeling spot. If you do not have a boat, it's catch as catch can,
depending on how crowded it is. The water clarity is there and
the lake has definite potential.

ELK LAKE   GRAND TRAVERSE COUNTY

Acreage: 7730 acres   **page 75 of the DeLorme Atlas**

Location: Take 72 west out of Kalkaska, Go north on Elk Lake
Road and right (east) on Park, which will take you directly to the
DNR access.

As is the story with all of the huge lakes, this is another one that
produces best results if you have a boat to seek out areas to
snorkel. The water is clear, so the lake has the potential, but it is
too large for the snorkeler to make any headway without a boat.
You can snorkel at the DNR accesses on both sides of the lake, but
there is not much to see at those two points.

ELLIS LAKE   GRAND TRAVERSE COUNTY

Acreage: 42 acres   **page 74 of the DeLorme Atlas**

Location: Take 31 south from Traverse City. Ellis Lake is on your
right, very close to the road. If you cross 137 you've gone too far.
It's just a half mile north of 31.

This is a great lake for those who like vegetation, which might not
be small children. Above the water, the scenery is staggeringly
beautiful--you'd never dream there was a busy highway so near.
The lake is in deserted, isolated wilderness.

You feel like Robinson Crusoe on your own private island. To the right of the lake entrance there are many shades of green and many different types of vegetation. At first you think the visibility is not that good, but it is actually excellent, once you adjust your eyes, which takes only a minute. Go straight out, gliding over the grasses until you get to a big open area with every kind of vegetation scattered everywhere--many types of pondweed, chara, watermilfoil, coontail, lilies--you name it--it's there. Lots of perch, bluegills, red eared sunfish, pike, black striped minnows. The vegetation comes right to the surface when you first get in but you really can glide right over it. Take your time, as there's lots to explore here.

FIFE LAKE   GRAND TRAVERSE COUNTY

Acreage: 617 acres   **page 75 of the DeLorme Atlas**

Location: Take 131 south of Kalkaska and go east on Fife Lake Road. The access is almost immediately on your right.

This is a good sized but not overwhelming lake with good visibility. It is especially good for the beginner due to its low weed structure. Sandy bottom with pondweed, fallen logs. I saw loads of baby largemouth bass, minnows, snails and clams. Fairly shallow.

FISH LAKE   GRAND TRAVERSE COUNTY

Acreage: 18.2 acres   **page 74 of the DeLorme Atlas**

Location: Take 31 southwest of Traverse City, then go south on 633. Fish Lake will be on your immediate left, right after crossing Center Road.

This is a small, intimate wilderness lake in a scenic setting surrounded by hardwoods. No cottages, very isolated. Sand and gravel bottom, with lily pads on both sides of the entrance. Sandy beach. There are also inviting weedbeds on both sides of the entrance--tall curly pondweed, big fields of chara. Good visibility. Go about 20 feet out, where the sand ends. There were plenty of perch, largemouth bass, very large black striped minnows and shad by the hundreds.

GREEN LAKE   GRAND TRAVERSE COUNTY

Acreage: 2000 acres   **page 74 of the DeLorme Atlas**

Location: Take 31 southwest of Traverse City--go south on 137 into Interlochen State Park--Green Lake public access will be on your right.

This is a very clear but very busy and commercial lake with its requisite number of jet boats and jet skis. Your only hope is to be lucky enough to hit a quiet day, or as an alternative, hire a boat and get away from the crowds and find your own snorkeling spot--the potential and the clarity is definitely here. The size and amount of activity is the drawback.

LONG LAKE   GRAND TRAVERSE COUNTY

Acreage: 2860 acres   **page 74 of the DeLorme Atlas**

Location: Take 610 south out of Traverse City. This becomes N. Long Lake Road. Then go south on Crescent Shores Road to the public access. You can also enter the lake at two township parks, either Gilbert or Taylor Parks. Both have good swimming beaches. Taylor Park has a big picnic area.

The lake is super clear, like Higgins Lake, but there's not much to see around the Parks. This is another very large lake where the choice snorkeling spots will be found by scouting in a boat.

SILVER LAKE   GRAND TRAVERSE COUNTY

Acreage: 600 acres   **page 74 of the DeLorme Atlas**

Location: go southwest out of Traverse City on 633, then go south on Silver Lake Road. The public access will be on your right.

Snorkeling here is a great experience, and my only regret was that I did not have an entire day to spend here. The lake is super clear, a real pleasure. It has a hard sand bottom, with a few stones and some chara and watermilfoil beds. There were perch, baby smallmouth bass, largemouth bass, and rock bass.

SPIDER LAKE   GRAND TRAVERSE COUNTY

Acreage: 459 acres   **page 74 of the DeLorme Atlas**

Location: Take 31 east out of Traverse City, then go south on Four Mile Road, east on 660 (Hammond Road) south on High Lake Road til it runs into East Arbutus. Spider Lake public access will be on the left hand side of E. Arbutus Road.

This lake is in a gorgeous setting. It has a picturesque shape, as does Arbutus Lake--it winds in and out. Not quite as interesting as Arbutus Lake, but if you are snorkeling Arbutus, you should also take a look at this lake--you never know in any lake what surprise is in store. There's a big log at the end of the dock and beds of wild celery. There were largemouth bass, black striped minnows, and bluegill. There's lots to explore here and I didn't begin to do it all. There's a little suspended sediment, but after a few minutes you don't even notice it. Tall pines and hardwoods surround the lake.

LONG LAKE   IOSCO COUNTY

Acreage: 493 acres   **page 70 of the DeLorme Atlas**

Location: Take I-75 north from Bay City and get off the expressway at West Branch. Go east on 55, then north on 65, west on Kokosing Road. The lake will be on your left.

This is a very big, commercial and busy lake with lots of wave runners and jet skis. If you could catch it on an off day you could have a good snorkel, as the clarity is there. Hard sand bottom with snails, pondweed and patches of chara. The lake meanders all over the place--a boat would be helpful.

LONDO LAKE   IOSCO COUNTY

Acreage: 176 acres   **page 70 of the DeLorme Atlas**

Location: Take I-75 north to West Branch, then 55 east, going north on County Line Road. Take a right at Riley Road which dead ends at the public access. There is no sign.

Good visibility. Lilies on both sides of the entrance. Nice weed structure of mostly chara, wild celery, curly pondweed, broadleaf pondweed. Perch, bluegill, largemouth bass and panfish. Cottages are only on the side you are on, so it feels like wilderness.

ROUND LAKE   **IOSCO COUNTY**

Acreage: 91.5 acres   **page 71 of the DeLorme Atlas**

Location: take I-75 north of Bay City, get off at West Branch and go east on 55 to the town of Sand Lake. Head north on Binder Road, take a left on Beck Road and keep to the right. You will run into the campground.

National Forest Campground in the Huron National Forest. Clear water here with a hard sand bottom. Sparse vegetation and the usual pan fish. This is one of the U.S. Department of Agriculture parks taken over by a private concession, so you could be charged a $3 fee, although I was not. But be prepared. It's an attractive lake and worthwhile.

BEAR LAKE   **KALKASKA COUNTY**

Acreage: 316 acres   **page 76 of the DeLorme Atlas**

Location: Take I-75 north to Grayling, then 72 west. Go north on E. Bear Lake Road and you will be at the public access, with the lake on your left.

An outstanding place to snorkel. It's a fairly big lake with quite a few cottages, most of which have boats. The water is super clear--I was not able to make the time investment to scout as much as I wanted, so this is definitely a lake I am returning to in the future. I went up and down the shore and out to the dropoff where I could see clearly about 30 feet below. There was pondweed, chara and lots of big boulders--just snorkel up and down the dropoff. Very relaxing. I also found hundreds of silver minnows near the shore by docked boats. 4PM on a Friday and no one is here but me.

BIG BLUE LAKE   KALKASKA COUNTY

Acreage: 114 acres   **page 76 of the DeLorme Atlas**

Location: Take I-75 north past Grayling, and go on 612, a great scenic wilderness road through the pines, until you come to Blue Lake Road. Go north on Blue Lake Road, cross Cameron Ridge Road and shortly after, the public access will be on your left.

A very scenic lake with a few cottages. A super clear lake with a very wide entrance. Enter the lake through a large flat area covered with wood chips, detritus, logs, stumps, wood planks, branches. The lake is shallow for a ways, then it slopes into deeper water. Go to the right where there is a big collection of planks and stumps. Largemouth bass are roaming around here. Lots to explore and the clarity in which to do it. Beds of chara to the right. Snorkel around the wood pillars that are sticking out of the water to the right. Hard sand bottom.

CUB LAKE   KALKASKA COUNTY

Acreage: 53 acres   **page 76 of the DeLorme Atlas**

Location: Take I-75 north to Grayling, go west on 72, go north on Bear Lake Road and the public access will be on your left.

This is a very clear lake with a hard sand/silt/gravel bottom. Although known for its smallmouth bass, I only saw the usual pan fish. I saw a few juvenile largemouth bass by the swimming raft. Sparse vegetation.

INDIAN LAKE   KALKASKA COUNTY

Acreage: 69 acres   **page 76 of the DeLorme Atlas**

Location: Take I-75 north to Grayling and the beautiful forest road 612 west. Go north on Blue Lake Road and west on Cameron Bridge Road (also called Twin Lake Road)--follow Twin Lake Road to the right (north), then take a right at Birch Drive, and Indian Lake will be on your immediate right.

A scenic lake with a few cottages. Lilies on either side of the entrance--a shallow lake with a maximum of 18 feet. Not as good clarity as Big Blue Lake but definitely good enough to enjoy the experience, and there are a cluster of lakes in this area to snorkel, such as Pickerel, Big Blue, Starvation and Twin.

Float over beds of soft chara--you can go right through the lily pads, as the stems are very tall and thin, leaving plenty of space in between to snorkel. Clams and some attractive white snails and a goodly amount of largemouth bass. The lake is surrounded by hardwoods, punctuated by lots of white birch.

PICKEREL LAKE   **KALKASKA COUNTY**

Acreage: 100 acres   **pae 76 of the DeLorme Atlas**

Location: Take I-75 north to north of Grayling, get off and go west on 612, a scenic forest road through the pines. Go north on Sunset Trail Road, and the lake will be on your left.

A State Forest Campground in the Pere Marquette State Forest. This is a great super clear lake with plenty of action. Sand/marl bottom. partially covered with big chara beds. It would take a long time to explore everything here. Go to your immediate left to a tiny reed covered channel. This area is loaded with schools of many different kinds of colorful minnows. Big and small perch, largemouth bass, big and small bluegills, small pike, rock bass, shad, big and small pumpkinseeds. Again, the clarity is spectacular, a total treat. I didn't begin to scratch the surface of what was here.

STARVATION LAKE   **KALKASKA COUNTY**

Acreage: 125 acres   **page 76 of the DeLorme Atlas**

Location: Take either 131 or I-75 north and go east (if 131) or west (if I-75) on Mancelona Road (C38). Go south on Cinder Hill Road and east on Starvation Lake Road. The public access will be on your right.

This is a busy lake with lots of boats and cottages and a wide entrance. Go to the right and just where it starts to get deep, there are grasses and some very tall weeds. There were good sized largemouth bass and perch in this area. Super clear water with a hard sandy bottom. The lake is deep, but it's so clear that the depth isn't so important.

BIG TWIN LAKE   KALKASKA COUNTY

Acreage: 215 acres   page 76 of the DeLorme Atlas

Location: Just south of Starvation Lake. Go north on I-75 north of Grayling, and go west through the town of Frederic, north on Kolka Creek Road, west on Cameron Bridge Road, north on Indian Lake Road (also called Twin Lake Road)—follow this around til it becomes N. Twin Lake Road, and the access site will be on the west side of the lake.

This is a busy cottaged lake that is not as busy on the weekdays. It is clean and clear with one spot that is 80 feet deep. The clarity is outstanding, every bit as good as Higgins Lake which is sort of the benchmark to many people. On a sunny Friday afternoon I had the lake to myself. Hard sand bottom with leaves, sticks and some grasses. Snorkel over to the raft, where I saw largemouth bass, clams, crayfish. Visibility is excellent even in the deep areas.

ARMSTRONG LAKE   LEELANAU COUNTY

Acreage: approx. 50 acres   page 73 of the DeLorme Atlas

Location: Go west out of Traverse City on 72. When 72 crosses 669, keep going straight, and you will hit the public access shortly thereafter. Just .8 mile off Armstrong Road.

This is clear and has a nice bowl shape. It's fun to snorkel the slopes. Attractive weed beds--tall pondweed to the right, low chara beds to the left. In the chara, I saw a good sized painted turtle and largemouth bass.

At the entrance there was a big school of black striped and gold minnows. Gravel/sand bottom. Lake is narrow, giving you the opportunity, if you have the time, to roam all around the lake.

CEDAR LAKE   LEELANAU COUNTY

Acreage: 252.5 acres   **page 74 of the DeLorme Atlas**

Location: Take 22 north of Traverse City, then left on Cherry Bend Road--the public access site is almost immediately on your right.

This is a good clear lake with a gray silt over everything. Hard sand/marl/stones/gravel bottom. The bottom is littered with clams and a few snails. It's easy to snorkel across the lake as it is so narrow. You will see many black eyes near the shore--they are bluegills whose bodies blend right in with their surroundings. The lake gets deeper only gradually--you can go out about 30 feet to the dropoff and snorkel along that.

DAVIS LAKE   LEELANAU COUNTY

Acreage: 30 acres   **page 74 of the DeLorme Atlas**

Location: Take 72 west of Traverse City, go south on Reynolds Road, then west on Davis Lake Road. The public access will be on your right.

A beautiful wilderness scenic lake. No cottages. Great swimming area for children, with a big sand beach. Bottom is sand/gravel. Very attractive underwater landscape. A big gill bed to the right, near shore. Spring-fed lake with acceptable but not outstanding visibility. Go to the right--there are logs and branches and the bottom is carpeted with the elodea plant. Saw medium sized painted turtle, red eared sunfish, bluegills. Turn over a small log at the entrance to see crayfish. Tall grasses. Good sized clams.

LAKE LEELANAU   LEELANAU COUNTY

Acreage: 5,370 acres   **page 74 of the DeLorme Atlas**

Location: Take 22 north of Traverse City--go west on 618 (Bingham) which will dead end into the public access.

This is a very clear lake, but as is the case with very large lakes, best results are obtained if you have access to a boat and can scout snorkeling spots--there was not much action at the public access, which is typical of a lake of this size.

ARCADIA LAKE   MANISTEE COUNTY

Acreage: 275 acres   **page 65 of the DeLorme Atlas**

Location: Head north on 31 towards Benzonia, then go west on 602 to a dead end, take 22 south and the lake will be on your right.

You can enter the lake either right by the side of the road or go into town and enter there. It is much less congested by the side of the road--usually just a couple of fishermen, and there is wide open space to roam without interference. In town there are a great many big pleasure boats going in and out. In town, I did see sights that were totally different than those by the road. In town, the water at the entrance is deep, but the visibility is adequate and it is loaded with fish from big carp to good sized largemouth bass to big rock bass, big perch, large size breeding bluegills and good sized pumpkinseeds. A lot of activity among the boulders, rocks and beds of chara, pondweed and watermilfoil. There are big clams; this was the first lake in which I saw zebra mussels--they literally encrusted the tops of the clams. The access by the side of the road was equally interesting, without quite as much activity, but with much more opportunity to roam over the numerous weedbeds without boat interference, which was very heavy in town.

BEAR LAKE   MANISTEE COUNTY

Acreage: 1744 acres   **page 65 of the DeLorme Atlas**

Location: Head north on 31 towards Benzonia. Upon entering the town of Bear Lake, go west on Potter Road and again north on Millarch Road which dead ends into the public access.

This is a shallow lake with a maximum depth of 22 feet. The large size of the lake is mitigated by the fact that the access is in a baylike area, so it is somewhat sheltered. Try to go on a weekday or before 10AM on a weekend before the boat traffic stirs it up. Good visibility. Go to the left past the point--you will see many yellow lilies--the area used to be a sawmill, so there are fallen logs in the area. There are sailing masts there also. I saw perch, bluegills, and juvenile largemouth bass.

HEALY LAKE   MANISTEE COUNTY

Acreage: 39 acres   **page 65 of the DeLorme Atlas**

Location: Take 115 northwest of Cadillac, then go west on 13 mile road (county road 600), go north on Healy Lake Road, then right at Plagany, and a right at Hendrickson, which will take you directly to the lake.

State Forest Campground in the Pere Marquette State Forest. Beautiful drive in through huge stands of tall scotch pines. The campsite settings here are gorgeous. Campsites 3, 4, 5, 6, 7, and 8 are particularly choice, 8 being closest to the lake. Each campsite is surrounded by skinny-trunked super high scotch pines. Great privacy and great beauty. The lake had no one on it on a Sunday, only fishermen on the banks. Good visibility. Lots of fish right at the end of the ramp and both right and left. The lake is thick with brown pondweed and chara, some elodea. Good bowl shape for snorkeling. Good sized largemouth bass, perch, bluegills.

MANISTEE LAKE   MANISTEE COUNTY

Acreage: 930 acres   **page 65 of the DeLorme Atlas**

Location: Take 31 north to Manistee and the public access is in the middle of downtown on the right hand side. There is also a public access on the opposite side of the lake in East Lake Park.

At the marine entrance in town, the visibility is excellent close to shore, not quite as good as you get out further. Lots of pondweed and elodea, tall grass--float over those to the open sandy areas. This area is worth a snorkel just to see the hundreds of clams on so many of the large rocks. Another entry point is at Holiday Park by the side of the road. Go out a short distance and see some nice perch, largemouth bass and sunfish.

PINE LAKE   MANISTEE COUNTY

Acreage: 156 acres   **page 65 of the DeLorme Atlas**

Location: Take 31 north to Manistee, then go east on 55, south on Bosschem Road, then west on Pine Lake Road to the access.

State Forest Campground in the Manistee National Forest. This is great for weekends, as there were no power boats. Lake is clean and clear with great weed structure. This lake is excellent for beginners, as it is not too deep, and it's easier to feel comfortable here. You can almost always see bottom. Clams were huge. Big spawning areas for largemouth bass. There is a brown mud bottom, but it is near very attractive weed structure. You can go way out in the lake without fear of jet boats or jet skiers.

PORTAGE LAKE   MANISTEE COUNTY

Acreage: 2164 acres   **page 65 of the DeLorme Atlas**

Location: Take 31 north to Manistee, going west at 8 mile road into the town of Onekama--there are accesses both on the north side on Portage Point Drive, and on the south side on Crescent Beach Drive.

Visibility is excellent in this very large and busy lake. Try to come during the week if possible to avoid the traffic. The lake entrance in town is much less congested. It has a hard sand bottom and is flat rather than bowl shaped. It has a very clean feeling to it. Go to the left among the bulrushes--there's lots of perch, bluegills, and black striped minnows.

GOOSE LAKE   MISSAUKEE COUNTY

Acreage: 100 acres   page 67 of the DeLorme Atlas

Location: Take 131 north to Cadillac, go east on 55, north on 66, west on Sanborn Road, south on Al Moses Road, west on Randall Road which you take to a dead end. Then take a right on Green Road and follow it around Goose Lake--the public access will be to your left.

State Forest Campground in the Pere Marquette State Forest. This is 100 acres of totally awesome underwater scenery. The entire lake is shallow, so you can roam over the whole lake and always find something interesting. Most of the lake has a maximum depth of 9 feet, perfect for snorkeling. There were no power boats, in fact, no boats at all the Saturday of a holiday weekend that I was there. It's a spring fed lake with excellent visibility. There's some bright and colorful vegetation here, orange and lime green, a combination of bladderwort, watermilfoil, chara and pondweed. It is especially colorful around 5-6PM when the sun is lower in the sky--superb light effects are created on a sunny day. If you go left, there are many lily pads and if you sneak up quietly, you can see some very large largemouth bass hiding in the lily pads. Lots of perch, big red eared sunfish, loads of black striped minnows, big bluegills. The lake has an intimate wilderness feel.

LONG LAKE   MISSAUKEE COUNTY

Acreage: 60.5 acres   page 87 of the DeLorme Atlas

Location: Take 131 north to Cadillac, go east on 55, north on 66, west on Sanborn Road, south on Al Moses Road, west on Randall Road which you take to a dead end.

Then take a right on Green Road and follow it all the way around Goose Lake--the public access for Long Lake is on the other side of the lake opposite Goose Lake. Long Lake will be on your right. This is a State Forest Campground in the Pere Marquette State Forest. There is no boat launch here, so you have to go into the camping area to get to the part of the lake that isn't weed covered. But when you get there it's worth it. Spectacular vegetation in orange, lime and yellow, colors that are not usually found in Michigan inland lakes. Although the weed beds are thick, they are always beneath you and never obstruct. There's every kind of pondweed, chara, watermilfoil and bladderwort. There are big pumpkinseeds, big bluegills and loads of perch. The lake has a maximum depth of 15 feet, so you can snorkel the entire lake. There are no power boats so it's a perfect place to spend a holiday weekend. It's a spring-fed lake with an intimate feel. The clarity is not outstanding but more than good enough. Altogether, a very fine experience.

LOON LAKE   MISSAUKEE COUNTY

Acreage: 20.6 acres   page 67 of the DeLorme Atlas

Location: Take 131 north ot Cadillac, east on 55, north on 66, east at Rhoby Road, north on Vandermullen Road, and when you come to the lake, take the first gravel road to the left. As soon as you turn in you will see a fork--take the left road and you will see the lake almost immediately.

This is a very natural and unspoiled environment. The visibility is not outstanding but more than adequate. The whole lake is only 19 feet deep with a sand/silt bottom. You can stand up when you are halfway across the lake, though it is about 10 feet deep when you are near shore. Loads of fish, lots of pumpkinseeds, largemouth bass, loads of perch, (some quite large), bluegills. There are tall weeds near shore--go out about 20 feet from shore for more great weed beds full of fish. Then go a little further and snorkel up and down the weed beds--a lady's boot is there to the left of the tiny protruding weed island. Lots of sago pondweed. It is fun and easy to cover the entire lake, as it is so small. There's a fairly good sized swimming beach which feels like the old swimming hole. A couple of small grassy islands in the middle. This is just a charming place and a very special snorkeling experience.

LAKE MISSAUKEE   MISSAUKEE COUNTY

Acreage: 1880 acres   **page 67 of the DeLorme Atlas**

Location: take 131 north to Cadillac, east on 55, north on 66--the lake is on your left right in the town of Lake City.

This is another very big lake which means if you go out very far to explore you are going to be right in the path of water skiers. And you need to go out far, because the lake is shallow. It is still, however, a lake with a good deal of potential due to its extreme clarity. It just means that, typical of big lakes, a boat is your best bet to finding the spot or spots that offer what you are looking for, whether it be weed structure, fish, etc. The lake is heavily cottaged with no shore above-water foliage except on the non-cottaged side.

LAKE SAPPHIRE   MISSAUKEE COUNTY

Acreage: 264 acres   **page 67 of the DeLorme Atlas**

Location: Take 131 north to Cadillac, go east on 55, north on LaChance Road, east on Jennings Road, and the public access site will be on your left.

This is a quiet, scenic lake, shallow with decent visibility. There is a point and an island to snorkel to, with plenty of the usual panfish, plus largemouth bass and pike. Scattered weed beds--a very good environment to snorkel in.

AVALON LAKE   MONTMORENCY COUNTY

Acreage: 372 acres   **page 84 of the DeLorme Atlas**

Location: Take I-75 north to Gaylord and 32 east to Atlanta. Go into Hillman and take 451 north. Go west on Cole Road and this will dead end into 459. Go right on 459 and the public access site will be almost immediately on your left.

Avalon Lake is what the limnologists (fresh water lake experts) call an oligotrophic lake--that is one that has little or no vegetation and nutrients and that is oxygen rich.

The good news is that this makes for an extremely clear lake, almost a paradise for snorkelers, but it usually means there is often not as much to see. I found this to be the case in my several visits to Avalon. I would still keep coming back because it is such a therapeutic pleasure to float in that super clear universe, but it does lack excitement. In the south end there are smallmouth bass, which others have seen but I have not. When they are there they are at the dropoff by the sign behind the party store on Lake Avalon Road. Hard sand bottom. Heavily cottaged lake. Similar to nearby Clear Lake, which is also oligotrophic, except there is much more activity in Clear Lake. Avalon is definitely worth the visit while you are in the area.

AVERY LAKE   MONTMORENCY COUNTY

Acreage: 180 acres   page 77 of the DeLorme Atlas

Location: Take I-75 north to Gaylord, east on 32, south on 491, to the town of Lewiston, east on 512 and north on Avery Lake Road which will take you to the lake.

State Forest Campground in the Mackinaw State Forest. This is another snorkeler's paradise. A flooded out valley, Avery Lake has large areas of logs, tree stumps, twisted shapes everywhere. The area around the shore is pretty solidly wood-covered, containing some good sized largemouth bass, and I was surprised to see smallmouths in only 3 feet of water near the shore. It seems inconceivable to me that everyone would not want to look into this wondrous world. Beyond the wooded area there are fields of chara and pondweed. An endlessly fascinating underwater landscape.

CLEAR LAKE   MONTMORENCY COUNTY

Acreage: 133 acres   page 83 of the DeLorme Atlas

Location: Take I-75 north to Gaylord, then go east on 32 to Atlanta, north on 33 and Clear Lake will be on your left.

There are 2 public access sites here, a day use area and a State Forest Campground, and both are excellent. Clear is an oligotrophic lake like Avalon, with incredibly clear water that has to be seen to be believed.

There is plenty of action here, just no weed structure to speak of. Sandy bottom with lots of pieces of broken wood. Many snails. Some largemouth bass, but it is the perch population for which Clear Lake is famous. I got caught in a school of perch that must have had several thousand perch in it. They were on all sides of me as far as I could see, and it was some time before they finally passed, quite an experience. Wonderful bowl shape so you can snorkel the slopes. Visibility seems endless, and even though it's some distance, I snorkeled across the lake, as I was too lazy to go around. I preferred the day use access site, if I had to make a choice. There's a wonderful beach and it's a great place for small children. Delightful in every way. A must.

CROOKED LAKE   MONTMORENCY COUNTY

Acreage: 48.5   **page 77 of the DeLorme Atlas**

Location: Take I-75 north to Gaylord, then go east on 32 to Atlanta, then south on 487. After passing Kohlman Road on your right, take your next left which will be the access site.

This is a long narrow lake that is just fabulous to snorkel back and forth across. I could have spent several days here continually exploring new areas. Right at the entrance to this access site (you can also enter in downtown Atlanta, and that is also worthwhile but is a little more congested than this site) are huge weedbeds well below the surface, so they're easy to snorkel over.There are hundreds of black striped minnows, shad, gold striped minnows, as well as various other types of minnows. There was a big 2-3 foot northern pike watching them, lying next to the big log. There are big patches of sand there and hundreds of perch feeding. Go either left or right--the snorkeling is great everywhere you go--it's impossible to go wrong. To the right, and before you get to the first cottage, there is an arrangement of two tires, logs and wood planks, around which there were several very large largemouth bass cruising as well as a huge crappy. I have never seen a crappy this size.

There were lots of large red eared sunfish, bluegills, rock bass, common shiners, bluntnose minnows, and crayfish. This is a scenic lake with cottages only on the side next to the boat entrance. There were no cottages visible on the opposite side, so it feels like wilderness.

DECHEAU LAKE   MONTMORENCY COUNTY

Acreage: 25.4 acres   **page 83 of the DeLorme Atlas**

Location: Go north on I-75 to Gaylord, then go east on 32 to Atlanta, north on 33 and west on Kellyville Road. The public access site will be on your right.

This is another fabulous snorkeling experience--the Atlanta area seems to be full of them. Almost an embarrassment of riches to have so many great lakes in such a small area. This is real therapy--incredibly relaxing. The entire lake is ony 5 feet deep, with thousands of lilies, but plenty of room to snorkel.

Lots of clams. The bottom is covered with chara and some sand. This is basically a bluegill lake--the spawning beds are everywhere. The lake underwater looks like a forest with cut off tree stumps everywhere, fallen logs scattered all over, and the water is so very clear. The sight of the largemouth bass sailing over the hundreds of tree stumps is an awesome sight. Lots of schools of minnows and the bluegills here are beautiful. This area is also the home of the Kirtland Warbler, all up and down M-33, only a mile away. This is big elk country also. So be on the alert.

ESS LAKE   MONTMORENCY COUNTY

Acreage: 114 acres   **page 84 of the DeLorme Atlas**

Location: Take I-75 north to Gaylord, then go east on 32 to Atlanta, then go north on 33, and after Jackson Lake, go east on 624. Go past Grass Lake Road, and following that there will be a left turn into Ess Lake.

State Forest Campground in Mackinaw State Forest. There are
beautiful campsites overlooking the lake in a scenic wilderness
setting. This is a super clear lake, almost like gin. Another
oligotrophic lake like nearby Clear Lake, with almost no
vegetation., though there are some bulrushes near shore. Silty
bottom with a maximum depth of 50 feet. You can easily snorkel
across the lake. Schools of perch, largemouth bass, and I saw a
pike circling near shore. Ess is a big pike lake. Snorkel to the right
where a log is sticking up above the surface. Below this are pallets
on the bottom which were attracting fish. This is also a big lake for
loons.

LAKE FIFTEEN   MONTMORENCY COUNTY

Acreage: 89 acres   **page 77 of the DeLorme Atlas**

Location: Take I-75 north to Gaylord, then go east on 32 to Atlanta,
go south on 489 to Lake 15 road, then take a left at Ryan Road
which will take you to the access site.

Lake 15 is super clear and clean. The sides slope to a dropoff with
watermilfoil, coontail, lily pads, elodea. Largemouth bass, perch,
minnows. Entire lake appears to be solid sand and gravel. To the
right, out from shore near the lilypads is a jungle of vegetation
with panfish circulating. No boats, no cottages and lots to explore
here.

JACKSON LAKE   MONTMORENCY COUNTY

Acreage: 25.3   **page 83 of the DeLorme Atlas**

Location: Take I-75 north to Gaylord, then go east on 32 to Atlanta,
then north on 33. The Jackson Lake public access will be the next
right after passing Rouse Road. M-33 is a beautiful paved road
through wilderness, one of the nicest roads in Michigan. The sign
does not say Jackson Lake--it just says State Forest Campground;
you have to know to turn in anyway.

State Forest Campground in the Pigeon River State Forest. The campsites here are fabulous, stretched out all along the lake, so you are at lake level and always have the close view and can just step into the lake from your campsite. Very convenient. Number 9 is especially good. Vegetation consists of pondweed, lily pads, watermilfoil, and low scrubby vegetation. Visibility is excellent. It's a very relaxing wilderness experience. Watch for sand darters near the shore. Small clams and snails. Organic and hard sand bottom. The lake is a maximum of 15 feet and you can snorkel across it and always see bottom. Black striped minnows, schools of perch. This is another of the exceptional lakes clustered around the town of Atlanta.

McCORMICK LAKE   MONTMORENCY COUNTY

Acreage: 100 acres   **page 77 of the DeLorme Atlas**

Location: Take I-75 north to Gaylord, then go east on 32, and after passing Gaylanta Lake (which is no good for snorkeling), you will go around a big curve. Right after curving, coming in on a sharp slant, is McCormick Lake Road--the access will be on your left. The lake is 2 miles south of M-32.

State Forest Campground in the Mackinaw State Forest. A beautiful, scenic lake with a wide entrance and surrounded by high hardwoods and pines. Hard sand and gravel bottom. Steep dropoff makes for a great snorkeling wall so you can stay as shallow or as deep as you want. Go to the right for the shallowest water. Big beds of coontail, watermilfoil and chara to the right. Pondweed and lilies both right and left. Look for sand darters on the sand and stones near the entrance. Lots of sunken branches and logs. Red eared sunfish, bluegills, perch, rock bass, clams, big crayfish.

PICKEREL LAKE   MONTMORENCY COUNTY

Acreage: approx. 45 acres   **page 83 of the DeLorme Atlas**

Location: Take I-75 north to Vanderbilt (north of Gaylord), go east on Sturgeon Valley Road, then north on Pickerel Lake Road which will dead end into the Pickerel Lake access.

State Forest Campground in the Pigeon River State Forest. This is
a beautiful narrow scenic spring-fed lake that is very clear and
perfect for snorkeling.   It's a shallow lake with a very wide
entrance and a great swimming lake with a nice beach, so come
and bring the family. If you go a very short distance off shore and
to the right there is a basin and you can free dive about 12 feet
down to the spring. The lake is only about 5 feet deep for quite a
ways out, and it is easy to snorkel across the narrow part in a few
minutes.   You can actually almost walk across the lake.   The
bottom of the lake is hard sand and marl. Vegetation is basically
chara and some scattered pondweed.   There are big largemouth
bass clearly visible in the deeper water--the bass are a pale color to
match the water, and they are beautiful to see. Visibility is 30 feet
or more in the few areas where the lake is that deep. Excellent
experience.

RUSH LAKE   **MONTMORENCY COUNTY**

Acreage: 224 acres   **page 84 of the DeLorme Atlas**

Location: go north on I-75 to Gaylord, then east on 32 to Atlanta,
north on 33 and east again on 624. Take the first road north (Rush
Road) and it will dead end into the public access for Rush Lake.

Very worthwhile snorkeling here. Excellent visibility. The sandy
bottom is littered with hundreds of snails and big clams, in fact
some areas are solid with clams. The lake is quite flat--you go way
out and it still isn't that deep, so avoid coming on a weekend when
you might run into boat traffic. Go straight out about 50 feet to the
weedbeds--I saw a big painted turtle, largemouth bass, a school of
perch and quite a few crayfish. The channel to the right is loaded
with fish.

SAGE LAKE   **MONTMORENCY COUNTY**

Acreage: 51.2 acres   **page 77 of the DeLorme Atlas**

Location: Take I-75 north to Gaylord, go east on 32, south on 491 to
Lewiston, west on 612, and a left into the Sage Lake public access.
Located in the Mackinaw State Forest.

This is a gorgeous scenic wilderness lake with perfect visibility. The lake is quite shallow--4-6 feet in depth but still very comfortable for snorkeling. Going straight out, there are 3 huge pipes and bluegill beds, with lilies and bulrushes on both the right and left sides. Along the left shore, I ran into 8 large largemouth bass and one northern pike, as well as very large bluegills and pumpkinseeds. The bottom is acres of chara and scattered pondweed. The lake is very spread out and winds in and out, so there's plenty to explore here, and the right environment to do it. The lake is narrow enough to easily snorkel across. You could easily spend an entire day or more here. Note the dozens of black and gold striped minnows swimming over the gravel. The lake looks yucky on top but is actually very clean and clear. No jet skiers or power boaters here and no cottages, making it an ideal lake to visit on a weekend, when other busy lakes are crowded. The lake is surrounded by high hardwoods.

EAST TWIN LAKE   MONTMORENCY COUNTY

Acreage: 830 acres   **page 77 of the DeLorme Atlas**

Location: Take I-75 north to Gaylord, east on 32, south on 491 to the town of Lewiston, west on 612. Take a left (south) on Kneeland St. which dead ends into the public access.

This is a super clear lake, but you do run into the problem with a lake of this size that a boat is going to be your best bet to find the best snorkeling spots, since the size of the lake precludes your having the time to discover them any other way. It is a fairly flat and shallow lake. The parts I saw were all sand with a hard bottom. The clarity is definitely there if you can commit the time to explore.

LITTLE WOLF LAKE   MONTMORENCY COUNTY

Acreage: 92.5 acres   **page 77 of the DeLorme Atlas**

Location: Take I-75 north to Grayling, go east on 72, north on 489. Take a right on Wolf Lake Road and another right on Park Road whch will take you right to the access site.

State Forest Campground in the Mackinaw State Forest. Beautiful campsites up on a bluff overlooking the lake. No boat launch here. This is an excellent lake with great visibility--it's like snorkeling in a big bowl of chara. On a Thursday, not a soul was there. Water is clean and very clear; this is definitely a place to spend a good bit of time. Lots of fallen logs, branches, stumps, and a rubber tire. I saw a few big clams, schools of juvenile largemouth bass, perch, and black striped minnows.

AMBROSE LAKE   OGEMAW COUNTY

Acreage: 43 acres   **page 69 of the DeLorme Atlas**

Location: Take I-75 north to West Branch, then north on F7 and west on Houghton Creek Road which will dead end into Ambrose Lake.

State Forest Campground in the Au Sable State Forest. There are some nice campsites overlooking the lake. This is a peaceful uncottaged lake surrounded by high hardwoods. It's a very shallow lake with a maximum depth of 10 feet. The setting is spectacular. There's a wide easy entrance, and the visibility is good though not outstanding.

The bottom is sand/silt and there is vegetation of chara, wild celery and pondweed. I saw largemouth bass, shad and hundreds of baby bullheads only about an inch long. Lots of snails and big clams. To the right of the entrance are sunken logs with snails on them. I found the larger bullheads here to be friendly and curious. This campground is surrounded by mountain bike trails and was popular with 10-12 year old well behaved young bikers.

AU SABLE LAKE   OGEMAW COUNTY

Acreage: 271 acres   **page 70 of the DeLorme Atlas**

Location: Take I-75 north to West Branch, then go north on F7, east on F28 (Rose City Road) (stop in Rose City and have the hot dogs and great ice cream of one of the best Dairy Queens in Michigan!), go north (left) on Sumac Trail just a short distance to the access site.

This is a busy, commercial lake and one to snorkel only if you are in the area, snorkeling other lakes. It is heavily cottaged with lots of jet ski activity. If you can catch it on an off day during the week, you can have a decent snorkel. There are lilies on both sides of the entrance, nice beds of chara, pondweed, and wild celery, populated by rock bass, bluegills and blackstriped minnows.

BUSH LAKE   OGEMAW COUNTY

Acreage: 51.5 acres   **page 70 of the DeLorme Atlas**

Location: Take I-75 north to West Branch, go east on M-55, south on Rifle River Trail to a dead end, left at Greenwood, left at Turner Pine Road, right at Sanderson Road, go one block to a dead end, turn left, go a short distance and the DNR access is at the curve on the right hand side.

This is a cottaged lake with outstanding visibility. It has a nice bowl shape with chara all over. Marl bottom. Near shore to the left are dozens of pumpkinseeds and bluegills--was surprised to see a juvenile pike only about a foot long that was totally white. This is absolutely great snorkeling, and I didn't begin to scratch the surface of what was here. This lake deserves a good bit of time.

CLEAR LAKE   OGEMAW COUNTY

Acreage: 171 acres   **page 69 of the DeLorme Atlas**

Location: Take I-75 north to West Branch, then north on Dow Road which becomes Clear Lake Road and dead ends into Horseshoe Lake Road. Take a right and the access is almost immediately on your left.

This is a busy commercial lake, so try to come during the week. It's as good as its name--very clear. Go to the left of the entrance to weed beds of wild celery, grasses and chara--you should see bluegills, perch, largemouth bass, the usual pan fish. The bottom is sand and gravel. This is an excellent snorkeling lake but busy.

DEVOE LAKE   OGEMAW COUNTY

Acreage: 130 acres   **page 70 of the DeLorme Atlas**

Location: Take I-75 north to West Branch, north out of West Branch on F7, east on Rose City Road (F28) and after passing through Rose City (try the great Dairy Queen there-maybe the best in Michigan), you will shortly see the Rifle River State Recreation on your right. Stop at the entrance and get a map of the area, as there are several lakes here--follow the signs to DeVoe.

There are no cottages here, just a gorgeous wilderness lake, with a great beach, swimming area, picnicking, canoeing, camping, everything.   A great place for a family vacation.   Pristine children's playground.   Boats with motors are prohibited here. Beautiful white birch everywhere. Great snorkeling, super clear water. It's bowl shaped so you will enjoy snorkeling the slopes. Marl bottom with fallen branches, chara, pondweed, coontail. A lovely experience.

GEORGE LAKE   OGEMAW COUNTY

Acreage: 186 acres   **page 70 of the DeLorme Atlas**

Location: Take I-75 north to West Branch, north out of West Branch on F7, east on Rose City Road (F28) and after passing through Rose City, you will shortly see the Rifle River State Recreation Area on your right. Take a right at Sandy Shores Drive, and a left at Forest Drive where you will find the public access. The access is next to the Shady Shores restaurant.

At first the lake doesn't look that clear--it looks a little cloudy, but in a minute or two your eyes adjust, and you can see everything around you very well. Beds of chara, curly pondweed, coontail, watermilfoil, pondweed and wild celery provide attractive vegetation. Quite weedy but very interesting. Bluegills, rock bass, pumpkinseeds and perch.

GREBE LAKE   OGEMAW COUNTY

Acreage: 72.5 acres   **page 70 of the DeLorme Atlas**

Location: Take I-75 north to West Branch, north out of West Branch on F7, east on Rose City Road (F28) and after passing through Rose City and passing the Rifle River State Recreation Area, take a right (south) on Brady Road and another right on Wiltse Road. The public access will then be on your right. Follow the sign that says "Lookout Tower"--there is no Grebe Lake sign. Stop at the Tower--the entrance is just beyond.

This is a tranquil and beautiful lake that is narrow enough so you can snorkel across it.   No motors are allowed here, always a godsend. Lots of white birches. It's a great beginning snorkeling area. Good visibility. Slightly to the left of the entrance is a fallen tree--not a branch but a tree, right at the shore.   I saw a pike here--also bluegills and perch. Vegetation consisted of wild celery, lily pads, coontail, elodea, hydrilla, curly pondweed and broad leafed pondweed.

GROUSEHAVEN LAKE   OGEMAW COUNTY

Acreage: 95 acres   **page 70 of the DeLorme Atlas**

Location: Take I-75 north to West Branch, north out of West Branch on F7, east on Rose City Road (F28) and after passing through Rose City you will find the Rifle River State Recreation Area on your right. Take a right into the recreation area and pick up a map of all the lakes. Grousehaven Lake will be the first one you come to.

This is an area similar to DeVoe lake with an excellent beach, good swimming, canoeing, picnicking area--outstanding for families. It's a beautiful wilderness lake with no cottages and no motors allowed.   Very clean and clear.   Marl bottom.   Many fallen branches and a great bowl shape. Not the vegetation that is in DeVoe Lake--just scattered pondweed. Very large clams.

HORSESHOE LAKE   OGEMAW COUNTY

Acreage: 37 acres   **page 69 of the DeLorme Atlas**

Location: Take I-75 north to West Branch, north out of West Branch on F7, west on Rose City Road (F28) and left (south) on Horseshoe Lake Road which will take you to the public access.

This is an uncommercial lake with only a few cottages. It's an excellent, clear lake loaded with fish. Vegetation is mostly curly pondweed, chara, hydrilla, tall grasses, and bulrushes. There is a hole at the entrance, then the bottom levels off, and the area is loaded with pumpkinseeds, perch, some large largemouth bass, rock bass, bluegills, red eared sunfish. Only a few fishermen and no jet boats, so it's a very relaxing laid-back place to snorkel. There's excellent depth, because everything is easy to see but for beginners, they are not brushing against any weeds. You can roam all over the lake, as it is only a maximum of 20 feet deep.

PEACH LAKE   OGEMAW COUNTY

Acreage: 208 acres   **page 69 of the DeLorme Atlas**

Location: Take I-75 north to West Branch, then east on M-55, north on Peach Lake Road which will dead into the public access.

This lake is crystal clear with a hard white sand bottom, patches of chara, and is known for its walleye. I found it to be rather featureless, but further exploration and more time might reveal more--the potential is certainly there.

RIFLE LAKE   OGEMAW COUNTY

Acreage: 183 acres   **page 70 of the DeLorme Atlas**

Location: Take I-75 north to West Branch, north out of West Branch on F7, west on Rose City Road (F28) south on Shady Shores Road (F17), left on Lakeside Drive, another left on Pine Ridge Road, and a left at Birch Point Drive where you will find the public access.

This is a heavily cottaged and busy lake but a great one for snorkeling. If you go to the right of the entry you'll have your own private wilderness and should be undisturbed. Good visibility and a great underwater landscape, with tall wild celery, chara, curly pondweed, broadleafed pondweed, Eurasian watermilfoil and elodea. Loads of fish—pumpkinseed, perch, bluegills, shad, rock bass, minnows. A very fine experience.

SAGE LAKE   OGEMAW COUNTY

Acreage: 785 acres   page 70 of the DeLorme Atlas

Location: Take I-75 north to West Branch, north out of West Branch on F7, west on Sage Lake Road, follow this around the curve, and the public access will be on your right.

This is a cottaged and fairly busy lake. Lots of wild celery, Brazilian elodea, tape grass. Lots of small pan fish when you enter. Loads of minnows, perch, bluegills, and red eared sunfish.

TEE LAKE   OGEMAW COUNTY

Acreage: 33 acres   page 69 of the DeLorme Atlas

Location: Take I-75 north heading toward West Branch. Get off and go west on Rau Road. Go left (south) on Tee Lake Road which dead ends into the public access.

This is a great lake for snorkeling. It might not be everybody's cup of tea, but I loved it. It's a clear spring-fed lake. The first 20 feet are cloudy, but then it clears right up. There is a nice path through the lily pads. It's a great wilderness lake—only a couple of cottages. There was absolutely *no one* on the lake, not even a fishing boat, and this was a holiday weekend. Lots of vegetation, pondweed, elodea, chara, coontail, thick with lily pads. Loads of big bluegills and blackstriped minnows. There's a big dropoff at the end of the lily pads. Don't be discouraged by the cloudy beginning—the visibility is very good and there's a lot to see! It's a beautiful underwater landscape. I want to spend a great deal more time here.

ISLAND LAKE   OSCODA COUNTY

Acreage: 65 acres   page 77 of the DeLorme Atlas

Location: Take I-75 north to West Branch, east on 55, north on 33 and left into the Island Lake campground.

This is a private campground in the Huron National Forest, so there is a fee of $3 per person. It's a short walk from the parking lot to the entrance to the lake. It's a scenic woodsy setting, peaceful, no boats, just picnickers. Good beach, so bring the family and come and swim. It's a narrow lake and easy to snorkel across. Snorkel to the right of the swimming area--there is a dropoff, where largemouth bass hang out. Bottom is sand with patches of chara.

LOON LAKE   OSCODA COUNTY

Acreage: 90.4 acres   page 77 of the DeLorme Atlas

Location: Take I-75 north to West Branch, east on 55, north on 33 and left for a quarter mile on 486 into the Loon Lake public access.

There's no boat launch here. Visiblity is good and there's much to see. Park in the lot and walk to the lake. Go to the right of the swimming area--there is a great spot loaded with stumps, branches, logs and fish--big bluegills, big largemouth bass (I counted 14 around me at once). This is just an outstanding snorkeling experience--there's a little sheltered shallow bay that is captivating. Loads of fallen logs and branches sheltering many fish. I saw a father holding a toddler--they both had snorkels and masks, and the father was gently pushing the toddler along. The child was delightedly viewing the big bass and other pan fish. The bottom has fields of chara and some pondweed, leaves and other organic material. I did not begin to scratch the surface of what this lake had to offer and plan to go back next summer for more visits.

PERRY LAKE   OSCODA COUNTY

Acreage: 34 acres   **page 78 of the DeLorme Atlas**

Location: Take I-75 north to Grayling, then east on 72 to Mio, where it becomes 33/72. At the point where 72 continues east, you will take 33 north (Abbe Road) until you come to Reber Road. Go left on Reber Road, and the public access will be on your left. Although there are no signs, the entrance is easy to see.

This lake has a fascinating underwater landscape. The ground has sunk, and it has created lots of caves and weird structures. Saw pike, lots of largemouth bass, big and small bluegills. Bottom is silt covered with chara. Go to the left in front of all of the water lilies. Also, look *in* the lilies for fish. There's a picnic area and beach here, so bring the family.

SMITH LAKE   OSCODA COUNTY

Acreage: 25.5 acres   **page 78 of the DeLorme Atlas**

Location: Take I-75 north to Grayling, go east on 72, and after passing through the town of Mio, take a left at Caldwell Road and the Smith Lake public access will be on your left.

This is a clear lake, good visibility, with a sand/marl bottom. You have to walk from the parking lot down a grassy area to the lake, where there is a nice beach. The lake is quite shallow for quite far out--it's only 3-5 feet, good for a beginning snorkeler. There's no boat launch, but it's a good place to bring the family with picnic tables, swings, etc. There were the usual pan fish, minnows, snails. There's lots to explore here and a good environment.

TEA LAKE   OSCODA COUNTY

Acreage: 216 acres   **page 77 of the DeLorme Atlas**

Location: Take I-75 north to Gaylord, east on 32, south on 491, passing through the town of Lewiston, where you take 489 south, with a left at Stickford Road, then a right at Mielke Way Road. Take this to a dead end, then a left at Tee Lake Road. The public access will appear almost immediately on your right.

This is a long narrow lake with very clear water in a beautiful scenic setting. The dropoff is very gradual, and the sloping bowl shape makes it a very pleasurable experience. There's tall pondweed, sunken logs, birch trunks, organic matter. Largemouth bass as well as the usual pan fish. Go to the right, where there's a big tire, an anchor and lots of logs. Plenty to explore and very worthwhile.

BIG BASS LAKE   **OTSEGO COUNTY**

Acreage: 70 acres   **page 77 of the DeLorme Atlas**

Location: Go north on I-75 to Gaylord, east on 32, south on Turtle Lake Road and east on Bass Lake Landing Road, which will dead end into the public access.

This is a true wilderness lake in an incredibly scenic setting with only a few cottages with pontoon boats. The lake has a peat bottom and outstanding visibility. Go to the immediate right for the vegetation and fallen logs. Plenty of sunfish, bluegills, largemouth bass, good sized clams.

BIG BEAR LAKE   **OTSEGO COUNTY**

Acreage: 350 acres   **page 77 of the DeLorme Atlas**

Location: Go north on I-75 to Gaylord, east on 32, south on Meridian Line Road. Then take a right (west) on Bear Lake Drive which will dead end into the campground.

State Forest Campground in the Mackinaw State Forest. Park at the public beach and go in there. This is a good place to bring the kids to swim or snorkel. The water is super clear, and the bottom is hard sand. I wish someone would clean up the cigarette butts underwater here--one of only a very few lakes where I've seen them in quantity. Near shore I saw largemouth bass, perch, black striped minnows and sand darters. Good for beginning snorkelers, as there is little or no vegetation except short grass. This is quite a busy and popular lake, even on a weekday.

BIG BRADFORD LAKE   OTSEGO COUNTY

Acreage: 228 acres   **page 76 of the DeLorme Atlas**

Location: Go north on I-75 to Waters (just north of Grayling). Get off at the Waters exit and go south on Old U.S. 27. Take a right at Bradford Lake Drive which will dead end into the public access.

This is a lake with good clarity and plenty of fish including bluegills, rock bass and largemouth bass, as well as crayfish, clams and snails. Lots of underwater tree trunks as well as many trunks sticking above the water. The lake is very shallow Go left, then go out to the dropoff--I saw smallmouth bass suspended. Lots of organic material on the bottom. Lily pads housed some bluegills.

CLEAR LAKE   OTSEGO COUNTY

Acreage: 35.5 acres   **page 77 of the DeLorme Atlas**

Location: Take I-75 north to Gaylord, go east on 32 into Johannesburg, south on Douglas Lake Road, west on Old State Road. Turn right (north) on Charlton Road and the public access will be on your left.

There is no boat launch here but it's a super clear lake not contradicting its name. The bottom is hard sand covered with chara. Lots of fallen logs and stumps. There is a particularly massive arrangement of logs and branches just to the left of the dive raft to the right of the entry. It is cover for some big largemouth bass, as well as bluegill beds. The lake starts out fairly shallow and deepens gradually to 20 feet or so, but you can still see bottom well. There are no DNR signs, so the directions are particularly important. You have to walk down from the bluff to the water. This is a small enough lake to allow you to easily explore, and it's well worth the time.

DIXON LAKE   OTSEGO COUNTY

Acreage: 80 acres   **page 76 of the DeLorme Atlas**

Location: Go north on I-75 and before reaching Gaylord, get off at Johnson Road and go east, then take a left on E. Dixon Lake Road.

The public access site will be on your left. The site is not marked.

Drive in through a lovely avenue of white birches. When I stared into the abyss of this lake, I found myself shocked by the incredible clarity. It's convenient to stay at the Dixon Lake Motel and snorkel from there. There were big largemouth bass, suckers, wallleyes, schools of perch, big clams, lots of brush and fallen logs though not much vegetation. Go to the right for weed structure and boom, you hit a major dropoff. Snorkel along this wall. There's great plant life here. It's a really remote lake with only one visible cottage and no jet boats or skis.

EMERALD LAKE   OTSEGO COUNTY

Acreage: 50 acres   **page 76 of the DeLorme Atlas**

Location: Go north on I-75 to Gaylord, east on 32, south on Big Lake Road, west on Ranger Lake Road, which will bring you to the public access site.

Gorgeous! Great visibility--at least 25 feet. You're snorkeling in very shallow water. Go straight out and a little to the right and then just wait, the fish will come--largemouth bass, bluegills, sunfish and perch.

GUTHRIE LAKE   OTSEGO COUNTY

Acreage: 128 acres   **page 76 of the DeLorme Atlas**

Location: Take I-75 north and get off at Waters (north of Grayling), east on Marlette Road. Go south on Fascination Drive and the public access site will be on your right.

This is a very oligotrophic (super clear with little or no vegetation) much like Clear Lake and Avalon Lake in Montmorency County. Near shore you can see the largemouth spawning beds. Lake is not too cottaged or busy. There is some debris on the bottom, but it's mostly white sand.

HEART LAKE   OTSEGO COUNTY

Acreage: 62.5 acres   **page 76 of the DeLorme Atlas**

Location: Go north on I-75 and get off at Waters (north of Grayling). Go north on Old U.S. 27 and east on N. Heart Lake Road which will wind all around the lake til it becomes Memorial Drive. The public access site will be on your right.

Fabulous! Stunning visiblity, like Avalon and Clear Lakes in Montmorency County. Great for beginners as you can see everything so clearly and there's no vegetation in your way. All sand bottom with a few patches of elodea. This lake is noted for its smallmouth bass, but I saw some beautiful largemouths as well. The lake is bowl shaped for perfect snorkeling. It was Labor Day, and there were no jet skis and few power boats. Heart Lake Resort is located on the lake.

LAKE MARJORY   OTSEGO COUNTY

Acreage: 40.5 acres   **page 76 of the DeLorme Atlas**

Location: Go north on I-75 and get off at Waters (north of Grayling). Go south on Old U.S.27, then east on Cottonwood Avenue and the public access will be on the left.

State Forest Campground in the Mackinaw State Forest. A very quiet situation, with only pontoon boats, so it is especially safe to snorkel. It's a real fairyland with water clear as crystal and tons of fish. Loads of bluegills with big largemouth bass hiding under the logs. The underwater environment is really out of this world--I could have stayed here forever. Lots of fallen trees and hiding places at the shore. Straw like stalks sticking up to the surface--otherwise there's nothing in the way but some picturesque lily pads.

OPAL LAKE   OTSEGO COUNTY

Acreage: 122 acres   **page 76 of the DeLorme Atlas**

Location: Go north on I-75 and get off at Charles Brink Road (north of Grayling).

Go east on Charles Brink Road, right (south) on Birch Drive which becomes Opal Lake Road. Stay left and drive around the northern side of the lake, still on Opal Lake Road. At this point you will be on the east side of the lake and the public access site will be on your right.

This was a strange lake--I felt like I was in the Arctic--everything was completely white. It looked like it had been snowing. White sand and marl bottom with only a few patches of elodea. Perfect for beginning snorkelers with its crystal clear water and lack of serious vegetation. It took me only 9 minutes to snorkel over to a little island where largemouth bass, stark white to match their environment, posed for my video. There were also schools of sunfish, bluegills and minnows. A busy lake on summer weekends, but I found it most worthwhile.

OTSEGO LAKE   OTSEGO COUNTY

Acreage: 1972 acres   **page 76 of the DeLorme Atlas**

Location: Take I-75 north beyond Grayling and get off at Old State Road at the southernmost part of Otsego Lake. Go north on Old U.S. 27. You can enter at the first public access site on your left, or go further north and enter at the Division Street access site or go all the way around to the west side of the lake and enter at the Beechwood Avenue access site.

This is a very large and busy lake, so try to confine yourself to weekdays if possible. Clarity is excellent, but like so many large lakes, it tends to lend itself more to those with boats who can scout out the best snorkeling spots.

LAKE 27   OTSEGO COUNTY

Acreage: 112 acres   **page 82 of the DeLorme Atlas**

Location: Go north on I-75 to Gaylord, west on 32, left on Hallenius Road, and the public access site will be on your right.

This lake has good visibility and the great bowl shape that makes it so desirable for snorkelers. It has a hard sand bottom covered with leaves and beds of chara.

Go either right or left and snorkel among the bulrushes. The usual pan fish as well as numerous clams and snails.

BEAR DEN LAKE   PRESQUE ISLE COUNTY

Acreage: 29 acres   page 83 of the DeLorme Atlas

Location: Take I-75 north to Gaylord, 32 east to Atlanta, north on 33, left (southwest) on Bear Den Road and the lake access will be on your right. Two miles southwest of 33.

This lake is a real delight. It has that desirable bowl shape so perfect for snorkeling, allowing you to snorkel the sides and decide quickly what depth you prefer. The shore area is flat, so you have to get beyond that to snorkel along the dropoff. The bottom is marl/sand, and in no time I had hundreds of panfish around me. Tall grasses, chara, pondweed, some very lovely greenery. Visibility is excellent. Loads of black striped minnows, perch, fat head minnows, shad. In the shallow flat area were good sized suckers and largemouth bass in only about a foot of water. Bluegill beds were just beyond the bulrushes. It's not a deep lake--only 15-20 feet at the maximum in the areas in which you would be snorkeling, 30 feet in the deepest part. The lake is small enough to go all around. This is easily worth a whole day. Or more. No cottages. The cry of the loons was present, almost sounding like a human's scream. There were three that were fairly close to me. Beautiful pine and birch drive in. Very worthwhile.

LAKE EMMA   PRESQUE ISLE COUNTY

Acreage: 115 acres   page 84 of the DeLorme Atlas

Location: Take I-75 north to Gaylord, 32 east to Hillman, north on 451 which becomes F21, west on 634, then right (north) on Lake Emma Road. Take a left on West Highway, and the access will be almost immediately on your right.

This is a gorgeous wilderness lake surrounded by hardwoods, many of them white birch. Silt bottom with a few fallen logs, fields of chara flattened out with individual tall pondweeds sticking up.

Saw pike on the right hand side in front of a broken and bent-in-half birch. Schools of perch and pumpkinseed. Good visibility.

LAKE FERDELMAN   PRESQUE ISLE COUNTY

Acreage: 33 acres   **page 84 of the DeLorme Atlas**

Location: Take I-75 north to Gaylord, 32 east to Hillman, north on 451, left (west) on Hubert Road, north on Royston Road, a right on Lake Emma Road, and the lake access will be on your right.

Welcome to your own private paradise. This is another true wilderness lake surrounded by tall hardwoods including many white birch. This is a lake that has everything--excellent underwater clarity, the wilderness setting and an interesting landscape. Lots of parking in spite of the wilderness setting. Not a sign of anyone on a Tuesday in August. There are a couple of docks but you can't see the cottages and the only sound is the birds. The lake has a silt/sand bottom and is only 5-8 feet deep. Be careful not to kick up the silt. Lots of fallen branches and logs. Go left to the lilies--lots of largemouth bass of all sizes, as well as bluegills. Schools of black striped minnows near shore. Pondweed, chara and large lilies with thick stems to provide cover for the fish. There were 8-9 largemouth bass in front of my camera lens at once.

GRAND LAKE   PRESQUE ISLE COUNTY

Acreage: 5660 acres   **page 85 of the DeLorme Atlas**

Location: Go north on U.S.23 to Alpena, continuing on 23 past Long Lake. The Grand Lake public access will be on the right after passing North Grand Lake Highway,

This is a huge lake that is best scouted by boat. The clarity is definitely there, and there's lots of potential if you can invest the time. The clarity is not as outstanding as Torch Lake, but it is still more than acceptable. Rocky/sand bottom. There's no vegetation anywhere near shore. Black and gold striped minnows.

Don't come to a big lake like this on a windy day, as it is too choppy to enjoy. Try to come during the week, as there's lots to explore and it is too busy on the weekends.

LOST LAKE   PRESQUE ISLE COUNTY

Acreage: 104 acres   **page 84 of the DeLorme Atlas**

Location: Take I-75 north to Gaylord, 32 east to Hillman, north on 451 which becomes F21, west on 638 (W. Hawks Highway), left (south) on Lost Lake Road. The public access will be on your right.

There are two areas to snorkel here--the beach area and the boat launch on the other side of the lake. On the beach side, you walk across a grassy area to the sandy beach. The bottom is silt over hard sand around the entrance. Around the entrance I saw black striped minnows, largemouth bass and pumpkinseeds. Go out to the raft where I saw schools of small largemouth bass. Scattered low vegetation, grasses and curly pondweed. There is decent clarity--about 10-15 feet. The change of depth is gradual. There is some suspended sediment but it doesn't interfere that much with the visibility. You quickly learn to ignore it. The boat entrance is more interesting to snorkel because of its bowl shape. Silty bottom. Go in the shallows to the right to the big lilies with thick stems (in contrast to the many lilies there with long thin stems). There I saw perch, schools of pumpkinseeds, largemouth bass and some logs and branches.

LAKE MAY   PRESQUE ISLE COUNTY

Acreage: 161.2 acres   **page 84 of the DeLorme Atlas**

Location: Take I-75 north to Gaylord, go east on 32 to Hillman, north on 451, west on 634 which will become Lake May Road--the public access site will be on your left.

The boat access is also a big swimming beach, so this offers the opportunity of coming with the family. It's quite a busy lake with water skiiers, jet boaters, etc. in addition to quite a few cottages.

There is some suspended sediment but it is clear enough to snorkel. Attractive beds of chara, curly pondweed and coontail, small snails and big Venus clams. Go to the right of the swimming beach. It gets deeper very gradually.

LAKE NETTIE   PRESQUE ISLE COUNTY

Acreage: 278 acres   **page 84 of the DeLorme Atlas**

Location: Take I-75 north to Gaylord, go east on 32 to Hillman, north on 451, west on 634 which will become Lake May Road. Go past Lake May, and the public access site for Lake Nettie will be on your left.

This is a good snorkeling lake with a wide entrance and lots of room to roam. There is a gradual dropoff, and it is bowl shaped which is always a big plus. There are only a few cottages. Visibility is very good, about 15 feet. There was no activity on the weekdays I was there.There are lilies on both the right and left sides, plus beds of chara, pondweed, elodea, coontail, bladderwort and 2 kinds of watermilfoil. There were loads of big clams, especially around the bottom of the stone covered ramp. I saw sand darters, schools of perch, black striped minnows, and largemouth bass.

OCQUEOC LAKE   PRESQUE ISLE COUNTY

Acreage: 130 acres   **page 84 of the DeLorme Atlas**

Location: Take I-75 north to Gaylord, go east on 32, north on 33 to Onaway, then continue on north out of Onaway on 211 to Onaway State Park. Take 489 north out of Onaway State Park, take 646 east to U.S.23, go south on Ocqueoc Road, west on Cheboygan Road and right (north) on Domke Road which will dead end into the public access site.

This is an enormously worthwhile lake which bears repeating and is deserving of a good bit of time. You enter on the road of the same name, one of the most attractive paved forest highways in Michigan, reminding me a good bit of the wilderness of Scotland.

This is an isolated "no wake" lake surrounded by white birch and other tall hardwoods. There are a few cottages, but they are well hidden so the wilderness experience is preserved. The lake is a little cold, so dress accordingly. Attractive vegetation consists of curly pondweed, elodea, big fields of chara, coontail, watermilfoil. Immediately on entering the water I saw numerous large rock bass, small crappies, perch by the hundreds. The weed structure is so picturesque, a pleasure to look at due partly to the varying heights from very tall to the low fields of chara, but you are always floating over the top, never touching. There are many, many big clams in the shallow areas. The weed structure is to the left, the lilies are on the right. The lake is bowl shaped with a sandy bottom.

PRESQUE ISLE HARBOR*   PRESQUE ISLE COUNTY

Bay of Lake Huron   **page 85 of the DeLorme Atlas**

Location: Take I-75 north to Gaylord, go east on 32 to Alpena, then north on U.S. 23, east on Rayburn Highway, north on Grand Lake Road, and the public access site will be on your right.

Strictly speaking, this is of course not an inland lake, but the locals were so enthusiastic about the snorkeling here that I felt it worth including. Go to the left of the long blue walkway--the water is very clear. You can stand on the walkway and look down into the water and see the big carp swimming around. The rocky shore and bottom are covered with stones and boulders. There were 5 big gold colored carp swimming with me--very exciting. The water is, of course, cold, as you are in one of the Great Lakes, but if you wear even a medium weight wet suit you are fine. Walk further down the pathway to the lighthouse. There are shoals out in front of the American flag where I saw walleye. In the morning, on the inside of the breakwater, the brown trout come in looking for minnows.

SHOEPAC LAKE   PRESQUE ISLE COUNTY

Acreage: 45 acres   **page 83 of the DeLorme Atlas**

Location: Take I-75 north to Gaylord, go east on 32 to Atlanta, north on 33, east on 634, and a right on Shoepac Lake Highway.

The campground will be on your right.

State Forest Campground in the Pigeon River State Forest. You
come in along an incredibly scenic birch lined drive to the boat
entry. The water is very clear with a hard sand bottom. It's a
gorgeous wilderness lake with no cottages, You have to snorkel
through a weedy area to get through to the lake proper. If you
don't want to snorkel through this area, you can go in from a
campsite if it is free and go directly to the beach. I found
snorkeling through the weedy area very pleasurable--it was clean
and clear, and I saw 2 very large crappies, a medium size northern
pike and many good sized bluegills and largemouth bass. There
are a dozen or so gill beds to the right of the weedy entrance. This
is a drop dead beautiful setting and a spectacular place to camp.
Tall pines and hardwoods everywhere--this definitely feels like
Hiawatha country!

TOMAHAWK FLOODING   PRESQUE ISLE COUNTY

Acreage: 604 acres   **page 83 of the DeLorme Atlas**

Location: Take I-75 north to Gaylord, go east on 32 to Atlanta,
north on 33, east on County Line Road (the road *before* Tomahawk
Lake Highway) and this will dead end into the public access.
Drive *past* the Tomahawk Flooding signs and go further on to get
to the lake entrance.

Great snorkeling here! Water is super clear with big boulders
around the shore. Lake has a maximum depth of 15 feet. Loads of
northern pike here. Lots of tree stumps, black striped minnows,
perch, gills. Great vegetation to snorkel over--beds of chara, wild
celery and pondweed. High grass on one side and tall hardwoods
and pines on the opposite side.

BIG TOMAHAWK LAKE   PRESQUE ISLE COUNTY

Acreage: 40 acres   **page 83 of the DeLorme Atlas**

Location: Take I-75 north to Gaylord, go east on 32 to Atlanta,
north on 33, east on Tomahawk Lake Highway and the
campground will be on the right.

Drive *past* the Tomahawk Flooding signs and go further on to get to the lake entrance.

State Forest Campground in the Pigeon River State Forest. This is a beautiful wilderness lake with no cottages in an extremely scenic setting surrounded by pines. There's a lovely sandy beach, and the lake bottom is sandy near shore and silty further out. There are some big clams among the clumps of chara and pondweed. It's a flat lake that gets deeper very gradually. Excellent visibility. Wide and attractive entry. Very uncommercial. During the week I was completely alone.

HIGGINS LAKE   ROSCOMMON COUNTY

Acreage: 9600 acres   **page 68 of the DeLorme Atlas**

Location: Take U.S.27 north and get off at the Higgins Lake exit. There are public access sites at Higgins Lake State Park on the north side on Roscommon road, on the west side on Old U.S. 27, and on the south side on Pine Drive (104). In each case, the public access sites are adjacent to the road.

This is a lake that is well known with divers and snorkelers--noted for its outstanding visiblity. I took my son on his first snorkel here, and he loved it. He felt totally comfortable, as he could see so well in every direction and the vegetation was minimal--just scattered patches of chara. The fish I saw were mostly small, just minnows and small perch, but it was still a relaxing and fun experience. Flag Point is one of the recommended snorkeling spots--lake maps are available at the Higgins Lake Dive Shop, which is also well equipped for all of your other snorkeling needs.

HOUGHTON LAKE   ROSCOMMON COUNTY

Acreage: 20,044 acres   **page 68 of the DeLorme Atlas**

Location: Take U.S. 27 north and get off at the Houghton Lake exit (M-55). Heading east for a small distance, you will see Old U.S. 27. Go north on Old U.S. 27 to Bradford Drive (300). Take a right, and the public access site will be almost immediately on your right. Or, another access site can be used if when traveling east on M-55 you stop at Sturgis Road.

The public access site will then be on your left. Or continuing on M-55 to the easternmost part of the lake, head north on Houghton Lake Drive East, and after crossing N. Cut Road, the public access site will be on your left.

This huge lake is not as clear as Torch Lake but it's still plenty clear. The task here is to find the best spots in a lake this size, a job that is best suited for a boat. It's a substantial time investment, but the clarity and the weed beds are there. It is of course a very busy and commercial lake, but the boat action takes place pretty far out, so you are quite safe if you just stay alert to your surroundings.

LAKE ST. HELEN   ROSCOMMON COUNTY

Acreage: 2390 acres   **page 69 of the DeLorme Atlas**

Location: Take I-75 north past West Branch. Get off and go north on F97 and west on Airport Drive which will dead end into the public access.

There is an excellent beach with good swimming and sunning possibilities here. It's a busy lake, but the jet skis stay quite far out due to the size of the lake, so they don't really bother you. Avoid the lagoon which is very murky because of all the boats. But you can walk along the grass to the end of the lagoon and enter there where I saw bluegills and largemouth bass. It's a very shallow lake, only about 5-10 feet deep.

HODENPYL DAM   WEXFORD COUNTY

Acreage: 1680 acres   **page 66 of the DeLorme Atlas**

Location: Take 115 northwest out of Cadillac, and after passing through the town of Mesick, go southwest on Beers Road (598). The public access site will be on your left opposite 3 and a Half Road.

A very large and very clear lake. Go to the RV public beach. At the edge of the swimming area are weed beds with largemouth bass and smaller pan fish. There are many areas along the shoreline to try. As in any lake as large as this, there is an investment of time involved to cover this large a body of water.

LONG LAKE   WEXFORD COUNTY

Acreage: 190 acres   **page 67 of the DeLorme Atlas**

Location: Take 131 north of Cadillac and go east on Long Lake Road. The campground and public access site will be on your right.

State Forest Campground in the Pere Marquette State Forest. There's a gorgeous three mile drive in to get to this total wilderness lake. This is really the place to get completely away from civilization--a drop dead scenic environment that reminds me a great deal of the wilderness of Scotland. Beautiful campsites overlooking the lake. Visibility is good, bottom is silty. Lots of small panfish, minnows and gills. Nothing that exciting but the setting is worth it.

MEAUWATAKA LAKE   WEXFORD COUNTY

Acreage: 94.5 acres   **page 66 of the DeLorme Atlas**

Location: Take 115 northwest out of Cadillac. Go north on No. 27 Road, east on No. 26 Road, north on No. 27 and a Quarter Road, west on No. 24 Road, and south on No. 27 Road which will dead end into the public access.

This lake environment took some getting used to but proved to be an excellent experience which I have repeated--the ultimate test. The bottom is solid with lots of detritus. Go to the left of the public beach where there's lots of habitat among the fallen logs and branches. Pondweed, both narrow and broad, as well as some attractive watermilfoil. The area is loaded with large snails, some clams, large rock bass, baby largemouths as well as full size, lots of bluegills and small sunfish. I saw medium sized painted turtles and snapping turtles (remember, snapping turtles will NEVER bother you unless you should grab them and attempt to restrain them in some way. Grabbing a snapping turtle would be close to impossible, since they swim so swiftly, they wouldn't give you the chance). This is a fairly quiet and not heavily boated lake.

LAKE MITCHELL   WEXFORD COUNTY

Acreage: 2580 acres   **page 66 of the DeLorme Atlas**

Location: Take 115 into Cadillac, then go west on M-55. The
public access site will be on your right opposite No. 35 Road. Or,
for a second access site, take a right off M-55 onto Pole Road, and
after passing 33rd Road, the public access site will be on your
right.

There is a huge public area here with a nice beach and a good
family environment. It's a busy, commercial lake with excellent
clarity, but I found no weed structure near shore. It's great for
beginners, as the bottom is solid sand and gravel, and it is so
shallow you can wade out very far. By doing so, you must be on
the watch for the boat traffic. Try to stick to weekdays here.

CENTRAL LOWER PENINSULA

ARNOLD LAKE   CLARE COUNTY

Acreage: 19.12 acres   **page 68 of the DeLorme Atlas**

Location: Take U.S. 27 north to Harrison and continue on to Arnold Lake Road, where you will go east. The public access site will be on your right.

This lake offers a beautiful experience. Although there are lots of cottages, I still found it very quiet on a holiday weekend. The underwater landscape is exceptional with just the right depth for snorkeling. The vegetation is thick but always below you. There are hundreds of fish right off the dock--shad, black striped minnows, largemouth bass, bluegills, crappie, and rock bass. Take the time to really explore here--it's well worth the effort.

BUDD LAKE   CLARE COUNTY

Acreage: 175.4 acres   **page 68 of the DeLorme Atlas**

Location: Take U.S. 27 north to Harrison. Take the Harrison exit and go into town on business 27 which will join with 61. In the middle of town, go right on 61 to a dead end, go left on S.Lake Road and the public access site will be on your immediate right. Or you can enter at the Wilson State Park entrance on the north side of the lake. There is also another access site on the south end of the lake.

This is an excellent family area, with a wide beach area and plenty of space for picnicking and swimming. Though heavily cottaged, this is still a real fairyland with good visibility and acres of attractive vegetation--elodea, hydrilla, a little pondweed, coontail, watermilfoil, tape grass and wild celery. The underwater esthetics are great due not only to the quantity of plant life but to the variety in heights. Hundreds of fish, both big and small are swimming through this setting--both large and small bluegills, red eared sunfish, good sized largemouth bass, big perch, black striped minnows.

There is a bay section right at the access that is perfect for snorkeling, and it has that great bowl shape that makes the whole experience so pleasurable.

CRANBERRY LAKE   CLARE COUNTY

Acreage: 106 acres   **page 68 of the DeLorme Atlas**

Location: Take U.S. 27 north to Harrison and continue on to Arnold Lake Road, where you will go east, pass Arnold Lake on your right and continue on to Eberhart Road, where you will take a right, then a left at Hamilton Drive, then a right at Flashing Site Road which will dead end into the public access site.

This lake provided an excellent snorkeling experience. The water was clear with good though not great visibility. The bottom was littered with large and small snails, as well as big crayfish. I was surprised in late August to see the big breeding male bluegills, along with lots of perch and black striped minnows. There was every kind of vegetation right around the shore--elodea, tapegrass, pondweed, coontail, Eurasian watermilfoil and chara. Go either right or left for a rich experience. To the right I found some tree stumps with snails on them, as well as big crayfish. I also found it profitable to go to the right, where the buoys are--a good place to find fish. The lake is in a beautiful setting among hardwood trees.

EIGHT POINT LAKE   CLARE COUNTY

Acreage: 387.5 acres   **page 57 of the DeLorme Atlas**

Location: Take U.S. 27 north to Clare, go northwest on 115, then west on 10, then south on W. Eight Point Lake Road--then go left on South Shore Drive and the public access site will be on your left.

There's a public access for swimmers and one for boaters, but it's awfully busy. The best bet is the north shore access. This is a lake that locals rave about for clarity, and indeed it is, and though the visibility is there, this is a hard lake to appreciate because of the large number of power boaters.

It has the potential to provide a good experience, with lots of bays and intimate coves, if you can be lucky enough to hit it on an off day for boating activity. Try to come during the week, either before 10AM or after 6PM.

LAKE GEORGE   CLARE COUNTY

Acreage: 134 acres   **page 58 of the DeLorme Atlas**

Location: Take U.S. 27 north past Harrison, then go west on Mannsiding Road, take a right on Cedar Road, a left on Arthur Road and a left on Lake George Street. The public access site will be on your left.

Very good visibility here with some interesting and varied vegetation--tape grass, curly pondweed, northern watermilfoil, wild celery, coontail and chara. A spring fed lake with plenty of red eared sunfish, bluegills, pumpkinseeds--30-40 of these were hanging off the end of the dock at the entrance.

LILY LAKE   CLARE COUNTY

Acreage: 209 acres   **page 58 of the DeLorme Atlas**

Location: Take U.S. 27 north to Harrison, then west on 61, then south on Harding Ave. The public access site will be on your left, after passing Cherry Grove Avenue.

This is a spring fed lake that is unusually clear. Just great snorkeling here with a perfect depth. The vegetation is plentiful but low. The gravel and sand bottom is mostly covered with chara. Go left about 15 feet out--I saw loads of big perch, pumpkinseeds and bluegills. This is a lake to repeat with an outstanding underwater landscape and the visibility to appreciate it, as well as a picturesque setting to frame it. Very few cottages.

LITTLE LONG LAKE   CLARE COUNTY

Acreage: 43 acres   **page 68 of the DeLorme Atlas**

Location: Take U.S.27 north to Harrison, then east on Townline Lake Road. Go south on Lakeview Drive and take the first left which will dead end into the public access site.

This lake is a good example of not letting a holiday weekend keep you from checking out a lake. Although this lake has everything going for it, on the Friday of Labor Day weekend, this heavily cottaged lake had *no one* on it--really amazing. Good visibility with acres of chara, pondweed, a little elodea, lots of wild celery. Go to the left where the tall grasses are--there's lots of rock bass, bluegills and black striped minnows. Plenty of good sized snails. Lots of places to explore here. Don't forget to look for fish at the end of the boat ramp.

LONG LAKE   CLARE COUNTY

Acreage: 210 acres   **page 68 of the DeLorme Atlas**

Location: Take U.S. 27 north through Harrison, and get off at Old U.S.27 heading north. Take a right at Forest Road and a left at Breeze Road which will dead end into the public access site.

There are a number of cottages here, but it's not too busy to snorkel. Good but not great visibility. Lily pads on either side of a very wide entrance. Gorgeous hardwoods fill the access site, and the entire lake is surrounded by high hardwoods. There's lots of vegetation, but you can snorkel around it. Big fields of curly pondweed, tall grasses, brown broadleaf pondweed, northern and Eurasian watermilfoil. It's only a few minutes snorkel over to an off shore island. Lots of bluegills, crappies, largemouth bass and black striped minnows.

NESTOR LAKE   CLARE COUNTY

Acreage: 15 acres   **page 58 of the DeLorme Atlas**

Location: Take U.S. 27 north through Harrison and get off at the Mannsiding exit. Head east on Mannsiding Road.

Take the first left after you have passed the lake. This left will dead end into the public access site.

This is a small intimate spring fed lake with good though not great visibility. Vegetation is mainly chara, coontail, northern watermilfoil, but it is the elodea that dominates and gives the underwater landscape its distinctive look. Lots of vegetation here but it doesn't get in your way. Lilies on the left with bluegills, the usual pan fish and black striped minnows.

PIKE LAKE   CLARE COUNTY

Acreage: 14 acres   **page 57 of the DeLorme Atlas**

Location: Take U.S. 27 north to Clare, go northwest on 115, south on Lake Station Road, and the public access site will be on your right.

This lake looks mucky but it isn't. It has a sandy bottom, is clear, and has good weed structure to float above. I saw only small pan fish but I didn't stay as long as I wanted to. There was *no one* there, even though it was a weekend. It has a very picturesque setting--what you imagine the old swimming hole to be like.

SILVER LAKE   CLARE COUNTY

Acreage: 55 acres   **page 57 of the DeLorme Atlas**

Location: Take U.S. 27 north to Clare, go northwest on 115, take a right on Ashard Road, go right on Hemlock, left on North Road, and a right on Silver Lake Road. The public access site will be on your right. There is no sign--the entrance is basically down a long alleyway between two cottages.

This lake was really bizarro. You wade in and it's very shallow --barely up to your knees--for quite a ways out. Then suddenly boom, there is a 52 foot drop! It's like walking to the edge of a cliff that you didn't know was there and suddenly looking out on a huge deep vista. This is a gin clear and very fascinating lake. The hard sand bottom is littered with snails. Go out to the right about 50 feet--that is where the dropoff is.

There I saw tons of bluegills, largemouth bass, perch, pumpkinseeds. The vegetation is very picturesque with pondweed, northern watermilfoil and chara in many beautiful shades of green. A spring fed lake that offers a fine snorkeling experience.

WINDOVER LAKE   CLARE COUNTY

Acreage: 50 acres   page 68 of the DeLorme Atlas

Location: Take U.S. 27 north to Clare, go northwest on 115, take a right on Twin Lakes Road, another right on Monroe Road, another right on Strawberry Avenue, a left on Spring Avenue, and a right on Spring Road. The public access site will be on your left.

A great snorkeling experience! No power boats--only pontoons. Very quiet, even on weekends. The lake is clear, flat and shallow with lots of snails and huge clams everywhere. It's good either going left or right. Big largemouth bass, perch, bluegills and rock bass.

MYERS LAKE   GENESEE COUNTY

Acreage: 32 acres   page 40 of the DeLorme Atlas

Location: Take I-69 between Lansing and Flint, and go southeast on Grand River Road. Take a left at Lehring Road which in the town of Byron becomes Silver Lake Road. Take a right at Murray Road and the campground is on the immediate right hand side.

Methodist campground--there are some beautiful campsites up on the bluff. Walk down the steps from a campsite to the lake. Nice children's play area. Very scenic, somewhat cottaged lake with a nice beach. Visibility is good but not great. Hard sand bottom with sparse vegetation--mostly scattered chara. Quite shallow--you have to go out quite a ways before it's deep enough to enjoy. Snorkel out to the raft where pan fish are located.

SILVER LAKE   GENESEE COUNTY

Acreage: 41.21 acres   **page 40 of the DeLorme Atlas**

Location: Take I-69 northeast of Lansing and after passing the Swartz Creek exit, go south on Linden Road into the town of Linden. Take Silver Lake Road east out of Linden, and the access is on your right, next to the road.

You pay $3 to park at the Water Sports Marina and snorkeling is permitted. It's a busy commercial lake that is loaded with boats, but on the right hand side is a little shallow bay that is way out of the way of the boats (but take care with the boats entering and leaving). You can stay in the shallow area near the lilies and weeds--lots of bluegills and gill beds. All the usual pan fish as well as gold striped minnows. Bottom is hard sand where you can always stand up. Water is extremely clear. Vegetation consists of chara, curly pondweed, wild celery, and northern watermilfoil. Another entrance is next to the Silver Spray Sports where it is $5 to park. It is a little better at this entrance, as the vegetation is thicker and the water is deeper.

LAKE FOUR   GLADWIN COUNTY

Acreage: 35 acres   **page 69 of the DeLorme Atlas**

Location: Take I-75 north from Detroit, take F-18 (Greenwood Road) west, go south on Maple Valley Road (F-97), go east on Hilts Road and north on Lake Four Road which dead ends into the public access.

This is a great spring fed lake with fine visibility. Near shore is cloudy--you have to go out about 15 feet before it becomes clear. There are a few cottages here but otherwise it is uncommercial--just a few fishermen. No jet skis or power boats. The water gets deep very fast. Very tall weeds in deep water. Vegetation is largely northern watermilfoil with some pondweed and lily pads on both sides. Loads of bluegills, largemouth bass and black striped minnows.

LITTLEFIELD LAKE   ISABELLA COUNTY

Acreage: 183 acres   **page 58 of the DeLorme Atlas**

Location: Take U.S. 27 north through Mt. Pleasant, then go west on Stevenson Lake Road, south on Gilmore Road, west on Woods Road, and north on Littlefield Road which will dead end into the public access.

This was a fascinating little lake full of surprises, at least for me. Clarity is excellent, but I spent about 20 minutes with nary a sign of life, and I was about to give up when as I came near the shore I saw an unusual sight—a number of cigarette butts. My immediate thought was how unfortunate it was that someone had despoiled the environment with these unattractive butts. But no sooner had my brain formed the thought when out of nowhere came two large white suckers that vacuumed up all the butts in a few seconds. I was simply stunned at their speed and that they would even eat such things. It was also a startling moment because prior to that there had been nothing moving, not even a minnow. The suckers were accompanied by a big largemouth bass. So you see, you have to stick around, if the clarity is there, be patient, and give the lake a chance to provide some excitement for you. There's a nice little bay at the entrance that is perfect for snorkelers. Lots of fallen logs on both sides with detritus and organic matter. It has a sloping bowl shape, with lily pads on the left, a little pondweed, otherwise only sparse vegetation. This is a no wake lake, and the bay has buoys to divide it off so jet skiers can't come in.

BASS LAKE   KENT COUNTY

Acreage: 184 acres   **page 47 of the DeLorme Atlas**

Location: Take U.S. 27 north to Ithaca, then go west on 522 (Stanton Road which becomes Lake Road), go south on Larsen Avenue, east on 21 Mile Road, then south on Bass Lake Road. The public access site will be on your right.

This feels like a clean and healthy lake with good but not great visibility. There are good weed beds in front on both right and left sides. Schools of perch, many schools of bluegills including one blind one. Painted turtle and black striped minnows.

Vegetation consists of tape grass and fields of watermilfoil patrolled by perch and very tiny minnows. Bottom is white sand and mud in parts.

CAMP LAKE

KENT COUNTY

Acreage: 125.3 acres   **page 46 of the DeLorme Atlas**

Location: Take I-96 west to Grand Rapids, then go north on 131. Go west on 14 Mile Road (M-57) to a dead end, then go south at Lymburner, west at Broman and north at Division Avenue. The public access site will be on your right.

This lake provides a very worthwhile snorkeling experience with good visibility. Go straight out from shore and the weedbeds are endless--chara, coontail, watermilfoil. Big patches of white sand on the way out to the dropoff, approximately 250 feet from shore. Saw one large painted turtle, along with largemouth bass, bluegill, big sunfish, and grass pickerel. Schools of small minnows and blackstriped minnows. It is not thick with fish but it's still very interesting and very esthetic. Lots of cottages but saw only a little boating, and there were no jet skis, even on a Sunday. That is, of course, the luck of the draw.

CAMPBELL LAKE

KENT COUNTY

Acreage: approx. 46 acres   **page 37 of the DeLorme Atlas**

Location: Take I-96 heading west towards Grand Rapids, go south on Morris Lake Avenue, west on 84th Street and the public access will be on your left.

This lake was really fabulous, and though it was a bit busy, all the action is near the shore anyway, so jet skiers do not really interfere. Head left and go back and forth along the shore. The water is quite deep but very clear. Weed beds are very tall and thick and loaded with largemouth bass, perch, pumpkinseeds and bluegill. This lake is not for a snorkeler who does not like vegetation, as you are really surrounded by it. But I think that just adds to the attraction. It's a lake to return to and if you can go during the week, so much the better.

CLEAR LAKE   KENT COUNTY

Acreage: approx. 9 acres   **page 46 of the DeLorme Atlas**

Location: Take I-96 west to Grand Rapids, then go north on 131, take Cedar Springs exit and go west on 46, then north on Division Avenue and the public access will be on your right.

This lake is adjacent to Spring Lake, and as is so often the case with Clear Lakes, the visibility is absolutely outstanding--gin clear. Quite incredible. It's extremely remote with just one house. There is some good weed structure on the shore opposite the DNR entrance, and because the lake is so small, it's easy to cross to the other side in just a few minutes. Fallen logs and detritus on the hard bottom. What vegetation there is is mostly decayed watermilfoil and pondweed, as well as some lilies and bulrushes. I saw some rock bass, medium size largemouth bass, some decent sized bluegills and black striped minnows. A fine and relaxing experience--it's a feeling of being in your own private lake.

COUNTY LINE LAKE   KENT COUNTY

Acreage: approx. 43 acres   **page 47 of the DeLorme Atlas**

Location: Go west on I-96 heading towards Grand Rapids, then go north on 66, then west on 57, south on Mills Avenue, left on Simpson Street. The first right hand turn will take you to County Line Lake.

A small lake on the Kent County Line. Sloping slides good for snorkeling and decent visibility. Fallen logs on the slopes, small and medium-sized largemouth bass, bluegills, sunfish, black striped minnows.

LIME LAKE   KENT COUNTY

Acreage: 36 acres   **page 46 of the DeLorme Atlas**

Location: Take I-96 to Grand Rapids, go north on 131, west on 46, south on Lime Lake Drive which dead ends into the public access.

This is an interesting glacial lake with a wide and easy entrance. The sides near the boat ramp are sloping and a good place to see a good deal of fish. I saw a big logperch here, as well as grass pickerel, largemouth bass, shadow bass and sunfish. There's tons of vegetation here--big columns of northern watermilfoil, coontail, loads of lilies, and pondweed. Excellent weed beds both to the left and right. Bottom is sand/soft muck/gravel.

LINCOLN LAKE   KENT COUNTY

Acreage: 411 acres   **page 47 of the DeLorme Atlas**

Location: Go west towards Grand Rapids on I-96, then go north on 66 and west on 510 (Sidney Road). Go south on Lincoln Lake Avenue, west on 18 Mile Road and north on Meddler Avenue. The public access will be on your right.

This is a clean and quite clear lake with decent visibility, a sandy and rocky beach, with all the usual pan fish as well as largemouth bass. This is a very busy lake with lots of speed boats, so try to come during the week. Scattered watermilfoil beds. The big drawback here is the high degree of activity.

MURRAY LAKE   KENT COUNTY

Acreage: 320 acres   **page 47 of the DeLorme Atlas**

Location: Take I-96 west towards Grand Rapids, then go north on 66 and west on 44 through the town of Belding. Continue on and go south on Lincoln Lake Avenue, going east on 4 Mile Road and south on Nash. Go west on Lally Street and take a right turn at Causeway Drive which will take you to the public access.

This is another lake that has the clear water and nice vegetation but is so developed that you have to pick an off day to be able to enjoy it. The potential is there, so try to go early in the morning on a weekday to avoid the rush. The south access off of Lally Road is the only acceptable access, as the north side is too dirty, and the weeds are too close to the surface to enjoy the snorkeling.

SPRING LAKE   KENT COUNTY

Acreage: approx. 12 acres   **page 46 of the DeLorme Atlas**

Location: Take I-96 west to Grand Rapids, then go north on 131, get off at the Sand Lake exit and go west on 22 Mile Road, go south on Albrecht, west on 20 Mile Road, and the very first dirt road to the left will take you to the public access.

This is a spring fed lake that is quite cold, but if you come prepared, it has a lot to offer. Clarity is outstanding along the sides, not good in the middle, simply because the middle is too deep. The lake is very shallow along the sides, and since it's such a tiny lake, what I found to be very successsful was to just snorkel all along the sides of the lake, and since it is narrow, you can go down one side, go across the end of the lake and come back to shore along the other side. There are many indentations, almost like mini caves along both sides with plenty of fish dodging in and out. I saw one northern pike here and he was so still that I was able to reach gently in front of him and lift away a piece of vegetation that was blocking my view, and he didn't even move a muscle. This lake is loaded with big carp, and as I was getting *out* of the lake, right by the shore, I stumbled over one. Gravel and sand bottom. This lake is extremely remote with just a narrow dirt road in. I saw thousands of perch, bluegills and black striped minnows in numerous schools. The largemouth bass were so big I at first thought they were carp. Very tall watermilfoil in the deep water. Some vegetation was flaming yellow. There are no cottages here or any signs of human activity. I was the only one on the lake. Spring fed and you can feel it as you move about the lake, and the cold spring water comes up and hits you from underneath.

WABASIS LAKE   KENT COUNTY

Acreage: 418 acres   **page 47 of the DeLorme Atlas**

Location: Take I-96 west towards Grand Rapids, go north on 66, west on 44, north on Wabasis Avenue. The public access will be on the right in Wabasis State Park.

This is a chain of lakes near Grand Rapids that is part of Wabasis Creek. Although the visibility is only average, there's a lot to see--largemouth bass, bluegills, schools of perch, sunfish, black striped minnows. Sometimes there is a little tinge of red tannic acid in the lake. It's an interesting jungle underneath with feathered watermilfoil everywhere. Large rocks dot the underwater landscape.

ELBOW LAKE   LAKE COUNTY

Acreage: 60.8 acres   **page 65 of the DeLorme Atlas**

Location: Take I-96 to Grand Rapids, go north on M-37, west on 10 Mile Road, north on Merrillville Road, west on Harvey Road, south on Bass Lake Road and the public access site will be on your right.

I do not suggest going in at the public access, as though it looks terribly inviting, when you wade in where it is extremely shallow, it suddenly gets soft underneath you and your feet could get stuck. Instead, drive to the opposite side of the lake and see if you can get permission to enter at the end of Turner Street at the spot where all the rowboats are lying around and people are tenting. You have to go through some weeds to get through, but it's well worth it. Head straight across the lake, then turn right and go to almost the end of the grassy area where the creek comes in. There are great weed structures here with caves and bizarre formations. I saw big friendly largemouth bass, a huge snapping turtle the size of a bushel basket, northern pike and hundreds of bluegills. Two big blue heron were perched in the bulrushes on the lake, and I could snorkel right along next to them. The whole lake has a white marl bottom and looks white everywhere, like Opal Lake near Gaylord. Like snorkeling in the Arctic. You have to be willing to tolerate a good bit of shallow snorkeling to get over to the good stuff where the creek is, so if you think that might be a problem for you, it would be best to skip this lake. I found the rewards more than justified the effort.

HARPER LAKE   LAKE COUNTY

Acreage: 76 acres   **page 65 of the DeLorme Atlas**

Location: Take I-96 to Grand Rapids, go north on M-37, west on 10
Mile Road, north on Merrillville Road, south on Bass Lake Road,
east on Ten and a Half Mile Road and south on Granger Road.
The public access site will be on your right.

It's a beautiful drive through rugged untouched forest to arrive at
Harper Lake. It's a clean and clear, lovely lake to snorkel with lots
of inlets and lily pads. The bottom is studded with big snails.
Huge and medium sized largemouth bass, as well as sunfish and
big bluegills. Hug the shoreline and the boat traffic shouldn't
bother you. Look for largemouth bass among the lily pads, and
don't miss the snails perched on the lily pad stalks. Weed beds are
great and varied here.

IDLEWILD LAKE   LAKE COUNTY

Acreage: 105 acres   **page 56 of the DeLorme Atlas**

Take I-96 to Grand Rapids, go north on 131, west on 10 and south
on Broadway. Go west (right) on Pine which becomes Lake Drive
and the public access site will be on the left.

This is a super clear lake with an easy wide entry. Go left along
the shore for the best weed structure and small pan fish. Scattered
chara beds and patchy white sand bottom. There are many small
snails as well as 3-4 inch clams. Lots of bluegills and good sized
largemouth bass.

NORTH LAKE   LAKE COUNTY

Acreage: 48.5 acres   **page 56 of the DeLorme Atlas**

Location: Take I-96 to Grand Rapids, go north on M-37, east on
68th Street, south on James Road, east on 72nd Street and north on
Forest Road which will dead end into the public access.

This is a very clear lake that is perfect for beginning snorkelers. There were no jet skis or power boats, and the lake is very scenic with few cottages. The Plains Township sheriffs dive here. The sunken boats here make great habitats for fish. Gravel/sand bottom. Stay near the shore for best results. There were big logs, big clams and big snails. I saw a number of big largemouth bass, some medium sized and some large bluegills. There is a little side lake area that is cut off by a big board which makes a great little snorkel area. I saw huge carp, both blue and white, come speeding by--this lake is also known for its big northern pike. On the left hand side of the small side area is a huge rock covered with coral like structure. It sits alone. There are also some very bizarre looking formations in here, but the water is not as clear in the little side area. The water in this area offers good visibility if you keep facing toward shore.

REED LAKE   LAKE COUNTY

Acreage: 45 acres   **page 55 of the DeLorme Atlas**

Location: Take I-96 to Grand Rapids, go north on M-37, west on Carrs Road, south on Evergreen, and a right on Hayes Avenue. The public access site will be on your right.

This lake is a great one for beginners and to get comfortable with snorkeling. It has the clarity of the waters of Grand Cayman--you almost don't feel like you're underwater. It's like looking through air. It has a bowl shape, so you can't go out more than about 50 feet without hitting the dropoff. Since the visibility is so outstanding, you can go into the deeper areas and still see well. This lake is a perfect example of a lake that initially might look unexciting and empty, but which, if patience prevails, can provide a good bit of excitement. You have to wait a bit and search for the habitat. The lake has a hard sand bottom with big clams and small snails. For starters, go to the left where the branches are sticking out of the water--I saw big largemouth bass and a turtle there. Continue on over the scattered chara beds til you get to the docks in front of the cottages. Underneath the docks, I saw some big largemouth bass as well as oversized bluegills. The lake is small enough to cross and the potential is great.

SAND LAKE   LAKE COUNTY

Acreage: 50.5 acres   **page 65 of the DeLorme Atlas**

Location: Take I-96 to Grand Rapids, go north on M-37, west on 10 Mile Road, north on Merrillville Road, west on Harvey Road, north on Johnson Road, west on Sand Lake Road and north on Dexter Road. The lake will be on your right.

Federal campground with a $1 fee. Plenty of jet skiers on the weekend, but no one was there when I was there on a weekday. Good clarity here but no shoreline vegetation and it gets deep fast. Nevertheless, when I went to the right, by the buoys, I saw largemouth bass, bluegills, and sunfish.

SAUBLE LAKE   LAKE COUNTY

Acreage: 64 acres   **page 65 of the DeLorme Atlas**

Location: Take I-96 west to Grand Rapids, go north on M-37 and west on Loon Lake Road. The lake will be on your right.

This lake is very worthwhile, but you need to stay at the Jungle Haven Lodge to be eligible to enter the lake. It's a gorgeous lake, scenic and clear. Clams were 6-8 inches long. Lots of turtles, including one huge snapper, and I saw some smaller painted turtles. Of course, you know that you have no worry of snapping turtles ever bothering you. Just be smart, as you would with any other wildlife and do not attempt to touch or disturb it. Normally, the turtles are too busy heading in the opposite direction as fast as they can, which looks faster than a speeding bullet. Go to the left by the lily pads, and you have a chance to see dozens of bluegills, sunfish and good sized perch. There's lots of fish habitat in the remnants of boats, logs and fallen trees. Go to the fallen pines near shore--a great habitat for large rock bass, tons of bluegills, sunfish and perch. It's always solid ground under your feet. There's a great dropoff--it feels like diving Cayman. I saw few cottages, mostly trailers.

WOLF LAKE
LAKE COUNTY

Acreage: 418 acres
page 66 of the DeLorme Atlas

Location: Take I-96 west to Grand Rapids, go north on M-37 and just north of the town of Baldwin, the public access will be on the left hand side.

This is a clear beautiful lake with a nice sandy beach and public swimming access. It's rather flat without much vegetation. Go to the right of the entrance where I saw largemouth bass that were so big they looked like a child's inflated toys. I also saw big muskie and northern pike, close enough to get very good photographs. There were big carp and large catfish as well as one very large sucker. I went in every day for five days and I would just lie in the same area and wait. It would take about 3-4 minutes each day for the largemouth bass, pike and muskie to arrive, but arrive they did just like clockwork. The muskie and pike lined up right next to each other, and there were 9 big largemouth bass, very still, watchful and observing me. Quite a sight.

ALGOE LAKE
LAPEER COUNTY

Acreage: approx. 8 acres
page 41 of the DeLorme Atlas

Location: Take I-69 east to the town of Lapeer. Go south on 24, west on Brocker, south on Hadley and west on Sawmill Lake Road. The lake will be on the right.

Rustic state campground in the Ortonville State Recreation Area. Walk from one of the campsites down the steps (sometimes a little steep) to the lake. Crystal clear water in this very small lake. It's like a little garden of Eden with low soft green chara beds, coontail, pondweed and northern watermilfoil. Go either left or right—it's great either way—lots of largemouth bass, perch, bluegills, and black striped minnows. The vegetation is in varying heights and in many shades of green—the whole lake has a fresh clean feeling. Lots of lily pads, but there's so much space in between that you can easily see the bass hiding in there and you can explore without concern of getting tangled up. Just snorkel along the edges—the lake is small enough to snorkel the entire lake, and this is well worth a whole day of your time.

BIG FISH LAKE   LAPEER COUNTY

Acreage: 105 acres   **page 41 of the DeLorme Atlas**

Location: Take I-69 east to the town of Lapeer. Go south on 24, west on Brocker, south on Hadley, cross Big Fish Lake Road, and the next left will take you to the public access.

A busy cottaged lake with a small public beach in the Ortonville State Recreation Area. The water is not crystal clear but visibility is still very good. The shore is sandy and it slopes deeper very quickly. Very picturesque vegetation--northern watermilfoil (lots of good weed beds just off the ramp), Eurasian watermilfoil, elodea, wild celery, broadleaf   pondweed and chara beds. Cottages are on the opposite side of the lake, so keep off to the right and fairly near shore to avoid boat traffic. Go along the edge of the weed beds and water lilies to see all the usual pan fish.

DAVISON LAKE   LAPEER COUNTY

Acreage: 56 acres   **page 41 of the DeLorme Atlas**

Location: Take I-69 east to the town of Lapeer. Go south on 24, west on Brocker, south on Diehl, east on Sinroll, south on Diehl, west on Davison Lake Road, south on Cornell Road, west on Fish Lake Road, and the public access site will be on your right.

The entire lake is a no wake lake, great for snorkeling. Outstanding visibility with every kind of vegetation--elodea, wild celery, northern watermilfoil, coontail, chara and pondweed, but it is the way it is arranged underwater that makes it so pleasing to the eye. One side is cottaged, but this is basically a very quiet lake.

DUPEROW LAKE   LAPEER COUNTY

Acreage: 5.6 acres   **page 52 of the DeLorme Atlas**

Location: Take I-69 east going to the town of Lapeer. Go north on 24, east on Daley and north on Five Lakes Road. Go past Watts Lake on your right, and further up the road on the right hand side is the public access site for Duperow Lake, a lake not shown on the map.

The lake is 60 feet deep and shaped like a bowl with excellent visibility if you stay on the slopes of the bowl. Vast beds of solid chara, a little curly pondweed, a little bladderwort plus the usual pan fish.

FISH LAKE   LAPEER COUNTY

Acreage: 17.8 acres   page 52 of the DeLorme Atlas

Location: Take I-69 east to the town of Lapeer. Go south on 24, east on Daley, north on Five Lakes Road and west on Vernor. The access site will be on your right.

Enter at the right hand side of Vernor just before hitting the pavement. The lake has a maximum depth of only 17 feet, and though the visibility is only average, the lake is worth checking out if you are already in the area. Visibility is best if you're looking straight down. Lilies are on both sides of the entrance, along with northern watermilfoil, coontail, and broadleaf pondweed. All the usual pan fish are here. Limited parking.

MILLERS LAKE   LAPEER COUNTY

Acreage: 45 acres   page 51 of the DeLorme Atlas

Location: Take I-69 east to the town of Lapeer, go north on 24, west on King's Landing Drive, and the access site is on your left.

Ten miles north of Lapeer and named King's Landing R.V. resort. $1 entry fee weekdays, $2 on weekends. Quite a cottaged lake but no power boats or jet skis are allowed on the lake, so you find fishermen only. The lake is 48 feet at its greatest depth. This is a super clear lake--even the swampy area of the lake is clear. Lots of 2 foot pike, a big map turtle, lots of largemouth bass and bluegills. It's great for beginners as the vegetation is so low and the entry and beyond is a hard sand bottom. You can stand up even when you're out quite far. Plenty of vegetation, with beds of chara, broad leaf pondweed, northern watermilfoil and Eurasian watermilfoil.

LAKE MINNEWANNA   LAPEER COUNTY

Acreage: 60.6 acres   **page 41 of the DeLorme Atlas**

Location: Take I-69 east to the town of Lapeer. Go south on 24, west on Pratt Road and south on Hurd Road. The public access site will be on your left.

This lake is in the well developed Metamora Recreation Area. This is a slow no wake lake with a great public beach and no cottages. Bring the family, as all the amenities and recreational facilities are here. It's a beautiful unspoiled lake with a hard sand bottom. The water is crystal clear and shallow. The area to the left of the boat launch is littered with snails and all the usual pan fish. It's narrow enough to snorkel across easily. Vegetation consists mostly of chara, northern watermilfoil, coontail and pondweed.

NEPESSING LAKE   LAPEER COUNTY

Acreage: 414 acres   **page 51 of the DeLorme Atlas**

Location: Take I-69 east and just before arriving at the town of Lapeer, go south on Golf Road and east on Hunt Road. The public access site will be on your right.

The access is across the road from the Lapeer Country Club and Golf Course. This is a busy commercial lake, so come in the off hours. It's fairly shallow with a sandy bottom and good visibility. Vegetation is northern watermilfoil, chara and pondweed containing all the usual panfish.

TODY LAKE   LAPEER COUNTY

Acreage: approx 9 acres   **page 41 of the DeLorme Atlas**

Location: Take I-69 east past Flint, go south on 15 and east on Green Road, south on Washburn Road, east on Tody Road. The public access site will be on the left.

A gorgeous lake tucked into the Ortonville State Recreation Area. This is a real wilderness experience.

You have to watch carefully for the access site as it is not well marked. It's just after the last house on the left. You're unlikely to see power boaters here. The lake is small, shallow and extremely picturesque. Cottages are barely seen from the access site. It's easy to snorkel across the lake because of its narrow shape. It's shallow almost all the way across--I could find no deep areas. It's perfect for beginners as the foliage is low, and it's only about 3 feet deep. There are beautiful beds of chara, elodea, northern watermilfoil and curly pondweed. Look for the submerged brush and big fallen branches for fish habitat. Lots of perch, bluegills, and largemouth bass.

WATTS LAKE   LAPEER COUNTY

Acreage: 3.8 acres   **page 52 of the DeLorme Atlas**

Location: Take I-69 east to Lapeer, go north on 24, east on Daley Road and north on Five Lakes Road. After crossing Vernor Road, the public access site is on your right.

This is a super lake--awesome!! It's surrounded by tall dead trees and the water is fantastically clear. It has a hard sand/gravel bottom, with big beds of northern watermilfoil, coontail, chara, curly pondweed and loads of elodea at the entrance. It gets deep rather quickly and it's just great snorkeling along the edge of the lilies (and even *in* the lilies, as there is enough space in there). There are fallen logs and stumps, a big car tire at the left of the entrance. A beautiful underwater wilderness setting.

GUN LAKE   MASON COUNTY

Acreage: 219 acres   **page 65 of the DeLorme Atlas**

Location: Take I-96 west to Muskegon, go north on 31, east on Townline Road, and the public access site will be on your left.

A very clear lake with a nice swimming beach. Excellent for families. Go to the right among the bulrushes--I saw bluegills, black striped minnows. The usual pan fish appear immediately. Nice chara beds along with Eurasian watermilfoil, curly pondweed, broad leaf pondweed. Hard sand bottom.

HAMLIN LAKE   MASON COUNTY

Acreage: 4990 acres   **page 64 of the DeLorme Atlas**

Location: Take I-96 west to Muskegon, go north on 31, west on Fountain Road, and north on Victory Park, which will dead end into the public access.

This is the only lake in the book that I have not personally snorkeled--I was unable to reach it before dark, but I am including it because of the excellent feedback I have had on it from a DNR official who snorkels it regularly and who vouches for its clarity and opportunities to see fish and vegetation.

BERGESS LAKE   MECOSTA COUNTY
(also spelled BURGESS)

Acreage: 60 acres   **page 57 of the DeLorme Atlas**

Location: Take I-96 west to Grand Rapids, go north on 131, east on Sixteen Mile, north on 165th, and south on 160th. This will dead end into the public access site.

Clarity in this lake is excellent. Take an immediate extreme right to avoid heading into high vegetation. You will see a sand path that will lead you out into an open area. Because of the tight vegetation, this would be for a more experienced snorkeler who doesn't get irritated at being surrounded by thick vegetation. There are many lilies, bulrushes, coontail, broadleaf pondweed, chara, curly pondweed, Eurasian watermilfoil, elodea, loads of tape grass, along with perch, largemouth bass and bluegills.

BROCKWAY LAKE   MECOSTA COUNTY

Acreage: 14.2 acres   **page 47 of the DeLorme Atlas**

Location: Take U.S. 27 north to St. Louis, go west on 46, north on 597 through the town of Lakeview, west on One Mile Road and north on 100th Avenue. Access road will be on your left.

This is a great small lake with an amazing variety and constantly changing surroundings. Visibility blows hot and cold--I've visited it on occasion and found it very clear and on several other occasions I've found it just too milky to see well.

When it's good, it's very very good, so I would give it a try. The fish are everywhere in great profusion. The lake is very deserted, very clean feeling, and there are no cottages. I've only seen fishermen here--it's very quiet. The lake is loaded with fallen logs and trees--you have to watch where you're going or you'll bump your head. Loads of largemouth bass, perch, pumpkinseeds, large bluegills, good sized largemouth bass, speckled bass. This is a lake that's worth spending a day at and exploring the entire lake. There's an underwater island out in the middle, and it's startling to be in deep water and a couple of minutes later you're in the middle of the lake and it's only up to your knees.

CHIPPEWA LAKE   MECOSTA COUNTY

Acreage: 790 acres   **page 57 of the DeLorme Atlas**

Location: Take I-96 west to 66, go north on 66, west on 20 Mile Road and north on Lake Shores Road. The public access site will be on your left.

Very warm water in this lake, which at first doesn't appear that clear but after a minute or two you can see very well. Snorkel where the sand ends and the weed beds begin. Fish are gathered there in large numbers. Be very still and wait--they will start to crowd around. Large black striped minnows by the hundreds, plus bluegills, pumpkinseeds, perch and the occasional largemouth bass. Lots of attractive vegetation--coontail, northern watermilfoil, tape grass, wild celery, chara and pondweed.

CLEAR LAKE   MECOSTA COUNTY

Acreage: 130 acres   **page 57 of the DeLorme Atlas**

Location: Take I-96 west to Grand Rapids, go north on 131 and east on 20. The public access site will be on your left.

There's lots of action in this lake. Good but not great visibility. Good sized largemouth bass in the lily pads to the right. I saw a couple of painted turtles paddling around in here, as well as large bluegills and smaller perch.

A big blue heron was at the entrance when I arrived. He stayed the whole time I was there by the spectacular group of white branches sticking up on the left hand side. It's a striking setting with hundreds of white lilies in bloom (September) in the lake on both sides. You snorkel in the open area between the two sets of lilies. Unique among all the lakes I visited. The cabbage butterflies had just hatched before I arrived, and there were hundreds gathered in various puddles.

LOWER EVANS LAKE   MECOSTA COUNTY

Acreage: 52.6 acres   **page 57 of the DeLorme Atlas**

Location: Take I-96 west to 66, go north on 66, west on 20 Mile Road, south on 90th Avenue, east on 17 Mile Road (Milton). This dead ends into the public access site.

This lake originally looked rather dark, but after you are in the water a couple of minutes, it becomes very clear. Bottom is somewhat silty but is mostly covered with pondweed interspersed with wild celery, chara, elodea, and grasses. Largemouth bass, perch, and bluegills roam in a stunning wilderness setting. Thick lily pads on either side. Snorkel back and forth among these or just snorkel over the vegetation in the middle. The broad expanse of lily pads makes for a spectacular sight. There are no cottages, no power boats, only fishermen.

JEHNSEN LAKE   MECOSTA COUNTY

Acreage: 270 acres   **page 57 of the DeLorme Atlas**

Location: Take I-96 west to 66, go north on 66, west on 20 Mile Road, and south on 90th Avenue which will dead end into the public access.

Don't be discouraged if it initially doesn't look that clear--it is, so just let your eyes get used to the light. There are four picturesque islands to snorkel to. A big largemouth bass was sitting to the left of the dock in a big deep hollowed out area. The lake is a good depth for snorkeling, and though there is a lot of vegetation, it's not too much. It's mostly chara, northern watermilfoil and pondweed.

MECOSTA LAKE   MECOSTA COUNTY

Acreage: 297 acres   **page 57 of the DeLorme Atlas**

Location: Take I-96 west to 66, go north on 66 and west on 20, continue west on 9 Mile Road, south at 90th Avenue, west at Buchanan Road, north at 105th Avenue, which will dead end into the public access site.

Excellent visibility with a wide entrance and attractive vegetation, consisting of chara, wild celery and pondweed. I saw mostly bluegills, largemouth bass and pumpkinseeds.

MERRILL LAKE   MECOSTA COUNTY

Acreage: 86.6 acres   **page 57 of the DeLorme Atlas**

Location: Take I-96 west to 66, go north on 66 and west on Evergreen Road. Stay to the right and you will dead end into the public access.

This lake is located in a county park--just drive right in. There's great clarity here, and the lake is flanked by lovely purple flowered pickerelweed. The bottom is covered with pondweed, chara, elodea and too much Eurasian watermilfoil. Excellent depth for snorkeling--about 5 feet or slightly more. Perch, bluegills and largemouth bass everywhere but many are clustered in the lily pads. Also saw a big painted turtle. There are a few cottages here, but it's basically a very quiet lake, very peaceful with no power boats allowed traveling more than 10 miles per hour.

TOWNLINE LAKE   MECOSTA COUNTY

Acreage: 73 acres   **page 57 of the DeLorme Atlas**

Location: Take I-96 west to 66, go north on 66, west on 20, north at 165th Avenue, west at 16 Mile Road, north at 180th Avenue which will become Townline Lake Road. Follow this to 175th Avenue and the public access site will be on your left.

This is a super clear lake--very scenic, very beautiful with the trees mirrored in the water. There are cottages only on the same side as you (except for one), so it looks very unspoiled. In the hollowed out area at the end of the dock, there are perch, bluegills, redear sunfish. Go straight out about 50 feet, over the vegetation, to a big dropoff--there are large numbers of perch, bluegills, pumpkinseeds, and good sized largemouth bass. Sand and peat bottom, but it's mostly covered with elodea, chara, coontail, curly pondweed and Eurasian watermilfoil. Bowl shaped and a lovely snorkeling experience. Big clams too.

BASS LAKE   MONTCALM COUNTY
(also called NEWCOMB LAKE)

Acreage: 40 acres   **page 46 of the DeLorme Atlas**

Location: Go west to Grand Rapids, north on 131 and take the Cannonsville Road exit. Head east on Cannonsville and north on 605 (Bass Lake Road) and the public access site is on your right.

There is good roadside access to this attractive lake near Little Whitefish Lake. Visibility is good but not great and the weedbeds are excellent and plentiful. You can profitably go either right or left, where I saw bluegills, perch and smallmouth bass. This is well worth a lengthy exploration.

COLBY LAKE   MONTCALM COUNTY

Acreage: 13 acres   **page 47 of the DeLorme Atlas**

Location: Take U.S.27 north to Ithaca, go west on 522 (Washington Road which becomes Stanton Road), south on 66 (Sheridan Road) and the public access site will be on your right.

This lake in the Stanton State Recreation Area is real wilderness. No cottages and no people! Bulrushes and cattails are everywhere. Lake is surrounded by dead trees with purple flowered pickerelweed on both sides of the entrance. It's a real pristine wilderness experience--you won't find jet skis here! Good variety of vegetation with large chara beds, coontail, broad leaf pondweed, lilies and northern watermilfoil.

All of the panfish are here as well as big perch. The lake is narrow enough to snorkel across easily. This is a unique experience and a lake to come back to.

COWDEN LAKE   MONTCALM COUNTY

Acreage: 128 acres   **page 47 of the DeLorme Atlas**

Location: Take I-96 west, go north on 66, west on 44, north on 91, west on Cannonsville Road, north on Black Road, west on Coral Road.

A great wide entrance here where you enter a beautiful bay. Only a few cottages way off in the distance. Good though not great visibility. The lake gets deep right away, so you can go through the thick wild celery or snorkel closer to the shore where visibility is excellent. Snails litter the bottom everywhere. A small amount of northern watermilfoil along with bulrushes both right and left.

CRYSTAL LAKE   MONTCALM COUNTY

Acreage: 724 acres   **page 48 of the DeLorme Atlas**

Location: Take U.S.27 north to Ithaca, west on 522 (Washington Road which becomes Stanton Road), south on 565 (Crystal Road), west on Colby Road, south on Crystal Road, west on Sidney Road. The public access will be on your right.

This is a busy commercial lake, but the visibility is good, and the underwater landscape, vegetation and fish are all very attractive. Purple flowered pickerelweed on both sides of the entrance. Lots of black striped minnows greet you when you start out, and the underwater scenery consists of coontail, elodea, curly pondweed, chara, northern watermilfoil--it's all laid out in a very scenic way. There is excellent snorkeling close to shore. Try to come before 10AM and after 7PM to avoid the boat traffic. You can actually see extremely well in the early morning and after 7PM in the summer.

DERBY LAKE   MONTCALM COUNTY

Acreage: 118 acres   **page 47 of the DeLorme Atlas**

Location: Take U.S. 27 north to Ithaca, go west on 522 (Washington Road which becomes Stanton Road), south on Derby Road and the public access site will be on your left.

Excellent visibility with a great underwater setup, in which you start out snorkeling over a big sand area to the beginning of some tall weed beds. In the weeds and on the other side are pike and pickerel waiting vigilantly for fish to swim by so they can leap out and grab their prey. A big walleye came up and laid right next to me. There's a nice sloping dropoff here with big largemouth bass, big bluegills , rock bass, big and small turtles. Lots of cottages and boats, so it's nicer if you can go during the week. Easy access right next to the road.

DICKERSON LAKE   MONTCALM COUNTY

Acreage: 225 acres   **page 47 of the DeLorme Atlas**

Location: Take U.S. 27 north to Ithaca, go west on 522 (Washington Road which becomes Stanton Road), public access site will be on your left.

This lake is near Derby Lake and is very similar in its underwater landscape.   Every kind of vegetation--northern watermilfoil, pondweed and chara predominate. All the usual pan fish, and visibility is good.

HALF MOON LAKE   MONTCALM COUNTY

Acreage: approx. 95 acres   **page 47 of the DeLorme Atlas**

Location: Take U.S. 27 north to Ithaca, go west on 522 (Washington Road which becomes Stanton Road), south on 66, east on Sidney Road, north on Staines Road, and the public access site will be on your left.

This is a great lake with excellent visibility. It's a cottaged, busy lake, so come before 10AM and after 7Pm during the week. If you can do that, it's definitely worth trying to fit it into your schedule. When entering the water, if you want to avoid the high weeds that come almost to the surface, take an immediate left from shore, into the chara beds. There's also pondweed, elodea and loads of northern watermilfoil beds that are so beautiful they almost look ethereal. Saw bluegills, big largemouth bass, lots of huge black striped minnows. Many many big snails.

HORSESHOE LAKE   MONTCALM COUNTY

Acreage: 97 acres   **page 47 of the DeLorme Atlas**

Location: Take U.S.27 north to St. Louis, then go west on 46 through the town of Edmore. When 66 curves north, continue straight west on Almy Road. The public access site will be on the left.

A clear lake with a variety of vegetation, predominantly chara and broadleaf pondweed. All the usual pan fish.

LOON LAKE   MONTCALM COUNTY

Acreage: 63 acres   **page 48 of the DeLorme Atlas**

Location: Take U.S.27 north to Ithaca, go west on 522 (Washington Road which becomes Stanton Road), south on 575 (Vickeryville Road), east on Pakes Road, and the public access site is on your immediate right. There is no sign.

This is near Crystal Lake and outside the town of Ithaca. There are some cottages but they are not near the access site. Visibility is very good and there's lots of attractive vegetation, mostly curly pondweed, northern watermilfoil and chara beds. Small gold minnows as well as all the usual pan fish. This is a very tranquil and picturesque setting.

LAKE MONTCALM   MONTCALM COUNTY

Acreage: 68 acres   **page 47 of the DeLorme Atlas**

Location: Take U.S.27 north to Ithaca, go west on 522 (Washington Road which becomes Stanton Road), north on 66, west on Lake Montcalm Road, north on Hillman Road, and the public access site is your first left.

This is a good lake for snorkeling--the water is very clear. Lots of cottages, but the setting is still very scenic. The shore slopes to a steep dropoff, especially in front of the cottages. A very interesting underwater landscape in front of and to the left of the public access. Chara beds are everywhere on the bottom with occasional sand sections--very similar to Derby Lake. It gets very shallow to the left of center. You can stand up in 2 feet of water over an extensive area which is all solid sand and rocks near grassy islands. Very interesting underwater landscape with hills and valleys not commonly seen. Good sized and numerous perch, largemouth bass, bluegills, sunfish and minnows. You look out on an attractive setting of pondweed, northern watermilfoil, lilypads, tape grass and other tall grasses. Saw 6 map turtles and 2 large painted turtles.

MUSKELLUNGE LAKE   MONTCALM COUNTY

Acreage: 134 acres   **page 47 of the DeLorme Atlas**

Location: Take U.S.27 north to Ithaca, go west on 522 (Washington Road which becomes Stanton Road). Public Access site will be on your right (after passing Paris Road).

Good visibility in this worthwhile lake. It's a flat lake for about 300 feet out--then it slopes to a deep dropoff. Northern watermilfoil and pondweed predominate. I saw lots of perch, sunfish and bluegills and enjoyed a great experience.

NEVINS LAKE   MONTCALM COUNTY

Acreage: 53 acres   page 47 of the DeLorme Atlas

Location: Take U.S. 27 north to Ithaca, west on 522 (Washington Road which becomes Stanton Road), south on Nevins Lake Road and left (east) on State St. The public access site will be on your right.

Very similar to nearby Derby Lake with big sand patches ending with weed beds of northern watermilfoil, pondweed, coontail and chara. Visibility is excellent, and the underwater setting is superior. Lots of big largemouth bass, pickerel, perch and sunfish. This whole area has a chain of lakes that each offer a special experience.

SPRING LAKE   MONTCALM COUNTY

Acreage: approx. 106 acres   page 47 of the DeLorme Atlas

Location: Take U.S. 27 north to Ithaca, go west on 522 (Washington Road which becomes Stanton Road), north on 91. The next left after crossing Briggs Road will dead end into the public access.

This is a clean feeling lake with very good visibility and a nice sand bottom. There are no weed beds near shore, and the lake is rather shallow and flat. A small number of the usual pan fish.

TACOMA LAKE   MONTCALM COUNTY

Acreage: approx. 11 acres   page 47 of the DeLorme Atlas

Location: Take U.S. 27 north to Ithaca, go west on 522 (Washington Road which becomes Stanton Road), north on 91 and west on Briggs Road, and the public access will be on the right.

Located in Langston Park on a poor side dirt road, but the lake is interesting and worth the effort. You have to roam a little to find the weedbeds, but they are numerous and interesting.

Huge schools of black striped minnows as well as small minnows and small bass, all sizes in perch and good sized bluegill. White marl and sand bottom which is very hard near shore. Lots of lilies, bulrushes, scrubby watermilfoil, several varieties of pondweed. Visibility is good but not great. At first it seems a little cloudy but as your eyes adjust, you will find the clarity acceptable. It's shallow around the shore--the dropoff is about 20 yards out. Large and small clams and snails. Go left for the best viewing. The lake is in a beautiful setting surrounded by high trees with no people and no boats. There are only two cottages barely visible at the west end. You have the entire lake to yourself.

WEST LAKE   MONTCALM COUNTY

Acreage: 21.5 acres   **page 47 of the DeLorme Atlas**

Location: Take U.S.27 north to Ithaca, go west on 522 (Washington Road which becomes Stanton Road), north on 91, west on Briggs Road, and the public access will be on the right.

This is a marvelous wilderness picturesque small lake. There are only a few cottages at the far end which aren't visible at the entry area. There's excellent visibility and it's great for beginning snorkelers as there are no weeds in your face--they're all well below you. There are bulrushes on both sides, and the bottom is littered with good sized snails as well as a few clams. Underwater there's bladderwort, pondweed and chara, all at just the right depth. There's bluegills, black striped minnows and all the usual pan fish.

LITTLE WHITEFISH LAKE   MONTCALM COUNTY

Acreage: 181 acres   **page 46 of the DeLorme Atlas**

Location: Take I-96 west to Grand Rapids, go north on 131, west on Cannonsville Road, north on 605 (Bass Lake Road) and the public access site will be on the left.

This is a very clear lake with a number of cottages and a good public access. There were large white rock bass here, as well as perch, bluegills and big pumpkinseeds. It's a shallow lake--I went way out and it was still only about 5 feet deep. Lots of action here.

WINFIELD LAKE   MONTCALM COUNTY

Acreage: 121 acres   **page 47 of the DeLorme Atlas**

Location: Take U.S. 27 north to St. Louis, go west on 46, south on Master Road, west on Church Road, and the public access site will be on the left hand side at the corner of Church Road and Krampe Road.

Lovely white swans greet you here at this lake that is part of a park. It's a very solid footed entrance with a sand bottom. Very good visibility and attractive weed beds of broad leaf pondweed, big beds of chara, elodea, and northern watermilfoil. I saw a number of largemouth bass, bluegills, as well as the usual pan fish.

HALF MOON LAKE   MUSKEGON COUNTY

Acreage: 58 acres   **page 46 of the DeLorme Atlas**

Location: Take I-96 west to Grand Rapids, go north on M-37. After crossing 19 Mile Road, the public access site will be on the next corner on the right hand side.

This is a healthy clean lake with sensational weed beds, which provided me with much variety and surprises. Saw some monstrous largemouth bass as well as medium sized largemouth bass, perch and sunfish. The weed beds were quite breathtaking--you found yourself floating over flaming yellow chara, some unusual cactus-like plants (a type of elodea) watermilfoil and tall columns of coontail. There's a big dropoff, so you can snorkel along the wall, or just float over the beautiful flat weed beds spread beneath you. Allow several hours to snorkel all around the lake which zigs and zags in and out with cave-like structures to look at. This was a lake that kept me coming back.

BAPTIST LAKE   NEWAYGO COUNTY

Acreage: 86 acres   **page 46 of the DeLorme Atlas**

Location: Take I-96 west to Grand Rapids, go north on M-37. In the town of Grant, go east on 120th Street.

After crossing Butternut Avenue, take a right at Oak Drive and the public access will be on your right.

This was a fabulous lake with brown hard sand and a clean and healthy environment. Very good water clarity and lots of variation in weed height, which is key to a fine esthetic experience. Acres of flat palm-frond-looking plants lying flat and sprinkled with clumps of pondweed with big largemouth bass cruising above the so-called fronds. You are looking down on the fish and weeds, but everything is very clear and easy to see. Plentiful bluegill and perch. Very worthwhile.

BENTON LAKE   NEWAYGO COUNTY

Acreage: 33.3 acres   page 55 of the DeLorme Atlas

Location: Take I-96 west to Grand Rapids, go north on M-37, west at Pierce Drive (at the town of Broman). Pierce Drive becomes 8 Mile Road, and the campground is on the right hand side.

Outstanding visibility here and great weedbeds. Go straight out to the weedbeds where you will see bluegills, perch, largemouth bass and crappies. Try not to go in direct sunlight, as though the visibility is excellent, there is sediment in the water, and the sun lights up the sediment. Nothing worthwhile near shore--you definitely have to head out, but this is a super isolated lake, and you will not have to worry about jet skis or power boats bothering you here. There's a good chance you won't see another solitary soul, or at the most, the occasional fisherman.

BILLS LAKE   NEWAYGO COUNTY

Acreage: 204 acres   page 46 of the DeLorme Atlas

Location: Take I-96 west to Grand Rapids, go north on M-37, east on 82, west on 86th St. and south on Pear Road. The public access site will be on your left.

Excellent visibility here and a good lake for beginners. You can't snorkel the edges here, so go straight out from the DNR public access to the weedbeds.

It's only about 3 feet deep so for beginners it affords an easy opportunity to get used to using the snorkel and mask. Bottom is flat beige/brown sand. Weed beds are just average looking, not particularly esthetic, but rather brown watermilfoil and brown grasses. I saw schools of bluegills, medium sized largemouth bass, crappies and black striped minnows.

BLANCH LAKE   NEWAYGO COUNTY

Acreage: 63 acres   **page 46 of the DeLorme Atlas**

Location: Take I-96 west to Grand Rapids, go north on M-37. In the town of Grant, go east on 120th St. and north on Park Drive, which will dead end into the public access.

Three swans and Canadian geese greeted me here as I entered this easy access lake outside of the town of Grant. Many lily pads line the shore and though the visibility is only average, the lake is defiinitely worth a look for the attractive vegetation and fish. There were some very dark brown largemouth bass of huge size as well as some nice bluegills. Weedbeds were healthy looking and striking yellow and green.

DIAMOND LAKE   NEWAYGO COUNTY

Acreage: 171 acres   **page 56 of the DeLorme Atlas**

Location: Take I-96 west to Grand Rapids, north on M-37. After passing through the town of White Cloud (stop at Sally's Restaurant for whitefish and strawberry shortcake!) go west on Foss Avenue and north on Mundy. The public access site will be on your left.

A very pleasant lake outside of the town of White Cloud. It's flat at the shore, so go straight out to the nice weedbeds of short grass and pondweed. The clarity is excellent--a good 10-15 feet. There were good sized pumpkinseeds right at the dock as well as medium sized largemouth bass. It's shallow in many areas which makes it nice for snorkelers as you are closer to the fish. Good for beginners.

ENGLEWRIGHT LAKE   NEWAYGO COUNTY

Acreage: 54 acres   **page 46 of the DeLorme Atlas**

Location: Take I-96 west to Grand Rapids, go north on M-37, east on 128th Street. After crossing Butternut Avenue, the public access site will be on the right.

I *looooed* this lake, really paradise, like diving in an aquarium. Wall snorkeling both left and right with fields of northern watermilfoil, pillars of the striking black tipped coontail, --really all kinds of aquatic plants here. Healthy, in beautiful, vivid colors. Great variety in height and type of vegetation. There were big crappies and pike right by the entrance--fish were constantly swimming around you--big pumpkinseeds, perch, bluegills, big largemouth bass, white rock bass, black striped minnows. Even when the weeds were high and in tall pillars, the fish were swimming around me at eye level. Great visibility.

HIGHBANK LAKE   NEWAYGO COUNTY

Acreage: 20.55 acres   **page 55 of the DeLorme Atlas**

Location: Take I-96 west to Grand Rapids, go north on M-37, west on 11 Mile Road, north on Warner Avenue, west on 13 Mile Road, north on Osborn Avenue, east on Walkers Corners (16 Mile Road). The third road on the right will dead end into the campground.

State Forest Campground in the Manistee National Forest. An excellent lake with great water clarity, silty bottom with scattered pondweed and northern watermilfoil. Best to take a left and go into the dark corner where I saw a big school of largemouth bass, right by brush piles at the spawning beds and just to the left of the dock. It's a good lake for beginning snorkelers, as though there is quite a bit of vegetation, the weed beds are short and unobtrusive.

HUNGERFORD LAKE   NEWAYGO COUNTY

Acreage: 35 acres   **page 56 of the DeLorme Atlas**

Location: Take I-96 west to Grand Rapids, go north on M-37.

After passing through the town of White Cloud (stop at Sally's Restaurant for whitefish and strawberry shortcake!), go east on 20, north on Cypress Avenue, east on Hunger Drive. Follow the road all around the lake til you get to the north side--the public access site is there.

This lake looked like a Rousseau painting--very jungly with pillars of the black tipped coontail. The lake is fairly shallow and big largemouth bass were numerous. Some of the biggest bluegills I ever saw were here, and the perch were jumbo. Saw big brown carp. Great visibility, and the lake feels clean and healthy. Vegetation was lush--I came back and snorkeled by moonlight!

INDIAN LAKE   NEWAYGO COUNTY

Acreage: 34 acres   page 56 of the DeLorme Atlas

Location: Take I-96 west to Grand Rapids, go north on M-37 and at the town of Broman, go west on Pierce Drive and south on Nagek Drive which will dead end into the public access.

Near the town of White Cloud, this lake is situated in a picturesque setting, very isolated, with no cottages, no boats. Silty but solid bottom--you can stand up much of the time, which makes it nice for beginners. It's a long narrow dead end dirt road to get in, but the seclusion and setting make it worthwhile. It's a clean and very clear lake with broadleaf pondweed, lily pads and a small amount of northern watermilfoil. Go to the left, stay fairly near the shore. Head toward the small island of vegetation and you will come on brush piles and vegetation sheltering hundreds of bluegills, pumpkinseeds and bass. Public campground.

LODA LAKE   NEWAYGO COUNTY

Acreage: 16.6 acres   page 56 of the DeLorme Atlas

Location: Take I-96 to Grand Rapids, go north on M-37. Pass through White Cloud (stop at Sally's for a great whitefish lunch or dinner topped with strawberry shortcake!), then go west on 5 Mile Road, north on Felch Avenue which will dead end into the public access site.

This is a lake for advanced snorkelers due to the tremendous amount of vegetation. The water is clear but loaded with northern watermilfoil, lily pads. Saw tons of minnows and largemouth bass. There is a beautiful wildflower trail leading into the lake.

NICHOLS LAKE   NEWAYGO COUNTY

Acreage: 160 acres   page 55 of the DeLorme Atlas

Location: Take I-96 west to Grand Rapids, go north on M-37, west on 11 Mile Road and north on Jerome. This will dead end into the public access site on the south side of the lake. To get to the north side public access site, go west of M-37 on 11 Mile Road, north on Bingham and west on Cleveland. The public access site for the north side of the lake will be on your left.

This is an excellent lake offering a variety of experiences, depending on which access site you choose. On the north side of the lake, you have a large bay that makes for excellent snorkeling, going either left or right. Lots of organic material, oak leaves, etc. twigs and branches on the bottom, and there's every kind of vegetation from northern watermilfoil to broadleaf pondweed to scattered chara to tall grasses. You can head left toward the swimming buoys--I always saw schools of walleye in that area as well as good sized largemouth bass and big perch. Nichols is known for its jumbo perch which refuse to be caught. I also saw brown bullheads there in June guarding their eggs, and I was lucky enough to pass by one day when a big black bullhead was parked on what looked like a thousand young ones. I saw lots of map turtles here as well as snapping and painted turtles. There were a good number of rock bass and shadow bass with their marbled bodies, as well as bluegills, pumpkinseeds and black striped minnows. This can be a great lake for seeing pike. There are a gazillion crayfish. Late in the day, usually about sundown, all the crayfish come out, and the bottom simply comes alive with these creatures darting this way and that.

On the south side, the underwater environment is entirely different. There is a Department of Agriculture State Forest Campground in the Manistee National Forest. When you come into the lake from the campground, you will find the bottom filled with huge boulders, loaded with rock bass hiding in almost every crevice.

All of the other usual pan fish were here, and if you head off to the left and cross to the other side, you will no doubt see quite a bit of vegetation and fish life. I was lucky enough to see two different sets of turtles mating--quite a sight.

PETTIBONE LAKE   NEWAYGO COUNTY

Acreage: 44.35 acres   **page 56 of the DeLorme Atlas**

Take I-96 west to Grand Rapids, go north on M-37 past the town of White Cloud (for a big treat at a reasonable price, stop at Sally's restaurant for a whitefish dinner topped by strawberry shortcake!), go east on 15 Mile Road and north on Pettibone Road. The public access site will be on your right.

Just north of the town of White Cloud, this is another one of those lakes that initially looks dark, but once you are in the water, your eyes adjust and you suddenly find the visibility more than adequate. There are some weird formations here due to the decaying northern watermilfoil, which makes it very interesting. Plenty of big largemouth bass, the usual pan fish and attractive weed beds.

PICKEREL LAKE   NEWAYGO COUNTY
(Brooks/Garfield Townships)

Acreage: 318 acres   **page 46 of the DeLorme Atlas**

Location: Take I-96 west to Grand Rapids, go north on M-37. North of Newaygo, go west on 56th Street, south on Center Line Avenue, west on Pickerel Lake Drive. The public access site will be on your right.

This is a State Forest Campground in the Manistee National Forest. The lake has very good visibility and attractive weed beds, consisting mostly of chara beds, broadleaf pondweed and some northern watermilfoil. The lake is somewhat flat with a sandy bottom.

ROBINSON LAKE   NEWAYGO COUNTY

Acreage: 137 acres   **page 56 of the DeLorme Atlas**

Location: Take I-96 west to Grand Rapids, go north on M-37 and just before arriving at the town of White Cloud, go west on 8th Street (also called Echo Drive). Take a left (south) on McClelland Drive which will dead end into the public access.

This is a shallow lake-you have to go out about 150 feet from shore to get to the good snorkeling area. You will find a strip of attractive weed beds to snorkel along. Tall grasses and northern watermilfoil dominate the underwater landscape with schools of perch and bluegills.

WALKUP LAKE   NEWAYGO COUNTY

Acreage: 60 acres   **page 55 of the DeLorme Atlas**

Location: Take I-96 west to Grand Rapids, go north on M-37 and west on 11 Mile Road, north on Bingham and west on Cleveland. The public access will be on your right.

Just down the road from Nichols Lake, this makes an excellent lake to give your snorkeling additional variety. The visibility and weed beds are worthwhile, and there are plenty of pan fish here to make it interesting viewing.

CRYSTAL LAKE   OCEANA COUNTY

Acreage: 76 acres   **page 54 of the DeLorme Atlas**

Location: Take I-96 west to Muskegon, go north on 31, east on Taylor, south on 72nd Avenue. The public access site will be on the right.

This lake is not "Crystal" clear but the visibility is decent. Lots of stumps and logs near shore with bluegills, largemouth bass, both babies and full size, as well as snails and clams. Vegetation is basically beds of chara, wild celery and tape grass.

SILVER LAKE   OCEANA COUNTY

Acreage: 690 acres   **page 54 of the DeLorme Atlas**

Location: Take I-96 west to Muskegon, go north on 31, west on Taylor Road, which will dead end into the public access at Silver Lake State Park.

This is a wonderful lake for families, as all of the facilities of the State Park are at your disposal, along with the dune buggy rides and a developed tourism infrastructure. The lake itself is unusually clear, and you can enter either from the west side where the swimming area is located, or from the opposite side by first climbing the dunes. Although the clarity was outstanding, I saw only the occasional pan fish, and I think it would take some exploration to find the best that is in this lake. It is well worth the effort, however, and because of the lack of vegetation and the clarity, it is excellent for beginning snorkelers.

DIAMOND LAKE   OSCEOLA COUNTY

Acreage: 61.5 acres   **page 66 of the DeLorme Atlas**

Location: Take I-96 west to Grand Rapids, north on 131, west at 20 Mile Road, south at 200th Avenue, and the public access will be on your right after crossing 19 Mile Road.

Great lake! Incredibly clear, and it has the great orange and yellow weed structure of McCoy Lake. The day I was there I saw tons of tiny opening and closing blue jellyfish, about the size of a dime. Because of their size, it's easy not to notice them, so you have to pay attention. Once you start looking, they are floating all around you by the thousands. However, seeing them can be an iffy proposition, as a good wind can suddenly drive them all away, and the next day you can't see even one. Go right, left or straight out--it's all scenic and interesting. Lots of fish habitat with bluegills, perch and largemouth bass, as well as some sunfish. Only about 10 feet deep. There's bladderwort, northern watermilfoil and coontail, as well as the usual chara beds and some unusual elodea that looks like cactus.

McCOY LAKE   OSCEOLA COUNTY

Acreage: 18 acres   **page 67 of the DeLorme Atlas**

Location: Take I-96 west to Grand Rapids, go north on 131, east on 14 Mile Road and south on 170th Avenue. The public access will occur almost immediately after you get on 170th Avenue, and it will be on your left.

You can have a lot of fun in this lake! Visibility is excellent. Go to the left where there is a big log sticking up out of the water. When I was there there was a very tame largemouth bass that you could pet that hung around the log. All the locals knew about him, and he was quite a topic of converstion. All the usual pan fish are here, and you will enjoy it equally going either left or right. There's some gorgeous orange, lime and bright yellow vegetation that is quite startling. There's bladderwort, watermilfoil, coontail and chara.

ROSE LAKE   OSCEOLA COUNTY

Acreage: 340 acres   **page 67 of the DeLorme Atlas**

Location: Take I-96 west to Grand Rapids, go north on 131, east on 20 (Hayes Road) which becomes Rose Lake Road (18 Mile Road). The public access site will be on your right in Rose Lake County Park.

This has many tourist amenities and is excellent for families. It's a very easy entry and the visibility is excellent. All the usual pan fish are here as is outstanding weed structure. Go either left or right--the experience is worthwhile either way.

SUNRISE LAKE   OSCEOLA COUNTY

Acreage: 120 acres   page 67 of the DeLorme Atlas

Location: Take I-96 west to Grand Rapids, go north on 131, east on 14 Mile Road, north on 180th Avenue/Twin Lake Road, east on 15 Mile Road. The public access site is on the left.

This is a marvelous lake, and my only regret was that I didn't have as much time as I wanted to more thoroughly explore this lake of many possibilities. It has a great shape, bending in and out so you can explore little private bays. It's the ultimate wilderness lake--you feel you're the only person on earth. It's very scenic and intimate both above and underwater. Opposite the second beach on the right is a huge rock pyramid. The bottom is a big green carpet with a very colorful weed structure all around it. Huge boulders are strewn everywhere on the bottom. The lake is very deep, and there is a sunken airplane here, but of course you would have to be a diver to get down to it. I saw large largemouth bass, plenty of perch and the usual pan fish. There's a lot more here that I didn't get to explore, so plan plenty of time if you really want to get your money's worth out of this lake.

TODD LAKE   OSCEOLA COUNTY

Acreage: 75.5 acres   page 56 of the DeLorme Atlas

Location: Take I-96 west to Grand Rapids, go north on 131, go past Reed City and get off at 9 Mile Road. Go east on 9 Mile Road, and after passing Lincoln Lake on your right, the public access site for Todd Lake will be on your left.

This is an excellent, clear and clean lake. Very quiet--I was the only one here. The weeds here were very tall, big coontail and northern watermilfoil. Head straight out and get past the weeds--then take either left or right (I preferred the right)--then head back to shore--I saw nice perch, sunfish, good sized bluegills and many largemouth bass, 3 two-footers stayed near and watched with great interest. Lake has a nice sand bottom and has good visibility if you stay in 10 feet of water or less.

WELLS LAKE   OSCEOLA COUNTY

Acreage: 48 acres   **page 57 of the DeLorme Atlas**

Location: Take I-96 west to Grand Rapids, go north on 131, go
past Reed City and get off at 11 Mile Road going east. Go north on
170th Avenue (Cedar Road), then east on Glendale Road which
will dead end into the public access.

This is a nice quiet little lake--the clarity has varied on the
occasions I have been there. There's a big shallow spot to the right,
where I saw lots of largemouth bass, bluegills, perch, and the usual
pan fish.

SOUTHERN LOWER PENINSULA

BIG LAKE   ALLEGAN COUNTY

Acreage: 137 acres   **page 36 of the DeLorme Atlas**

Location: Take I-96 west to Grand Rapids, south on 131, west on 120th, south on Lake Drive which will dead end into the public access.

A very inviting lake that is not too cottaged. It was fairly busy while I was there, and because the lake has potential, it's worth coming in off hours and weekdays to keep from having the jet skiers spoil it. The visibility is good, and there's a nice little bay to snorkel in before you open on to the main lake. Cross the lake and go over to the point, where I saw some nice big largemouth bass, as well as the usual pan fish.

EAGLE LAKE   ALLEGAN COUNTY

Acreage: 225 acres   **page 27 of the DeLorme Atlas**

Location: Take I-96 west to Grand Rapids, go south on 131, west on 142nd, south on A37 into the town of Allegan, then out of Allegan south on 40, west on 102nd Avenue, south on Mary Road which will dead end into the public access site.

This is a great lake with good visibility, but it gets deep immediately and the deep area with the very tall weed structure is not productive as far as fish are concerned. Go to the right, next to the boat dock--I saw big largemouth bass, jumbo perch, big bluegills and minnows as well as snails and 3 painted turtles. Sandy bottom with a fair amount of northern watermilfoil and coontail.

MINER LAKE   ALLEGAN COUNTY

Acreage: 325 acres   **page 36 of the DeLorme Atlas**

Location: Take I-96 west to Grand Rapids, go south on 131, west on 128th Avenue, south on 28th Street, east on 118th , north on 26th and west on 120th Avenue. The public access will be on the right.

A very inviting lake near the town of Allegan. The lake has good visibility and a nice clean feeling, but it's busy on the weekends--worth making the effort to seek it out during the week. Go to either the right or left--they're equally good with all the usual pan fish. Attractive weed structure. Not too cottaged.

PIKE LAKE   ALLEGAN COUNTY

Acreage: 32 acres   **page 28 of the DeLorme Atlas**

Location: Take I-96 west to Grand Rapids, go south on 131, west on 142nd, south on A37 into the town of Allegan, then out of Allegan south on 40, east on 108th Avenue. Take the next left after Melodee Park Drive and that left will dead end into the public access site.

This is a very interesting lake with a varied underwater landscape consisting of elodea (the perfect vegetation for turtles), lots of northern watermilfoil and coontail. Go either left or right--both are great--the best largemouth bass are under the big willow tree on the opposite side of the lake. There is a big stretch of lily pads on both sides as you enter. Lots of turtles, lots of big sunfish, big suckers, jumbo perch, big bluegills and big bowfin. I didn't see pike, though this is what the lake is known for, so it's always a possibility.

SELKIRK LAKE   ALLEGAN COUNTY

Acreage: 94 acres   **page 36 of the DeLorme Atlas**

Location: Take I-96 west to Grand Rapids, go south on 131, east at 124th Avenue, south at 10th Street, east at 125th Avenue, and the public access site will be on your left.

This is a no wake lake between 7:30PM and 11AM, so it's ideal to come during those hours, though the lake is still doable at other hours, as the jet skiers tend to stay on the opposite side of the lake where the cottages are. Visibility is average--good enough to see what you want to see, but not notable. A great deal can be seen right at the concrete DNR entrance--I saw bluegills, sunfish and largemouth bass there. Then go left along the lily pads for all the usual pan fish in a setting of northern watermilfoil, grasses and pondweed.

SHEFFER LAKE   ALLEGAN COUNTY

Acreage: 12 acres   page 28 of the DeLorme Atlas

Location: Take I-96 west to Grand Rapids, go south on 131, west on 142nd, south on A37 into the town of Allegan, then out of Allegan south on 40, west on 108th Avenue. Your first left will dead end into the access site. Take the 2 track road to the left of the white house with black shutters.

A wonderful lake just north of the town of Gobles. Visibility is outstanding--the bottom can be seen easily. There's tons of great vegetation--tall northern watermilfoil in the center, giving a feathered look to everything, surrounded by a big carpet of elodea and tons of thick green tipped coontail with lily pads all around. A very woodsy feeling, both above and below the water. Plenty of largemouth bass, sunfish and bluegills. The lake was terribly scenic and secluded with no power boats. A real winner.

LAKE SIXTEEN   ALLEGAN COUNTY

Acreage: 35.2 acres   page 36 of the DeLorme Atlas

Take I-96 west to Grand Rapids, south on 131, east on 120th Avenue and the public access site will be on your right.

This is a very shallow lake that is great for swimming with its clear sandy bottom. It's a tranquil, inviting and unspoiled setting with very few cottages. Go straight out and a little to the left--there is a sunken boat and a ship's bell. Go to the right, around the point and you can see the remnants of an old boat.

It's great for little kids, and dive clubs also meet here to practice. Sloping sides good for snorkeling, and a nice little sand bar that surprises you out in the middle. No dogs allowed. Good visibility.

BASSETT LAKE   BARRY COUNTY

Acreage: 44 acres   **page 36 of the DeLorme Atlas**

Location: Take I-96 west, go south on 66 and west on 43 into Hastings. Out of Hastings, take A42 (Chief Noonday Road), north on Norris Road and the public access site will be on the right.

There's a long drive in off the main road, but a very scenic drive through a gorgeous stand of pines. The lake entrance looks like the old swimming hole with overhanging branches. Limited parking.

This is a lake that does not have the kind of clarity that dazzles, but as your eyes get used to the light, it's more than adequate. And I found plenty of action here. If you go to the left, you have a great many long branches outstretched in and on the water. I saw a turtle as big as a pieplate hanging down from one when I first entered the water. Lots of big and small largemouth bass roaming around, and I also saw several big bowfin and medium sized pike, as well as a couple of big white suckers. Many schools of perch, crappies, pumpkinseeds and other sunfish hanging around the various docks that jut out to the right of the entrance. The lake drops off almost immediately, so all the snorkeling is done along the walls which offer many ledges lined with some very attractive vegetation. This allows you to snorkel at more than one level. You have to feel comfortable with vegetation to enjoy this lake, as there is a gigantic weed structure here—a little bit of everything from broadleaf pondweed to tall thick watermilfoil to an abundance of the spectacular black or green tipped coontail. As you go past the last dock on the right, there are no more cottages, and you have a big stretch of sand and fallen logs which gives you the opportunity to sit on them and rest and take a break before continuing. There aren't many cottages here and no power boats—this lake is strictly for fishermen. I felt it was very worthwhile if the conditions suit you.

CLEAR LAKE   BARRY COUNTY

Acreage: 184 acres   **page 37 of the DeLorme Atlas**

Location: Take I-96 west, go south on 66 and west on 43 into Hastings. Out of Hastings, take 37 south past Dowling Road. The public access site will be on the right.

The lake, like its name, is good and clear and very scenic. It is not overrun with power boats and jet skiers and has some very attractive weedbeds. It's a flat lake—head straight out for views of perch, largemouth bass and bluegills. This is a good lake to repeat.

CLOVERDALE LAKE   BARRY COUNTY

Acreage: 58 acres   **page 37 of the DeLorme Atlas**

Location: Take I-96 west, go south on 66 and west on 43 into Hastings. Out of Hastings, take 43 south to the town of Cloverdale. The access site is on the right just at the edge of town.

You'll see the lake right away, but the access is not so obvious—it's just across from the store on the corner. Visibility is excellent, and there's all kinds of good weed structure, coontail, northern watermilfoil, broadleaf pondweed and chara, housing all the usual pan fish. Lots of space to explore here—a relatively flat lake.

DEEP LAKE   BARRY COUNTY

Acreage: 32.4   **page 36 of the DeLorme Atlas**

Location: Take I-96 west, go south on 66 and west on 43 into Hastings. Out of Hastings, take Gun Lake Road (37/43 430), then take Chief Noonday Road west to Yankee Springs Road, go left (south) and the public access site will be on your right.

This is a State Forest Campground, well developed and quite popular with groups of bikers, hikers, etc. It's just down the road from a horseback riding camp, so this is an opportunity to combine the two sports. I did not see power boaters or jet skiers here—it's a peaceful lake with most of the people-action taking place on the shore.

The water is very clear and it's a fine experience going either right or left. To the left, the lake gets deep rather quickly which means snorkeling along the ledge next to the shore, where lots of big crappies, pumpkinseeds and largemouth bass roam around. If you go to the right, there are gill beds, loads of turtles swimming among the lily pads (it's fun to watch them come to the surface for air), several bowfin (it sure is a shock to see one of these prehistoric monsters swim by you, or just stop and stare as they sometimes do) or big bluegills. This is a small enough lake that you can, if you give yourself several hours, snorkel all around it, and because there are several levels to snorkel at, I found it very rewarding. You can either snorkel in the shallow beds of chara, or move to the left and get deeper, where you can still see bottom very well. Keep going all the way to the right and then head toward the brown building that is in the right hand corner on the opposite side of the lake. It's easy to cross here because of the narrowness of the lake, and you never know what you might run into. There's lots of great vegetation--big fields of soft green chara, scattered lily pads, lots of elodea to attract the turtles, various types of pondweed and scattered northern watermilfoil. This is really a perfect size lake for snorkeling.

FISH LAKE   BARRY COUNTY

Acreage: 165 acres   **page 36 of the DeLorme Atlas**

Location: Take I-96 west, go south on 66 and west on 43 into Hastings. Out of Hastings, take 43 south , then take a right (west) on Guernsey Lake Road. The public access site will be on the right.

This is a super deep lake, so snorkeling has to be along the edges along the tall grasses, where the carp tend to follow along right behind you. The entrance is interesting, as it is a narrow shallow channel. Upon entering, take a right and you will go a ways before entering the lake proper. In this channel, I saw all the usual pan fish as well as some small white suckers. If you want to commit the time to it, and I do plan to do that this summer, there are two other small lakes you can access if you snorkel across Fish Lake. You then can reach Lime Lake and Horseshoe Lake at the northeast and southeast ends of Fish Lake. They are each 14 acres and so very easy to snorkel around--of course if you had a boat you could get there more quickly, but if you have the time, you can snorkel it. I will report on these lakes in a future update.

GULL LAKE   BARRY COUNTY

Acreage: 2030 acres   **page 29 of the DeLorme Atlas**

Location: Take I-96 west, go south on 66 and west on 43 into Hastings. Out of Hastings, take 43 south past the town of Delton. The public access site will be on the left in Prairieville Township Park.

This is one of those giant lakes that has unusually high clarity and is perfect for snorkeling if you don't need a lot of excitement. It's great for beginners who don't like a lot of surprises when they are just getting used to their equipment. The clarity is really dazzling, and along the shore there is an abundance of smaller perch and minnows which look very attractive cruising over the stony shore. The lake is flat and you have to venture out a ways to get into more activity and larger fish. If you stay around,and somewhat beyond, the swimming area there is an ice shanty below you--you have to look rather hard, as it is quite deep here, but a lot of divers are attracted to it. Just to the right of the shanty a lot of big largemouth bass hang out over scattered beds of chara.   The bottom is mostly sand, and there is a great deal to this lake, but like all large lakes, it requires a time commitment to get the most out of it.   Oddly enough, the jet boats, though they are plentiful, don't really interfere, as they stay further out in the lake.

GUN LAKE   BARRY COUNTY

Acreage: 2611 acres   **page 36 of the DeLorme Atlas**

Location: Take I-96 west to 66, go south on 66 and west on 43 into Hastings. Out of Hastings, take 43 south, then head west on Gun Lake Road (430) into the Yankee Springs Recreation Area. Two public access sites will be on your left, or continue on Gun Lake Road, take a left (south) at Patterson Road, and a third public access site will be on your left.

This is another big lake, even larger than Gull and very near Gull, a good bit of it being in Allegan County as well. The water is very clear, and the sand/stone beach contains many small fish and not much vegetation.   You almost need a boat to adequately explore this lake and find all the good spots. It's a busy commercial lake in the popular Yankee Springs Recreation Area.

HALL LAKE   BARRY COUNTY

Acreage: 46 acres   **page 36 of the DeLorme Atlas**

Location: Take I-96 west to 66, go south on 66, then west on 43 into Hastings. Out of Hastings, take 43 south, then head west on Gun Lake Road (430) and the public access site will be on your right.

The visibility here is variable--I have been here when it's excellent and I have been here when it's only fair. It's definitely worth checking out. It is rather an unusual lake for a snorkeler because of the three islands located so near shore. You can snorkel to any of them and I always found a variety of pan fish roaming around the islands. It's an extremely picturesque lake without boat traffic. I saw several large turtles, perch and largemouth bass, as well as a variety of minnows.

KIRKPATRICK LAKE   BARRY COUNTY
(also known as KILPATRICK)

Acreage: 19.3 acres   **page 37 of the DeLorme Atlas**

Location: Take I-96 west to 66, go south on 66, then west on 43, then east on 442 (Barnum Road). The public access will be on the left.

I found this to be a fun experience, though it might not be for everyone. There are a gazillion weed beds here, most of them in rather deep water, but it's still fun to mosey around among the very tall watermilfoil and coontail to see perch, largemouth bass, pumpkinseeds and bluegills. I looked over and thought I saw another snorkeler in a big yellow tee shirt. As I snorkeled over to say hello, I got closer and realized it was not a snorkeler at all but instead a huge yellow carp! I talked to people in the neighborhood and they were all aware of the venerable yellow fish that you can see easily from the road. The lake is by the side of the road and the public access is very tiny--there's only space for a couple of cars to park. There's a nice little island to snorkel to where the water is more shallow and fish are more easily seen. Try to stick to the sides of the lake for best results.

PINE LAKE   BARRY COUNTY

Acreage: 660 acres   **page 36 of the DeLorme Atlas**

Location: Take I-96 west to 66, go south on 66, then west on 43 into Hastings. Out of Hastings continue on 43, then go west on 412 (Pine Lake Road). Take a left on Boniface Point and another left into the Prairieville Township Park which is the public access site.

This is a very picturesque spring fed lake. It is not obviously accessible--you have to park on the grassy area near the pipe that protrudes. It's a very worthwhile experience, so don't be deterred. It's very scenic underwater with attractive vegetation of chara, broadleaf pondweed and northern watermilfoil housing the usual pan fish. The fish are very plentiful, and there is the occasional largemouth bass.

SHAW LAKE   BARRY COUNTY

Acreage: 4.6 acres   **page 36 of the DeLorme Atlas**

Location: Take I-96 west to 66, go south on 66, then west on 43 into Hastings. Out of Hastings, take 37, then go west on 436 (Shaw Lake Road) and the public access site will be on your left.

This is a picturesque lake that has a bit of a tough access, but it's worth it. It's very isolated with no jet skis or power boats--this is your own private lake. Gorgeous weedbeds housing pumpkinseeds, largemouth bass, and rock bass. Visiblity is superior.

STEWART LAKE   BARRY COUNTY

Acreage: 46 acres   **page 36 of the DeLorme Atlas**

Location: Take I-96 west to 66, go south on 66, then west on 43 into Hastings. Out of Hastings, take 43 south, then go west on Guernsey Lake Road, north on Otis Lake Road, and west on Keller Road, go right at Morris, right at Mullen, and the access is on the right hand side.

This is a worthwhile experience with all the ingredients you need to have a good snorkel--that's good visibility, plenty of fish, and very attractive and plentiful vegetation.

CARY LAKE   BRANCH COUNTY

Acreage: 79 acres   **page 21 of the DeLorme Atlas**

Location: Take U.S. 27 south, go west on 12, and the public access site will be on the left.

This is a gorgeous wilderness lake with only 3 or 4 cottages, which are hardly visibile. This is a lake for wall snorkeling, and the visibility is excellent if you keep your head turned toward shore, or toward the wall. Then you can see very well. This lake is a real keeper. There's plenty of space to roam and interesting vegetation as well as a great bowl shape. Go either left or right--there's plenty of fish and attractive scenery on either side. Lovely fields of chara abound. I saw a big silver sucker, big largemouth bass, plenty of perch and sunfish and a big bullhead. There were fantastic cattail ledges, and I studied them but couldn't quite figure what was holding them up. Very worthwhile.

CRAIG LAKE   BRANCH COUNTY

Acreage: 122 acres   **page 29 of the DeLorme Atlas**

Location: Take I-69 south to just south of Marshall, go west on 60, then go south on 9 Mile Road which dead ends into Union City Road. Continue on Union City Road, and the public access site is on the right hand side at Stevens Shores.

This is a nice lake that can, like many lakes, have an occasional algae bloom. There were plenty of fish here in the form of pumpkinseeds, small perch, and good sized largemouth bass. There's a nice mixture of tall and short weedbeds for esthetic viewing. A few fishermen but no power boats when I was there. Lots of territory to roam and lots of space to maneuver in. Hard sandy bottom--you can usually stand up.

LAKE GEORGE   BRANCH COUNTY

Acreage: 565 acres   **page 21 of the DeLorme Atlas**

Location: Take U.S. 27 south to Coldwater where you pick up business 69. Head south on business 69, then go west on Baker Road, north on County Road 150, and a right at Whaley Road which will dead end into the public access.

The visibility is good here and there's plenty to see. Go to the left and see the big red eared sunfish spawning if you are here in late June or early July. Bottom is solid sand and it's very shallow by the lily pads. You can easily stand up. It's a little work to get the best out of this lake, but you can have an adventure here, and it's worth the effort.

GILEAD LAKE   BRANCH COUNTY

Acreage: 130 acres   **page 21 of the DeLorme Atlas**

Location: Take U.S. 27 south, go west on 12, and right after Cary Lake, go south on Snow Prairie Road, west on Slisher Road, south on Orlando Road, west on Pleasant Hill Road, south on Riverson Road, and west on Booth Road. The access site will be on the left.

This lake is located in a park with good restrooms and an inviting appearance. It's a no wake lake between 7:30PM and 11AM, a partly cottaged lake in a lovely setting. There's lots to explore in this lake with an interesting oblong shape. It's quite a clear lake whose visibility gets better the longer you are in it. Some lily pads to the left for fish habitat, as well as fields of soft green chara and broadleaf pondweed. There's a nice dropoff as well as some large shallow areas. Saw largemouth bass, large perch and sunfish, as well as bullhead spawning. Great surroundings here and a lake worth repeating.

LAKE OF THE WOODS   BRANCH COUNTY

Acreage: 335 acres   **page 21 of the DeLorme Atlas**

Location: Take U.S. 27 south beyond Coldwater, then take Central
Road west, south on Fillmore Road, west on Grass Lake Road, and
a right on Pleasant View which will dead end into the public
access.

This is a definite yes, with good visibility, and an inviting
appearance above and below, with only a few cottages. Go to the
right into the shallow area--there's chara, broadleaf pondweed and
cattails, as well as largemouth bass, sunfish, minnows and clams.

LAVINE LAKE   BRANCH COUNTY

Acreage: 86.5 acres   **page 21 of the DeLorme Atlas**

Location: Take U.S.27 south beyond Coldwater, then take Central
Road west, south on Block Road, east on East Gilead Road, south
on Whaley Road and west on Fire Lane 54 which will dead end
into the public access.

This is a very inviting lake--picturesque, a wilderness setting and a
great place to meditate and recharge your batteries.   The
vegetation is varied and it's worth the trip just for this. The weed
beds are tall, short and in between. Many varieties of pondweed.
There are lily pads to the left, and all the vegetation is home to
largemouth bass, pumpkinseeds, bluegills, minnows and all the
usual panfish.   Lots of tall grasses, northern watermilfoil and
cactus-like elodea.

MARBLE LAKE   BRANCH COUNTY

Acreage: 780 acres   **page 22 of the DeLorme Atlas**

Take U.S. 27 south, go west on 12, south on Ray/Quincy Road and
west on Wildwood which will dead end into the public access.
There are two other public access sites. The second can be reached
by staying on U.S.12 and going south on Lake Boulevard which
will dead end into the public access.

The third can be reached by going past the first public access site on Ray/Quincy Road and continuing until you reach Fisher/Bennett Road. Take a right at Fisher which will become Bennett Road, and after crossing Brocklebank Road, the public access site will be on your left.

Wonderful, wonderful. Endless possibilities, limited only by the amount of time you have available. Visibility is excellent and there's so much room to roam, with all the usual pan fish, as well as good sized largemouth bass and pumpkinseeds. You can move from Marble into Middle Lake, which has a little bit of a rosy tinge but not enough to bother you. There's still a lot to see as you pass big boulders on your left housing lots of perch and sunfish, continuing on to the edge of the concrete breakway, where you will find many shellcracker beds that in June and July are simply loaded with these fascinating creatures who will let you get close and watch their spawning if you don't disturb. It's definitely Grand Central Station there at this time of year and their ritualized behavior is fascinating to watch. There were also bluegills spawning and spotted sand darters jumping around.

SILVER LAKE   **BRANCH COUNTY**

Acreage: 213 acres   **page 21-22 of the DeLorme Atlas**

Location: Take U.S.27 south to Coldwater. Out of Coldwater, take Business 69 (Angola Road). Take a left at Southern Road, and the public access site will be on your right.

On June 21, I was lucky enough to see the huge red eared sunfish spawning. These huge males only come in once a year--otherwise they're in the deep. They fan their tails to clean and clear the beds, and after the females have laid the eggs, the males fertilize them and then stay to guard them from harm. It's a sight well worth seeing and I found it lasted a couple of weeks. I saw 3 big bullheads next to the big wooden plank. There were many schools of large perch, as well as largemouth bass, bluegill and smaller sunfish. The lake is quite shallow and the visibility is good. The wooden plank is straight out from shore. There's a nice swimming area here, so it's a pleasant place to bring the family.

UPPER BRACE LAKE

CALHOUN COUNTY

Acreage: 70 acres   **page 30 of the DeLorme Atlas**

Location: Take I-69 south to Marshall--just south of Marshall, go west on Hughes Road which will dead end into Homer Road. Go southeast on Homer Road, then south on 18 and a Half Mile Road. The public access will be on the right.

This is a great lake--very clear and fairly shallow. There's a variety of topography that pleases the eye. There's the feathered look of the northern watermilfoil, the spectacular dark tipped coontail, lily pads, a little pondweed and the Elysian fields of chara. I saw a big map turtle as well as perch, the long eared sunfish, largemouth bass, bluegills and minnows in an underwater environment of great natural beauty. It's shallow almost everywhere, and in late May and early June the carp are bumping each other during the spawning process in the various lake inlets. You can actually stand on the shore and see it happening. The bottom is sand and slightly mucky. There's very little boat traffic and no power boats--just canoes and sailboats. This lake will show you as much as you have time for.

LANES LAKE

CALHOUN COUNTY

Acreage: 23.6 acres   **page 30 of the DeLorme Atlas**

Location: Take I-69 south to Olivet. In Olivet, go south on Old U.S. 27, west on N Drive North, and north on 16 Mile Road. The public access will be on your left.

This lake has a drop-dead gorgeous entrance. It's very secluded--it's 11AM on a Wednesday, and I am the only one there. Very picturesque. It gets deep fast, so go along the sides and to the right to get to the shallow end. If it's a sunny day, it's nice if you can go after 2-3PM so the sun will be in the right place over your shoulder. Of course if it is a cloudy day, it doesn't matter. Great wall snorkeling here. Vegetation is lovely--feathery northern watermilfoil, broadleaf pondweed and water lilies. I saw bluegills, crappies, largemouth bass, as well as the usual pan fish.

LEE LAKE   CALHOUN COUNTY

Acreage: 116 acres   **page 29 of the DeLorme Atlas**

Location: Go south on I-69, west on I-94, south on 11 Mile Road, west on I Drive South, south on 10 Mile Road and west on J Drive South. The public access site will be on your right.

This lake really blew me away--so much going on. Maybe I was lucky but I saw a big turtle tearing into a dead largemouth bass on the bottom as well as several hundred bluegills in the first 5 minutes. That was followed by a big bowfin, black crappies, white crappies and tons of largemouth bass, some so large they looked like toys. I saw 6 more turtles and huge pumpkin seeds. The visibility was outstanding, and the whole side of the lake where you enter is a sloping wall which lends itself beautifully to snorkeling. On my second visit, there was not nearly so much activity as there had previously been, which simply points up the importance of giving a lake a chance and not giving up on it.

NOTTAWA LAKE   CALHOUN COUNTY

Acreage: 116 acres   **page 29 of the DeLorme Atlas**

Location: Take I-69 south of Marshall, go east on F Drive South, south on 17 Mile Road, and west on N Drive South. The public access site will be on your right.

This is a good lake--go left of the public access for some great weed beds, walls and big patches of sand where fish gather--there were pumpkinseeds, good sized perch, largemouth bass, all in a lovely setting among northern watermilfoil and elodea. The lake is in a beautiful setting with only a few cottages and few or no boats, definitely not a busy lake.

BELAS LAKE   CASS COUNTY

Acreage: 58 acres   **page 19 of the DeLorme Atlas**

Location: Take I-69 south, go west on I-94, south on 40, west on Dutch Settlement Street, south on Savage, west on Quaker, south on Kirk Lake Road, and the public access site will be on your right.

It's a very scenic drive into what is a lake for experienced snorkelers only. This is because you have to enter through a pathway of lily pads in order to get out into the lake proper, and the average snorkeler is not going to want to do this. Once you have gotten used to foliage, this is not a big deal, which is why I really love this lake. It's in a gorgeous wilderness setting, completely isolated with nobody there, or at least not when I was. There was some very strange plant life—almost looked like a bryozoan animal with lots of eyes. Would love to have an expert identify it. It's growing in big stalks by the entrance. Visibility is good though not great. A big largemouth bass greeted me only a few feet from the entrance. Lots of bluegills and the other pan fish were swarming around. I plan to go back and spend a lot more time.

BIRCH LAKE   CASS COUNTY

Acreage: 295 acres   **page 20 of the DeLorme Atlas**

Location: Take I-69 south to I-94, go west on I-94, south on 40, west on Harvey Street, south on Lake Shore Road, and the public access wll be on your right.

Very good visibility here. Immediately to the right of the entrance is some weed structure worth checking out, but go out just a little further, both to the right and to the left and there's low pondweed and chara containing bluegills, good sized largemouth bass, and black striped minnows. Go straight out about 100 feet and there's much taller weed structure, broadleaf pondweed and northern watermilfoil containing large largemouth bass. The bottom is littered with clams and a gazillion snails. It's quite a busy and cottaged lake so try to come in the off hours and on a weekday.

COREY LAKE   CASS COUNTY

Acreage: 618 Acres   **page 20 of the DeLorme Atlas**

Location: Take I-69 south to I-94, go west on I-94, south on 40, east on Born Streeet, north on Corey Lake Road and the public access site will be on your right.

Good visibility here and quite a bit to see. There are many bluegill beds here, and if you hit it right for spawning--usually in June, you will be privy to quite a ritual, as the male cleans out the nest and waits for the female to come in and lay the eggs. It's fun to watch the female keep hitting her belly on the bottom to loosen the eggs, as the membranes are tight. She immediately leaves for deep water after laying the eggs, and the male takes over as the guardian. He fans the eggs and the nest endlessly to keep the eggs aerated and to ward off neighboring fish who get nosy. It takes about 2-3 weeks to spawn, so that gives you quite a bit of leeway to see the process, and the beds are usually in shallow water near shore.

DEWEY LAKE   CASS COUNTY

Acreage: 174 acres   **page 27 of the DeLorme Atlas**

Location: Take I-69 south, on I-94 go west, go south on 687, west on 94th, south on 152. Take a right at Garrett Road and a left at Huckleberry, which will dead end at the public access site.

Visibility is good but not great, with occasonally some suspended sediment. Huge rows of lily pads on both sides grace your entrance. I saw big turtles, largemouth bass, smallmouth bass, bullheads, perch, bluegills and sunfish. Water traffic may have roughened up the water a little, creating a little sediment, but it did not keep me from seeing the good that was there.

DONNELL LAKE   CASS COUNTY

Acreage: 246 acres   **page 19 of the DeLorme Atlas**

Location: Take I-69 south, go west on I-94, south on 131, west on 60, south on Main Road, east on Donnell Lake Road. Take a left at Donald Roadway, and the public access site will be on your left.

This lake is fabulous! Great clarity, and the only thing that makes it less than ideal is that it's a busy cottaged lake so you need to come during the week or before 10AM. Snorkel straight out about 30 feet and you will come to a small cliff or dropoff consisting of tall grasses, broadleaf pondweed, curly pondweed and just a little fluffy coontail.

Snorkel back and forth all along the cliff and there are loads of fish. I saw large and medium sized largemouth bass, good sized perch, bluegill, blackstriped minnows, big clams and snails. Hard sand bottom.

FISH LAKE   **CASS COUNTY**

Acreage: 340 acres   **page 28 of the DeLorme Atlas**

Location: Take I-69 south, go west on I-94, south on 131, west on 216, north on Finch Road, east on Steininger Street, and the public access site will be on the left.

This is a good quality lake with good visibility--the only drawback being the amount of traffic it generates. It is heavily cottaged and there are lots of pontoon boats, which do not interfere as much as power boats. It's a very scenic drive in and is well marked and well maintained. Attractive vegetation and all the usual pan fish are here--best to come during the week and before 10AM or after 7PM if possible.

HARWOOD LAKE   **CASS COUNTY**

Acreage: 122 acres   **page 20 of the DeLorme Atlas**

Location: Take I-69 south to I-94, go west on I-94, south on 40, east on Born Street, north on Corey Lake Road and the public access site will be on your left.

This is a wonderful lake--crystal clear. You can see 15 feet easily. There are fields of chara and broadleaf pondweed--all lovely to look at, and there are acres to roam around in. It's very shallow at first, but when it gets deeper you can still see very well. I saw largemouth bass, perch, sunfish, pumpkinseeds, rock bass and several turtles. Worth coming back to.

HEMLOCK LAKE   CASS COUNTY

Acreage: 63.8 acres   **page 28 of the DeLorme Atlas**

Location: Take I-69 south to I-94, go wet on I-94, south on 131, west on 216, north on Hemlock Lake Road. The public access site will be on the left.

This is an excellent clear lake with a nice and easy entrance. The only drawback is that it is quite cottaged, but it still manages to have an air of tranquility about it. The visibility, weed structure and fish life is here--try to come on weekdays for best results.

KIRK LAKE   CASS COUNTY

Acreage: 41.5 acres   **page 19 of the DeLorme Atlas**

Location: Take I-69 south, go west on I-94, south on 40, west on Dutch Settlement Street, south on Savage, west on Quaker, south on Kirk Lake Road, take a right at Pemberton, and the public access site will be on your right.

This is a case of a lake looking not at all inviting and then completely surprising you. Even so, I see this as a lake for a more advanced snorkeler due to a rather narrow entrance. Both sides are framed by purple flowered pickerelweed, and on the way through the narrow entrance, look on both sides.   I saw two bowfin peeking through the lily stalks. Some of the thick stalks had good sized snails perched on them. There were many big snails, and I saw a big musk turtle. Visibility is good but not great. I took some great video here of the bowfin peeking, etc. There were also big red eared sunfish, large bluegills, two good sized suckers, and lots of big largemouth bass. All in all, a very satisfying experience. There's a lot more here if you can commit the time to it.

PARADISE LAKE   CASS COUNTY

Acreage: 185 acres   **page 19 of the DeLorme Atlas**

Location: Take I-69 south to I-94, go west on I-94, south on 131, west on 60, south on Penn Road, east on Jeffries, south on Day Lake Road, and the public access site will be on the left.

This is a fabulous and super clear lake. Go out about 30 feet to the dropoff and snorkel the dropoff with its nice bowl shape. The vegetation is very scenic--broadleaf pondweed, soft green chara, a little fluffy coontail, and feathery watermilfoil. I saw loads of perch, largemouth bass, bluegills and blackstriped minnows. Head left toward the water lilies and snorkel that area--it's unlikely that you would have any traffic. There were very few cottages, and it was very much a wilderness feeling. The left area is like a little bay--perfect for snorkeling. Definitely a lake to return to.

SHAVEHEAD LAKE   CASS COUNTY

Acreage: 289 acres   **page 20 of the DeLorme Atlas**

Location: Take I-69 south to I-94, go west on I-94, south on 131, west on 12, north on Kessington Road, go right on Mt. Zion Street, left on Union Road, right on North Peninsula Drive, another right on Peninsula Drive West, and the public access will be on your right.

An excellent lake with good visibility. It's a heavily cottaged lake, so it's busy and you need to try to come in the off hours or at least on weekdays. You only need to go a short distance out to find wonderful scenic weedbeds of tall grasses, curly pondweed, broadleaf pondweed and picturesque beds of northern watermilfoil. I saw 4 turtles, 2 musk turtles, and 2 map turtles, lots of bluegills and largemouth bass and the ubiquitous black striped minnows.

LAKE INTERSTATE   EATON COUNTY

Acreage: Approx. 6 acres   **page 39 of the DeLorme Atlas**

Location: Take I-69 southwest of Lansing heading toward Charlotte, and the public access site is on the right.

This lake might seem a bit tame to some, but I can think of no better place to begin the snorkeling experience, if you just want to get used to the inland lake environment, than this delightful little lake with absolutely no boats—it's almost too small for any kind of craft. There usually are just a few little boys fishing from the side, and it's such an easy entrance off of I-69. It's like climbing into a big fish bowl. There's lots of chara spread out beneath you but nothing tall enough to get in your way, and the visibility is outstanding. Because of the small size, it's easy to cover the lake, although that would take 2-3 hours. There's no place in the lake you can't venture. The various pan fish, which are all here, will be closer to you as you stay near shore, but because the lake is fairly shallow everywhere, and you can always see bottom, there are no restrictions on where you can go. There's nothing startling here, but it is still very beautiful, very serene and a therapeutic experience. I strongly recommend it for those particular features.

BEAR LAKE   HILLSDALE COUNTY

Acreage: 117 acres   **page 22 of the DeLorme Atlas**

Location: Take U.S.127 south of Jackson, go west on Squawfield Road, north on Hillsdale Road, west on Card Road, north on Lake Wilson Road, and the public access will be on your left.

I include this lake because the clarity, vegetation and fish are here, but you have to snorkel a distance to get to it and not everyone will want to do this. If cottagers were agreeable to it, you could walk to the end of the road and enter right where the action is, but going in at the public access, which is the proper thing to do will require snorkeling a good distance. Hard sand bottom, and sparse vegetation around the entrance area and some distance out.

BIRD LAKE   HILLSDALE COUNTY

Acreage: 113 acres   **page 23 of the DeLorme Atlas**

Location: Take U.S. 127 south of Jackson, go west on Squawfield Road, north on Bird Lake Road, east on Lake Road, and the public lake access will be on your right.

This lake is a definite yes, with good clarity and a nice small public beach. However, it is heavily cottaged, and it is recommended that you try to come in the off hours. Morning is best if the day is sunny, so the sun will be on your subject while you are snorkeling. Go to the left of the beach for good sized largemouth bass, bluegills, sunfish and snails. Background is broadleaf pondweed, curly pondweed and chara.

CUB LAKE   HILLSDALE COUNTY

Acreage: 69 acres   **page 22 of the DeLorme Atlas**

Location: Take U.S. 127 south of Jackson, go west on Squawfield Road, north on Hillsdale Road, and the public access site will be on your left.

This lake is very worthwhile, and I suggest coming in the afternoon if the day is sunny, so you won't be looking against the sun while you are viewing. Here I saw the tallest elodea I have ever seen, vast fields of chara, northern watermilfoil, a jungle of coontail, all at varying heights to please the eye. The visibility is excellent, and you can go either left or right and find something interesting to see. It was in this lake that I found out how fast a turtle can move. As I was snorkeling by, I must have startled him, as all of a sudden, like a speeding bullet this serving-plate-sized flat turtle (probably a soft shelled female) shot past me--it was just amazing to witness this speed. In addition to the turtle, I saw numerous big perch, big largemouth bass, a painted turtle and numerous smaller pan fish. Three large brown carp repeatedly sailed back and forth next to me. Snorkel to the edge of the weedbed and then just float along. This is a lake one could profitably spend a day at, as I felt I hardly scratched the surface.

LONG LAKE Camden Township   HILLSDALE COUNTY

Acreage: 146 acres   **page 22 of the DeLorme Atlas**

Location: Take U.S. 127 south of Jackson, west on 12, south on 49 to the town of Camden, go west on Camden Road and the public access will be on your left.

This lake had good visibility and good weed structure but occasionally has an algae bloom, as a lake of course can. The lake needs to be rechecked but an algae bloom can clear up in a few days or a week. There are attractive lily pads to the left and a grassy area to the right. Good sized largemouth bass in the lily pads as well as the usual pan fish.

LONG LAKE Reading Township   HILLSDALE COUNTY

Acreage: 210 acres   **page 22 of the DeLorme Atlas**

Location: Take U.S. 127 south of Jackson, west on 12, south on 49, west on Bankers Road, and the public access site will be on your left.

This is a lovely spring fed lake with very good visibility. Heading to the right you'll find logs, fallen branches and stumps. Watch for largemouth bass shooting out from the shore. Heading to the left from the public access, make another immediate sharp left, go into the lily pads and broad leaf plants that rise above the water. There are many bluegill beds in there, which are very active from the middle of June for three weeks. At that time the large breeding males are so exciting to see, and sometimes they linger well after that time. I also saw very large perch, big red eared sun fish and long eared sun fish. It's important to be patient, as the first 15 minutes I saw very little and then, boom, it was payday.

LAKE LANSING   INGHAM COUNTY

Acreage: 452.5 acres   **page 39 of the DeLorme Atlas**

Location: Take I-69 to East Lansing (or come in on I-96 or 127), and go south at Lake Lansing Road, go north on Marsh Road, East on Lake Drive and follow it around the lake. The public access site will be on your right.

This was the only lake in Michigan where I was constantly shooed out when I tried to snorkel at the edge of the swimming area. A pity too, as the visibility is excellent, and I know the potential is here. It is always patrolled in the Lake Lansing Park area--I'm hoping that will change to open up this fine lake to snorkelers. Snorkeling is possible on the opposite side of the lake at the public access area, but it is a busy commercial lake, so it means coming out before 11AM on a weekday, or after 7PM. Stony/rocky, hard bottom with scattered vegetation and the usual pan fish.

CLARK LAKE   JACKSON COUNTY

Acreage: 580 acres   **page 31 of the DeLorme Atlas**

Location: Take U.S.127 south of Jackson, go east on Jefferson Road, north on Hyde Road, and the public access site is on your right.

Just outside the town of Brooklyn, this busy commercial lake is heavily cottaged but is still a good bet for beginning snorkelers, due to its great visibility and its sparse vegetation, as nothing seems to intimidate the beginning snorkeler like tall vegetation. The bottom is marl/sand and is littered with clams, snails and zebra mussels. The usual pan fish are here roaming over the wild celery, broadleaf pondweed and chara. The lake is also heavy with gold striped minnows.

CLEAR LAKE   JACKSON COUNTY

Acreage: 136 acres   **page 31 of the DeLorme Atlas**

Location: Take U.S. 127 south towards Jackson, go east on I-94 and north on Clear Lake Road. Clear Lake County Park access will be on your right.

This is where it all started for me--the first Michigan lake I snorkeled, and the one that inspired me to check further to see if there were any more at home like this. While my 13 year old hung out with his friends, I put on my mask and was startled to find that Michigan had inland lakes this clear. I have since returned to this lake a number of times and it has never disappointed.

It has exceptional visibility, as its name implies, and the entire lake seems to be carpeted with chara, always below you; nothing is ever sticking up. Along the left hand side, I suggest snorkeling down to the water lilies, next to which I saw many bluegills, one very tame bullhead, largemouth bass (though not plentiful) and many small sunfish. There's also elodea here and turtles were exceedingly common. There's endless space to roam here, and it is so relaxing and therapeutic. There is an occasional fishing boat, but there is not really a launch--you'd have to carry it overland, so basically you have peace and quiet. Highly recommended.

CRISPELL LAKE   JACKSON COUNTY

Acreage: 82.5 acres   **page 31 of the DeLorme Atlas**

Location: Take U.S. 127 south of Jackson, go west on Jefferson Road, south on Springbrook Road, east on Crispell Road, south on Adams Road, and the public access site will be on your right.

The drive in is almost worth the trip--a one mile trip down Adams Road between Crispell and Liberty, a canopy of hardwood trees, just spectacular. It's a semi-cottaged lake that has everything going for it. The water is extremely clear, and there's great vegetation everywhere--beautiful chara beds, broadleaf pondweed, curly pondweed, wild celery, and the feathery northern watermilfoil. The depth is perfect for snorkeling, though it is a little bit shallow until you get out 20-30 feet.

The bottom is a combination sand and gravel, is pretty much covered with vegetation and is littered with good sized clams and snails. The usual pan fish were here as well as good sized largemouth bass and black striped minnows. Definitely a lake to spend a day in and to come back to.

GILLETTS LAKE   **JACKSON COUNTY**

Acreage: 350 acres   **page 31 of the DeLorme Atlas**

Location: Take U.S. 127 east of Jackson and get off at Michigan Avenue, heading east. Go north (left) at Ambs Shore Drive which will dead end into the public access site.

This is a great lake if you can come when it's not too crowded, preferably during the week, early or late day, if possible. There's a lovely sheltered bay at the entry where you can snorkel unbothered (always looking out, of course, for boats entering or leaving). The vegetation is varied and very attractive--northern watermilfoil, wild celery, chara, broadleaf pondweed and a great area of tall grasses. Go straight out or angle slightly to the left toward the big water lily beds where there are lots of perch, largemouth bass and bluegills, as well as some good sized clams. I also found fish hanging around the end of the dock. Very worthwhile.

GRASS LAKE   **JACKSON COUNTY**

Acreage: 348 acres   **page 31 of the DeLorme Atlas**

Location: Take U.S. 127 east of Jackson and get off at Michigan Avenue, heading east. Take a left (north) at County Park Road and another left at Simpson Street which will dead end into the public access site.

This is just a great lake--the clarity really startles you and is likely due to the great numbers of zebra mussels, which have a way of clearing up a lake in a big way! The lake is very shallow and is loaded with largemouth bass, many big schools of perch, and bluegills. Plant life consists of wild celery, curly pondweed, but is mostly big beds of chara amid patches of silty sand. This lake is very productive and is worth coming back to.

LIME LAKE   JACKSON COUNTY

Acreage: 96 acres   **page 31 of the DeLorme Atlas**

Location: Take U.S. 127 south heading towards Jackson. Go west on I-94, southwest on 60, south on Teft Road. After passing N. Lime Lake, continue on Teft Road and the public access site will be on your left.

This lake is well worth a visit with one of the widest entrances I have ever seen. The local dive club was here which was certainly a good recommendation for clarity, and indeed the visibility was excellent. It's a complete wilderness, and with a very narrow shape, it's easy to snorkel across in only a few minutes. The stony entry is surrounded by low vegetation, consisting of chara, the pink tinged northern watermilfoil, broadleaf pondweed, curly pondweed and wild celery. Lots of fish, too--black striped minnows, bluegills, perch and largemouth bass. I know in the short time I had available, I didn't even scratch the surface, so I look forward to returning.

N. LIME LAKE   JACKSON COUNTY

Acreage: 75 acres   **page 31 of the DeLorme Atlas**

Location: Take U.S. 127 south heading towards Jackson. Go west on I-94, southwest on 60, south on Teft Road. When Teft makes a sharp right hand turn, the public access site will be on your left.

Outside the town of Spring Arbor, this is a gorgeous little wilderness corner with good though not great visibility. The environment is mostly northern watermilfoil, broadleaf pondweed and lots of fallen logs along the shoreline. There are no visibile cottages, and the lake is quite shallow--you have to go out a ways to get to a good snorkeling depth. I saw plenty of largemouth bass, bluegills, and black striped minnows as well as a good sized musk turtle.

MICHIGAN CENTER LAKE   JACKSON COUNTY

Acreage: 850 acres   **page 31 of the DeLorme Atlas**

Location: Take U.S.127 south to Jackson, go west on Page Road, south on 9th Street and west (left) on Napoleon Road. Go right on Edgewater Drive which will dead end into the public access.

This is not a lake to drive a great distance for, but if you are in the area, it's worth checking out. There are no cottages in sight, and the visibility is only good in the shallower areas. There's lots of area to explore here and the underwater environment is very picturesque with the pinkish northern watermilfoil, blacktipped coontail, curly pondweed and lots of wild celery. The usual pan fish are here along with the ever present black striped minnows. The lake is surrounded by low shrubs and low grasses, backed by high hardwoods. It's so near Jackson, it can be quite busy, but the lake is so large, you can usually make your own space. The silty bottom keeps the visibility from being as perfect as you might like.

PLEASANT LAKE   JACKSON COUNTY

Acreage: 296 acres   **page 31 of the DeLorme Atlas**

Location: Take U.S.127 south towards Jackson, go west on Berry Road, north on Hankerd Road, west on Styles Road, and Pleasant Lake County Park access will be on your left.

This lake is in a park and has all of the family facilities with picnic tables, playground equipment and a big swimming beach. It has a hard sand bottom and outstanding clarity--go to the edge of the swimming area to the vegetation, which is where I saw the usual pan fish. Either to the right or the left is equally productive.

SWAINS LAKE   JACKSON COUNTY

Acreage: 69.5 acres   **page 30 of the DeLorme Atlas**

Location: Take U.S. 127 south towards Jackson, go west on I-94, then south on Concord Road, west on Warner, south on Albion Road into the town of Concord. Go south out of Concord on Pulaski Road—there are two public access sites, both on your right.

Entry is right in a public park with all of the usual park amenities. There are some cottages, but the public access site has its own little wilderness area, and there are very nice places there for snorkeling. The vegetation is very attractive—beds of chara, Brazilian elodea, northern watermilfoil, curly pondweed, and broadleaf pondweed. Water lilies are on either side. Visibility is very good. The lake is a little on the shallow side but still comfortable for snorkeling. I saw a small snapping turtle, bluegills largemouth bass and black striped minnows.

AUSTIN LAKE   KALAMAZOO COUNTY

Acreage: 1090 acres   **page 28 of the DeLorme Atlas**

Location: Take I-94 west to Kalamazoo and go south at Portage Road. The public access site will be on your left.

This is an outstanding lake I would like to have spent much more time at. It's clear with great visibility, gorgeous underwater with great weed beds and an easy access. It's fairly shallow—the whole lake is a maximum of 11 feet deep. Take a left and go to the lily pads—stay shallow—there's hundreds of perch, sunfish and bluegills. In addition, I saw a school of 25-30 big largemouth bass, marching like soldiers, one behind the other—a really amazing sight. It was in front of the first two cottages, almost at the end. Unfortunately, this is a huge and busy lake, so try to come during the week in off hours.

BARTON LAKE   KALAMAZOO COUNTY

Acreage: 347 acres   **page 28 of the DeLorme Atlas**

Location: Take I-94 west to Kalamazoo, south on 131, east on XY
Avenue, north on Portage Road, and the public access site will be
on the right.

This lake is excellent, with a few conditions. It has a great entry
and sandy/gravel/stony bottom. The downside is that you have
to go way way out to get to the weed beds and the fish action. It is
there if you are willing to take the time to get there. The place to
be is the opposite side of the lake, so for best results you need to
snorkel to the other side of the lake. If you're willing to make this
effort, it's very worthwhile.

HOGSETT LAKE   KALAMAZOO COUNTY

Acreage: 81 acres   **page 28 of the DeLorme Atlas**

Location: Take I-94 west to Kalamazoo and take the Portage Road
exit, going south on Portage Road, west on U Avenue. Take a
right at Pineview Lane which wil dead end into the public access
site or continue on U Avenue around the lake to the opposite side
where there is another public access site.

This is a lovely lake that you enter by going into Prairie View Park
(pay a nominal county fee). You can literally walk across the
entire lake. There are no power boats during the week, and the
attractive recreational park makes for a nice family outing. The
lake is very shallow and the bottom has some broadleaf pondweed
but the northern watermilfoil predominates. There are tons of big
clams and small snails. Go to the right—there I saw a big group of
large orange perch, largemouth bass and bluegills. The water is
exceptionally clear. A very nice experience.

LEFEVRE LAKE   KALAMAZOO COUNTY

Acreage: 18.7 acres   **page 29 of the DeLorme Atlas**

Location: Take I-94 west (south of Battle Creek), go south on 40th Street, west on MN Avenue, south on 38th Street, east on P Avenue, and the public access site will be on the left.

This is a very small, intimate, isolated and picturesque lake with no cottages. At the entrance, you have to get past a few easy weed beds, then you're home free. Head to the right, but the center is also good. It's mostly 5 feet deep everywhere, and there's lots of room to maneuver and lots to explore. The visibility at first seems to be only fair, but after your eyes become accustomed to it, it gradually looks very clear. There's wall to wall elodea and broad leafed pondweed beneath, intermingled with big patches of sand and very interesting formations. Bluegills were plentiful, as well as sunfish, largemouth bass, musk turtles, painted turtles and one turtle with the strangest markings on its carapace--almost like a second shell on top. All in all, a very interesting lake.

PAW PAW LAKE   KALAMAZOO COUNTY

Acreage: 126 acres   **page 28 of the DeLorme Atlas**

Location: Take I-94 west to Kalamazoo, south on 131, west on Q Avenue, south on 2nd Street, and go right (west) at Paw Paw Lake Drive. The public access site will be on your left.

North of the town of Schoolcraft, this is an extremely scenic lake with an easy entry. No muck and great visibility. Lots of room to roam here, and the weed beds are large with a great variety of plant life. Very unspoiled, at least it felt that way during the week. There were no jet skis or power boats, only fishermen. Just a few cottages. The fish I saw consisted of northern pike, largemouth bass, perch, bluegills and gold striped minnows.

RUPPERT LAKE   KALAMAZOO COUNTY

Acreage: 28 acres   **page 28 of the DeLorme Atlas**

Location: Take I-94 west to Kalamazoo, go north on 131, west on B Avenue, and the public access site will be on your right.

This is a beautiful small lake with only a couple of cottages with excellent visibility. The left side is best as there are interesting cliff formations made of dirt. The lake has a great bowl shape, so snorkel along the sloping sides--I saw lots of big largemouth bass and bluegills. I want to come back and snorkel a good deal more, as I could easily see the potential. It's also fortunately a no wake lake.

SUGARLOAF LAKE   KALAMAZOO COUNTY

Acreage: 148 acres   **page 28 of the DeLorme Atlas**

Location: Take I-94 west to Kalamazoo, go south on 131, north on Shaver Road, and the public access site will be on the left.

This lake in the Gourdneck Recreation Area has good but not great visibility, and best results are achieved by going after 5PM due to the crowds of fishermen. Go to the left in the perfect little bay. I saw big gar pike and bowfin. Unfortunately my snorkeling was a bit hampered by running into a tournament of 40 bass fishermen (July 11).

ALLEN'S LAKE   LENAWEE COUNTY

Acreage: 63 acres   **page 31 of the DeLorme Atlas**

Location: Take U.S.127 south of Jackson, go east on 12, and the access site will be on your right (after crossing 50).

This is a gorgeous wilderness lake surrounded by high hardwoods. I happened to be here in the fall when it was just spectacular. There's nothing like snorkeling with that orange, red and yellow foliage mirrored in the water. There's just one hidden cottage.

The visibility is outstanding, and the weedbeds are eyecatching, with large beds of chara, tape grass, and northern watermilfoil. Go out about 40 or 50 feet, and there is a wonderful wall of grass with loads of bluegills, largemouth bass, perch, and I also saw a small northern pike, in addition to one musk turtle and one small snapping turtle. Go beyond the wall of grass, and there is a dropoff, also sheltering many fish. The clarity is such that you can easily see bottom at 20 feet and more. A memorable experience.

DEEP LAKE   LENAWEE COUNTY

Acreage: 65 acres   **page 31 of the DeLorme Atlas**

Location: Take U.S. 127 south of Jackson, go east on 12, south on Lake Highway, east on Vischer Road,, north on Prospect Hill Highway, and east on Laird. The public access site will be on your right.

The drive into this lake in the Onstead State Game Area is down a "natural beauty" road--really sensational. There are cottages on the opposite side of the lake, but this still feels very much like a wilderness area in the place where you enter. There's a great bowl-shaped entrance, and the water is absolutely gin clear--you can see bottom clearly at least 20 feet down. There are great chara beds, lots of wild celery, tape grass, curly pondweed, and all the usual pan fish. There are different levels of ground to look at--a real esthetic delight. Hard sand bottom, and bluegill and perch predominate.

ONE MILE LAKE   LENAWEE COUNTY

Acreage: 29 acres   **page 31 of the DeLorme Atlas**

Location: Take U.S. 127 south of Jackson, go east on 12, south on Miller Road, east on Prospect Hill and north on Grassy Lake Road. The public access site will be on your left.

This is a tiny but gorgeous wilderness lake surrounded by high bulrushes. No cottages on this hidden lake. The entrance is spectacular as you walk down a very long wooden dock.

Important: to keep from getting muddy, enter the lake to the far right of the dock where you see a short path through the low grass. Here it is hard sand versus the mud by the entrance. Once you are in the lake, the bottom is hard sand, and you can stand up in the spots where it isn't over your head. (always test the bottom first with your hand, to be sure.) I found no area of the bottom that wasn't hard. The bottom is mostly sand with scattered beds of chara and curly pondweed. The lake is shallow for about 50-60 feet out, then it becomes a big bowl, where you can snorkel all along the chara beds at the dropoff--just a great experience. Some clams and snails on the bottom, along with schools of big largemouth bass, blue gills and other pan fish. The whole area is a complete scenic knockout, and you definitely know you are in the middle of nowhere. This is definitely for people who say they want to get away from it all and mean it.

SAND LAKE   LENAWEE COUNTY

Acreage: 440 acres   **page 31 of the DeLorme Atlas**

Location: Take U.S. 127 south of Jackson, go east on 12, south on Pentecost Highway, and the public access site will be on your right.

This is a heavily cottaged and busy lake--that's the down side. The upside is that the visibility is good, the weed beds (wild celery and chara) are attractive, and all the usual pan fish are here. The bottom is a combination of sand and gravel. Try to come during the week in the morning or late in the day.

APPLETON LAKE   LIVINGSTON COUNTY

Acreage: 56 acres   **page 40 of the DeLorme Atlas**

Location: Take I-96 toward Brighton, go south on Grand River Road, west on Brighton Road, south on Bauer Road, west on Bishop Lake Road and the public access site will be on your right.

This lake in the Brighton State Recreation Area is a good clear lake that is just the right size for snorkeling--i.e. small. It has that perfect bowl shape with a wide entry and lots of parking.

The whole area is wild and scenic, with just a few cottages at the other end of the lake. The section where you enter is wilderness and untouched. Go left for the most scenery and the most interesting vegetation--lots of spectacular coontail and vast areas of the pink tinged northern watermilfoil, as well as Brazilian elodea, broadleaf pondweed and chara. There's a State Campground here with a ballfield, concession stand, big riding stables, and horseshoe courts. Gorgeous scenery at the entrance. Plentiful perch, good sized largemouth bass, bluegills, gold striped minnows and black striped minnows. A fine wilderness experience.

BISHOP LAKE   LIVINGSTON COUNTY

Acreage: 119 acres   page 40 of the DeLorme Atlas

Location: Take I-96 toward Brighton, go south on Grand River Road, west on Brighton Road, south on Bauer Road, west on Bishop Lake Road and the public access site will be on your left.

This is a scenic lake in the Brighton State Recreation Area with a public campground. Lots of paved parking and a beautiful public beach area with lots of recreational facilities. Reminds me a good bit of the Holly Recreation Area, and that can only be good. In this lake, you, like many of the fishermen, have to troll for the hot spots but they are there if you have the patience. Visibility is good but not great. It's a shallow entry--go out about 50 feet to get to the best snorkeling depth. Go straight out to the edge of the pink tipped northern watermilfoil--there's a long weedbed there that contains bluegills and good sized largemouth bass. Go left toward the water lilies for more good scenery and a few clams. A small painted turtle swam right up to my mask and seemed so startled--I think their eyesight must be poor, as this has happened to me several times, and when they get close they get terrified and make a hasty exit. Comical to see.

LAKE CHEMUNG   LIVNGSTON COUNTY

Acreage: 310 acres   **page 40 of the DeLorme Atlas**

Location: Take I-96 east towards Howell. Just beyond Howell, take the Grand River exit and head south. Take a left (north) on Hughes Road, and the public access site is on your left.

This is a big heavily cottaged lake, so by all means, come during the week. The lake is outstandingly clear with an environment of broadleaf pondweed, chara and northern watermilfoil. Lots of bluegills, largemouth bass, perch, and gold striped minnows.

WOODLAND LAKE   LIVINGSTON COUNTY

Acreage; 290 acres   **page 40 of the DeLorme Atlas**

Location: Take I-96 east beyond Howell, get off at the Grand River Road exit, go north on Grand River Road and east on Hilton Road. The public access site will be on your left.

This is a big, heavily cottaged lake so do come during the week for best results. The visiblity is good but not great. There's excellent vegetation and fish in the area to the left of the entry ramp, with very picturesque pink tipped northern watermilfoil, tape grass, wild celery, chara and broadleaf pondweed. The bottom was littered with snails. Fish were mostly bluegills, largemouth bass and medium sized perch.

BIG 7 LAKE   OAKLAND COUNTY

Acreage: 170 acres   **page 41 of the DeLorme Atlas**

Location: Take I-75 north from Pontiac, go west on Grange Hall Road, north on Fish Lake Road, west on Tinsman Road, and enter Seven Lakes State Park. Follow the entry road west and south. The public access site will be on your left.

This is an attractive lake in a lovely park area that is perfect for families, with a big picnic area, concession stand and excellent beach.

The concession stand closes September 1, but the area stays open until November 1. It's a very scenic lake with good visibility and all the usual pan fish plus black striped minnows.

No power boats or jet skis here. Enter at the boat launch and head to the left over large beds of solid elodea. Eventually you will arrive at the big beds of broadleaf pondweed and northern watermilfoil. This lake offers spectacular fall color. While you are here, you can take in the other high quality lakes in the Seven Lakes State Park, making it into a longer vacation.

CASS LAKE   OAKLAND COUNTY

Acreage: 1280 acres   **page 41 of the DeLorme Atlas**

Location: From Pontiac, go west on Orchard Lake Road, go north on Cass Lake Road, west on Cass-Elizabeth Lake Road and south on Parkway Drive, which will dead end into the public access.

Enter Cass Lake at Dodge Park, with its recreational opportunities. This lake was a real surprise, as somehow in a big industrial area, one doesn't expect a wilderness underwater experience, but that is exactly what it was. This is a large, busy and commercial lake, but if you keep alert to boat traffic, you can have a very pleasurable experience. Go to the left, which is away from all the traffic, and there is a sheltered area with hundreds of large perch, big largemouth bass and baby suckers--right near the entrance. Snorkel near the bulrushes which is out of the way of the boat traffic. The clarity is great, and you look out over big beds of coontail, curly pondweed, chara, wild celery and Brazilian elodea. The entrance is wide and the entry area is surrounded by low brush, giving it a wilderness feel. Definitely a lake to come back to and to spend considerable time exploring.

CEDAR ISLAND LAKE   OAKLAND COUNTY

Acreage: 144 acres   **page 41 of the DeLorme Atlas**

Location: Take 59 west from Pontiac, go south on Teggerdine Road which becomes Oxbow Lake Road, and the public access site is on your left.

Here's a lake with easy access and good visibility, which though heavily cottaged, still offers plenty to see. There are a number of power boats, but they do not interfere.

It's a fairly shallow lake with a rocky/stony bottom and sparse vegetation (mainly northern watermilfoil). I enjoyed seeing smallmouth bass, small perch, bluegills, a northern pike, a few good sized largemouth bass, two kinds of darters, and huge schools of black striped minnows. Very worthwhile.

CROCHET LAKE   OAKLAND COUNTY

Acreage: 29 acres   page 41 of the DeLorme Atlas

Location: Take I-75 north from Pontiac, go west on Grange Hall Road, take a right (north) on Fagan Road, a right on Shields Road, and the public access site will be on your right.

This is a very picturesque lake in the Holly State Recreation Area and one to include while you are there visiting Wildwood, Heron and Valley Lakes. Visibility is decent and it's easy and pleasant to snorkel across. Watch for some big largemouth bass and perch swimming in the broadleaf pondweed and northern watermilfoil.

DICKINSON LAKE   OAKLAND COUNTY

Acreage: 44 acres   page 41 of the DeLorme Atlas

Location: Take I-75 north from Pontiac, go west on Grand Hall Road, north on Fish Lake Road, west on Tinsman Road, and enter Seven Lakes State Park. Follow the entry road southeast and the public access site is on your left.

One of several lakes in Seven Lakes State Park. It's a gorgeous no wake lake in absolute wilderness, with no cottages and surrounded by high hardwoods and tall grass. This is worth spending the whole day snorkeling the entire lake. The water is crystal clear. Go straight out a very short distance to very appealing weed structure, mostly broadleaf pondweed. This area is chock full of largemouth bass, bluegill and tons of perch. There are hundreds of gill beds on either side in the shallow water.

Snorkel the edge of the dropoff, which feels like snorkeling the slope of a bowl--just awesome. Try to come here in the latter part of June and/or early July to witness the bluegills spawning--quite a sight. This was excitement and therapy at the same time, a real treat.

E. GRAHAM LAKE   OAKLAND COUNTY

Acreage: 11 acres   **page 42 of the DeLorme Atlas**

Location: go south from Lapeer on 24, east on Oakwood Road, south on Lake George Road, west on Predmore Road, and the public access will be on the right.

Yes, Yes, Yes! Spend a whole day here. The lake is just the right size to snorkel the whole lake. You can see bottom at 10 feet very clearly. All the usual pan fish were here--largemouth bass, perch, bluegills, etc. The above water environment is just as spectacular--no cottages, just complete wilderness. Plenty of parking. A sublime experience.

HERON LAKE   OAKLAND COUNTY

Acreage: 132 acres   **page 41 of the DeLorme Atlas**

Location: Take I-75 south from Flint, go east at Grange Hall Road/Groveland Corners which becomes McGinnis Road. The public access site will be on your right.

Because this lake is inside Holly State Park, you get the benefit of all of the recreational facilities and enjoy the wilderness and lack of cottages. The lake has good but not great visibility and attractive weed structure, consisting of broadleaf pondweed, chara, striking coontail, and northern watermilfoil, as well as lily pads for the big largemouth bass to hide in. There's a great beach and no motorboats or waterskiers. The weed formations are particularly attractive.

KENT LAKE METROPARK

Acreage: 1000 acres

OAKLAND COUNTY

page 41 of the DeLorme Atlas

Location: Take I-96 east towards Detroit and get off at the Kensington Metropark exit, heading north. The public access site will be on your right. For a second access site, follow the road around the lake to the opposite side.

This area can really stun the visitor just by virtue of its tremendous size, not only of the lake but of the entire area. It's the first park I've seen that has a McDonald's Restaurant *inside* the area. Thousands of acres of hiking trails, snack spots, visitors' center and all of the amenities you would expect when you are this close to the metropolis of Detroit. Because there is so much room to roam, it still manages to be very uncrowded. The lake visibility was only fair, but I did not sample every area, which I plan to do in the future, as the lake winds around and around, and there are so many places in which you can enter. There was adequate visibility where I entered across from the visitors' center, some pan fish and decent vegetation--this just needs further exploration, and I will give you an update in time.

LAKEVILLE LAKE

Acreage: 460 acres

OAKLAND COUNTY

page 42 of the DeLorme Atlas

Location: Go south from Lapeer on 24, east on Oakwood Road, south on Lake George Road, east on Lakeville Road, and the public access site will be on the left.

Though there are a few cottages here, it's a slow no wake lake with a beautiful little bay at the entry which is just perfect for snorkeling.   The depth of about 5 feet is just perfect. There's excellent water clarity and tons of perch, largemouth bass, and bluegills.   The lake is known for its northern pike.   There are wonderful pinkish northern watermilfoil beds right at the entrance. Head straight out or go to the right where the big tire is--there's lots of fish habitat here along with appealing elodea and curly pondweed beds. Don't miss this one.

LOON LAKE   OAKLAND COUNTY

Acreage: 243 acres   **page 41 of the DeLorme Atlas**

Location: go north from Pontiac on Oakland Road (business 24). Take a right at Forner Street, and the public access site will be on your right.

This lake immediately startled me. I thought for a moment I was in Grand Cayman, the water was so clear. We can thank the multitude of zebra mussels for that as they are off to the right of the entrance, covering the fallen logs and branches. The whole underwater scene had a brightness and vividness to it that was exceptional. I reached for what I thought was a bright blue rubber flipper someone had dropped--instead a bright blue carp emerged and quickly swam away. The brightest colored and largest crayfish were here. I saw big turtles, a small pike, big largemouth bass, loads of perch and bluegills. Watch for the spotted darters near the shore. Loads of attractive coontail and bladderwort.

LAKE OAKLAND   OAKLAND COUNTY

Acreage: 255 acres   **page 41 of the DeLorme Atlas**

Location: Go north from Pontiac on 24, east on Walton Boulevard, and left on Dill Road which will dead end into the public access.

This is a worthwhile lake with good clarity in the shallows. All of the usual panfish are here, along with largemouth bass. The bottom is a combination of sand, boulders and gravel. Weed structure is good with chara beds, coontail, and wild celery.

ORCHARD LAKE   OAKLAND COUNTY

Acreage: 788 acres   **page 41 of the DeLorme Atlas**

Location: Take 24 south through Pontiac, go west on Orchard Lake Road, and the public access site will be on your right.

This is a lake that doesn't initially seem to have good visibility but turns out to be very clear the longer you are in, especially in the shallower areas.

I saw big shadow bass and all the other usual panfish, along with quantities of black striped minnows. There were nice beds of chara, wild celery, broadleaf pondweed, curly pondweed and northern watermilfoil. It is particularly good in the sheltered bay area and out beyond the buoys, but it is a busy, heavily cottaged commercial lake, so come during the week if possible.

LOWER PETTIBONE   OAKLAND COUNTY

Acreage: 69 acres   **page 41 of the DeLorme Atlas**

Location: Take 59 east from Howell, south on Milford Road, east on Reid Road, and the public access site will be on your left.

This very worthwhile lake is in the Highland Recreation Area. The environment both above and below is very picturesque. The bottom is a combination of marl and dark sand, pretty solid, allowing you to stand up and not hit muck. Head to the left and stay quite close to shore--watch out for the branches that can stick out quite far from shore. The lake is very shallow with sloping sides making for some nice wall snorkeling. Watch for big perch, some huge pumpkinseeds and other sunfish, as well as crappies and largemouth bass. Go out to the point where it is so shallow you can almost walk across the lake. The northern watermilfoil fields are about 50 feet out from shore. I came out here several times and was never disappointed.

LOWER TROUT LAKE   OAKLAND COUNTY

Acreage: approx. 70 acres   **page 42 of the DeLorme Atlas**

Location: Take 24 south from Lapeer through the town of Lake Orion, go west into the Bald Mountain State Recreation Area. The public access site will be on your right.

This lake in the Bald State Recreation Area outside of Lake Orion has absolutely gorgeous scenery and no cottages in a well developed park. It feels like total wilderness. It's doubtful you would ever find jet skiers here. The water is extremely clear in this slow no wake lake. It's loaded with gorgeous vegetation, displaying many different subtle shades of green.

The pinkish northern watermilfoil dominates, along with some broadleaf pondweed. There are big holes down to the sandy bottom, perfect for fish to hide in. This is a real gem, both above and below. There's a beach and park recreation for the entire family.

UNION LAKE   OAKLAND COUNTY

Acreage: 465 acres   **page 41 of the DeLorme Atlas**

Location: Go east on 59 out of Howell, heading south on Williams Lake Road to a dead end. Go east on Cooley Lake Road, south on Union Lake Road. The public access site will on your left.

Though the lake is heavily cottaged, this is nevertheless an excellent lake with good visibility and shallow enough to enjoy. It is so incongruous to look down into a wilderness, yet lift your head and only a few feet away see bumper to bumper traffic go by. There are schools of largemouth bass and big schools of perch swimming among the beds of northern watermilfoil, tall grass, broadleaf pondweed and bluegills. This is a very popular lake with a steady flow of power boats and water skiers, so it would be wise to try to make your visit during the week in off hours.

VALLEY LAKE   OAKLAND COUNTY

Acreage: 37 acres   **page 41 of the DeLorme Atlas**

Location:Take I-75 south from Flint and take the Dixie Highway Exit. Go south on the Dixie Highway and east on McGinnis Road. On the right, enter Holly State Park. Head southwest, with Heron Lake on your right. The road dead ends into the Valley Lake public access site.

This lake is totally bizarre and well worth the time. The setting itself, in Holly State Park, is simply dropdead. I just couldn't stop running my video camera to try to capture the scenic beauty. No cottages of course--just wilderness scenery. You need to enter the water and snorkel from the boat launch--there's no beach. This spring fed lake is totally covered with weed structure. There's great clarity--you can see bottom at approximately 20 feet very clearly.

There are lily pads on both sides, and most areas are shallow. The weed formations are fascinating, with caves, dropoffs, overhanging dirt formations, you name it and it's there. There are cliffs of unusual vegetation surrounded by big yellow perch and big pumpkinseeds. This lake is well worth your time.

WILDWOOD LAKE   OAKLAND COUNTY

Acreage: 47 acres   **page 41 of the DeLorme Atlas**

Location: Take I-75 south from Flint, taking the Dixie Highway Exit. Go south on the Dixie Highway and east on McGinnis Road. On the right, enter Holly State Recreation Area. Head southwest with Heron Lake on your right. The public access site is on your left.

There's a great beach here and schools of bluegills, pumpkinseeds and crappies, many, many large largemouth bass, as well as many varieties of minnows. There's a very long shoreline, so give yourself plenty of time, at least several hours. The weeds extend very far out, and besides water lilies, you will find northern watermilfoil and lots of spectacular coontail. This is scenic, clean and picturesque--even the dirt looks clean. Bottom is hard sand. No motor boats or water skiers here.

WOLVERINE LAKE   OAKLAND COUNTY

Acreage: 241 acres   **page 41 of the DeLorme Atlas**

Location: Take I-96 heading east. Go beyond Brighton and take the Wixom exit, heading north on Wixom. Turn east on Glengarry Road, and the public access site will be on the right.

This is a heavily cottaged, busy commercial lake with lots of jet skiers, but if you snorkel near the shore and stay alert, you can still have a good experience. Good but not great visibility--look down for best results, rather than to the side. There's a great arrangement of vegetation--lots of the pink tipped northern watermilfoil, lovely chara beds, broadleaf pondweed, great fish habitat. I saw lots of bluegills, largemouth bass, and perch. A slow no wake lake from 7:30PM-11AM.

MOON LAKE

SHIAWASSEE COUNTY

Acreage: 35 acres

page 39 of the DeLorme Atlas

Location: Take I-69 northeast from Lansing and after passing East Lansing, angle right and take Old 78 Road east. Take Colby Lake Road north, and the public access site will be on the left.

This is a great little lake that is part of a trailer camp, so it is necessary to ask permission to use the lake, and I told the owners that I would be including it in my book. The vegetation is marvelous--extensive chara beds, northern watermilfoil, coontail and elodea. Go out to the dropoff and then snorkel along the weed beds. The lake is shaped like a bowl with a hard sandy bottom near the shore and an easy entry. The vegetation offers a lot of variety in height, and though initially the lake does not look inviting, you look underwater and it's great. I saw bowfin, bluegills, largemouth bass and perch. Lots to explore here and I didn't begin to scratch the surface, so a repeat visit is in order.

CLEAR LAKE

ST. JOSEPH COUNTY

Acreage: 240 acres

page 20 of the DeLorme Atlas

Location: Take I-94 west to Kalamazoo, south on 131. Go west on Coon Hollow Road. The public access site will be on your right.

Clear Lake is absolutely that--just as clear as Higgins Lake and it doesn't get much clearer than that. There's a good swimming beach here, so bring the family. Go either left or right--I preferred the left--and snorkel straight out to the weed beds and float along the edges. Among the broadleaf pondweed and chara I saw good sized perch, largemouth bass, rock bass, pumpkinseeds, bluegills and a few clams.

COREY LAKE

ST. JOSEPH COUNTY

Acreage: 630 acres

page 20 of the DeLorme Atlas

Location: Take I-94 west to Kalamazoo, south on 131, west on 60, north on Corey Lake Road, and the public access site will be on your right.

This is a definite yes, with good but not great visibility. Bluegill beds are on the left side and in late June I was able to witness the spawning activity, when it is like Grand Central Station, with the female lying on her side to lay the eggs, periodically hitting the bottom to help loosen the membranes that hold the eggs, so they will drop. The male also bumps the female to stimulate her to drop her eggs. The male then takes over and constantly fans his tail back and forth over the nest to keep off the silt and debris, as the eggs need to be aerated in order to hatch. This is a fascinating process to see, and this is a good lake to see it in.

FISH LAKE   ST. JOSEPH COUNTY

Acreage: 275 acres   **page 20 of the DeLorme Atlas**

Location: Take I-94 west to Kalamazoo, south on 131, east on Withers Road, south on Constantine Road, east on Banker Street. Take a left on Pine Drive which will dead end into the public access site.

This lake has good visibility and all the usual panfish but is busy with powerboaters and skidoos on the weekends so come in the early morning or after 7PM. There is a wonderful avenue of lily pads to snorkel through with lots of fish habitat.

FISHERS LAKE   ST. JOSEPH COUNTY

Acreage: 327 acres   **page 20 of the DeLorme Atlas**

Location: Take I-94 west to Kalamazoo, south on 131, east on Heimbach Road, south on 60, west on S, Fisher Lake Road, north on Seekle which will dead end into the public access site.

This is a heavily cottaged lake which must be avoided on the weekend. The lake is flat with excellent visibility and harbors small panfish over a white marl bottom.

KLINGER LAKE   ST. JOSEPH COUNTY

Acreage: 830 acres   **page 20 of the DeLorme Atlas**

Location: Take I-94 west to Kalamazoo, south on 131 past the town of Constantine, then east on 12, take a left at Crooked Creek Road, and the public access site will be on your right.

This is a flat, shallow, and incredibly clear lake. It's also a very busy lake, so try to come on a weekday, although I did successfully snorkel on a Sunday. Big bass tournaments are held on this lake, so that gives you a good idea what this lake is known for, and I did indeed see many of them, as well as crappies, bluegills, pumpkinseeds, gizzard shad and black striped minnows. Go to the right by the lilies or straight out to about 8 feet of water for the big bluegills. The bottom is littered with snails and some clams.

LEE LAKE   ST. JOSEPH COUNTY

Acreage: 30 acres   **page 21 of the DeLorme Atlas**

Location: Take I-94 heading west toward Battle Creek. Go south on 66 past the town of Sturgis, then go east on Fawn River Road, and the public access site will be on your right.

Just outside the town of Sturgis, this lake has fabulous visibility plus fields of chara and long spindly pondweed. I could see bottom in great detail at 15-20 feet. There were schools of perch, largemouth bass, bluegills, pumpkinseeds and black striped minnows.

LONG LAKE   ST. JOSEPH COUNTY

Acreage: 222 acres   **page 20 of the DeLorme Atlas**

Location: Take I-94 west to Kalamazoo, south on 131, west on Spence Hoffman Road, north on Hoffman Road, west on Hoffman Street, south on Day Road, west on Locas Road. Go left on County Line Road and the public access site will be on your left.

The public access has a murky channel, but after you get through that, the lake is very clear, with all the usual fish and spectacular vegetation. I saw good sized perch, bluegills and largemouth bass. To avoid going through the murky channel, you could ask permission to park at the bait shop, as there are usually a few extra parking spots there, and you can then enter there and go immediately into the clear water and the weed structure right at the end of the dock.

PALMER LAKE   ST. JOSEPH COUNTY

Acreage: 448 acres   **page 21 of the DeLorme Atlas**

Location: Take I-94 heading west toward Battle Creek. Go south on 66, east on Colon Road through the town of Colon, continuing on the same road (State Road or 60), heading south on Sprowl road which becomes Burr Oak Road. The public access will be on the right at Palmer Lake Road.

This is a flat, very shallow lake with very good visibility and good vegetation. I saw largemouth bass and smaller sunfish, as well as clams and snails. Hard sandy bottom. This is a great place to have a picnic, as there are 5 sheltered picnic tables and a public beach.

PLEASANT LAKE   ST. JOSEPH COUNTY

Acreage: 262 acres   **page 20 of the DeLorme Atlas**

Location: Take I-94 west to Kalamazoo, south on 131, west on W. Broadway Road, north on Stoldt Road and a right at Fishing Site Road which will dead end into the public access site.

This is a beautiful spring fed lake--a real paradise. Four huge largemouth bass were at the entrance when I first went in. There were numerous huge bass, big perch, pumpkinseeds, bluegills, and a variety of minnows. The vegetation was very appealing--on both the right and the left were spectacular coontail structures--it felt like being in a jungle, but there was still plenty of free space to move around. There were giant lily pads, the biggest I've ever seen. Beautiful fields of soft green chara rounded out the vegetation.

The bluegill beds were on the left hand side just beyond the lily pads. There are some cottages here but it is, nevertheless, still a wilderness feel.

PORTAGE LAKE   ST. JOSEPH COUNTY

Acreage: 510 acres   **page 28 of the DeLorme Atlas**

Location: Take I-94 west to Kalamazoo, south on 131, east on W Avenue out of Schoolcraft, south on 24th Street out of Vicksburg. Continue on 24th Street which becomes Silver Street. Silver Street, when it makes a sharp turn to the east, becomes Michigan Avenue, and the public access site is on the left.

This is a good but not great lake--still worthwhile if you are in the area. Go to the left at the boat dock and stay near the lily pads--there are interesting weed beds there as well as bluegills, perch, largemouth bass and many large snails. I also saw a big map turtle. If instead of entering at the boat dock, you enter at the swimming area, it is much clearer and very pleasant. All of the usual park amenities are there. Go to the left of the swimming area and there will be elodea below you--I saw a big female bowfin, largemouth bass, decent sized perch, and bluegills. You are not bothered by power boaters as you are on the sides, and they are in the middle. I'd like to come back and cross the lake--it looked very interesting over there. This is a county park so you pay a $4 entrance fee--well worth it.

PRAIRIE RIVER LAKE   ST. JOSEPH COUNTY

Acreage: 136 acres   **page 20 of the DeLorme Atlas**

Location: Take I-94 west to Battle Creek, go south on 66, and the public access site will be on the left at the corner of Featherstone Road.

What an incredible wilderness setting! Complete tranquility here, towering trees and not a cottage in sight. I saw only one tiny boat. It's worth a visit just to see the setting, much like you imagine the old swimming hole to be.

This is a no wake lake with just average visibility--best near shore with the usual panfish spread out through the appealing black tipped coontail and broadleaf pondweed.

THOMPSON LAKE   ST. JOSEPH COUNTY

Acreage: 150 acres   **page 20 of the DeLorme Atlas**

Location: Take I-94 west to Kalamazoo, south on 131 to the town of Constantine. Out of Constantine, take Mintdale Road east, south on Shimmel Road, then east on Airline Road. Go north on Stubey Road, and the public access site will be on your left.

What a beautiful experience this is! A spring fed lake with outstanding visibility. I saw pumpkinseeds, bluegills, largemouth bass, perch, and a big black bullhead. This is one place that it's not necessary to stay close to shore, as it is so shallow, and you need to get out where there is some depth. Go straight out to the beautful fields of chara and scattered broadleaf pondweed.

BANKSON LAKE   VAN BUREN COUNTY

Acreage: 217 acres   **page 28 of the DeLorme Atlas**

Location: Take I-94 west to Kalamazoo, south on 131 to the town of Schoolcraft, west out of Schoolcraft on 352, north on 23rd, west on 80th Avenue. The public access site will be on your left.

An excellent lake with great weedbeds and great visibility. There's an easy DNR entry, and there were nothing but a few fishing boats during the week when I was there. It's a flat lake with lots of room to roam and plenty of beds to explore. There were plentiful perch, largemouth bass and bluegills.

CEDAR LAKE   VAN BUREN COUNTY

Acreage: 269 acres   **page 28 of the DeLorme Atlas**

Location: Take I-94 west to Kalamazoo, south on 131, west on 216, north on 40 (Jones Road). The public access site will be on the right.

This is a super clear lake with a large area to explore. It's scenic, very natural looking and very unspoiled, with no cottages anywhere around the entry. Great weed beds here, and they are all below you, soft green chara with patches of sand and rocks. All the usual pan fish are here. Very busy on the weekends.

CLEAR LAKE   VAN BUREN COUNTY

Acreage: 69 acres   **page 28 of the DeLorme Atlas**

Location: Take I-94 west to Kalamazoo, north on 131, west on 388, north on 653 which runs into 2nd Avenue. The public access site is on the right hand side of 2nd Avenue.

This is another one of those Clear Lakes that really is just that. It is truly fabulous with super visibility and gorgeous foliage. The vegetation offers so many different shades of green over a hard sandy bottom. There's chara, wild celery, northern watermilfoil, broadleaf pondweed and many water lilies on either side, so you can snorkel in the big path between the lilies out to the end of the lily pads. You will then see the end of the tall weed beds and the beginning of more shallow water with a big area of sand. Snorkel all along the edge of these weed beds--there's lots of fish and it's just beautiful to look at. Some very big largemouth and average sized perch. There are a few cottages, but they're all on the access side, so you are always looking straight across at wilderness.

LAKE CORA   VAN BUREN COUNTY

Acreage: 197 acres   **page 27 of the DeLorme Atlas**

Location: Take I-94 west of Paw Paw, north on 51, west on Arrow Highway, south on 46th Street, east on West Street which will dead end into the public access.

This is a crystal clear lake--just great visibility. Go left near the lily pads--I saw big largemouth bass, some bluegills, a few perch, some snails and a few clams. Hard sand bottom. A lot of Eurasian watermilfoil here.

EAGLE LAKE   VAN BUREN COUNTY

Acreage: 198 acres   **page 27 of the DeLorme Atlas**

Location: Take I-94 west of Paw Paw, south on 51, west on 70th Avenue, and the public access will be on your right.

This is a scenic, spring fed, semi-cottaged lake that has great visibility. Go either right or left--to go straight ahead is to run into high weeds. It's a very clean lake, and although I saw no large fish, the usual pumpkinseeds, bluegills and perch were there, along with a great many snails and clams.

LAKE FOURTEEN   VAN BUREN COUNTY

Acreage: 69 acres   **page 27 of the DeLorme Atlas**

Location: Take I-94 west to Paw Paw, head north on 40, west on Mill Lake Road, another left on 12th Avenue into the town of Bloomingdale, heading out of Bloomingdale on 10th Avenue. This dead ends into 46th St. Go left on 46th Street and right on 12th Avenue. Take the next right after 47th Street and that will dead end into the public access.

No cottages and no people, even on weekends! Or such was my own personal experience. The visibility here was good and I saw big perch and big bluegills. The only possible objection with some people is that it is a pretty weedy lake except near the entrance. I feel it is worth the effort.

GRAVEL LAKE

VAN BUREN COUNTY

Acreage: 296 acres

page 28 of the DeLorme Atlas

Location: Take I-94 west to Kalamazoo, south on 131 to Schoolcraft. At Schoolcraft, go west on 352 and southwest on Shaw Road which becomes 92nd Avenue. Go south on Lake Shore Drive and an immediate right (south) on Grave Lake Drive which will dead end into the public access.

This lake has a great wide open entry, and a very clean feeling. Visibility is excellent. and the weedbeds are very appealing. I saw big largemouth bass and all the usual panfish. Though the lake is large, I found it very quiet during the week with only a few fishermen.

HUZZY'S LAKE

VAN BUREN COUNTY

Acreage: 80 acres

page 28 of the DeLorme Atlas

Location: Take I-94 west to Kalamazoo, south on 131, west on 354, south on 652 which will dead end at the public access.

This is a great clear clean lake with an easy entrance, a pontoon lake with no jet skiers. It's very picturesque, quiet and scenic. It's quite flat--you have to go out a ways to get to the dropoff where the snorkeling is best. The weedbeds are extremely attractive, and I saw big largemouth bass, as well as the usual smaller panfish. This is well worth a visit.

UPPER JEPTHA LAKE

VAN BUREN COUNTY

Acreage: 57 acres

page 27 of the DeLorme Atlas

Location: Take I-94 west beyond Paw Paw, north on 673, east on 380, and the public access site will be on the right.

This is a lake with a great deal to offer, and I did not begin to spend all the time I wanted to here. It is definitely a lake you will want to return to. The visibility is exceptional, and the cottages are mostly on the access side, so you look across at attractive high hardwood trees.

I was startled but not in any danger when an airplane quietly landed right in the water next to me. Fun! Go to the left and snorkel along the long row of thick lily pads. Several times, big carp slid down the sandy hill one behind the other, between the lily pads, a comical sight. That's their hiding place, as I found them there several times. There's a great carpet of elodea containing big largemouth bass, pumpkinseeds, perch, turtles, and a few snails in the shallows. There's a lovely island that's quite near that you can snorkel to--I didn't get there, but on my next visit I will, and I could tell it had much potential.

REYNOLDS LAKE   VAN BUREN COUNTY

Acreage: 87.5 acres   **page 27 of the DeLorme Atlas**

Location: Take I-94 west beyond Paw Paw, north on 51, west on Red Arrow Highway, angle left on Territorial Road, south on 46th Street, and the public access site will be on your right.

This is an exciting lake with tremendous variety both in fish life and in vegetation. All the plant life seems to be a different height and the fish life is equally varied. The clarity is outstanding. A muskrat swam toward me as I entered, but of course he was timid and immediately swam away. In the shallow area near shore there were juvenile largemouth bass and a great many colorful bluegills. To the right as you enter there were many water lilies and on the edge were some very large black striped minnows looking spectacular against the bright green vegetation. If you snorkel around to the other side of these lily pads you enter a large open area where I saw on several occasions a school of blue suckers. I also saw shadow bass with their striking marbled bodies and a very few perch. There were more lily pads on the other side, housing some very large largemouth bass. Beyond those lily pads, if you go nearer to shore, the bottom has some spectacular sized snails resting on the leaves and other organic matter.

ROUND LAKE   VAN BUREN COUNTY

Acreage: 194 acres   **page 27 of the DeLorme Atlas**

Location: Take I-94 west beyond Paw Paw, south on 681, west on 352, south on 690, west on 152, and the public access site is on the left.

This is an excellent but busy lake, which is still O.K. even on weekends if you stay near shore. The clarity is outstanding, and there is good weed structure, though it is a little thick. Go to the right, then head south along the retaining wall, then go around the corner to the right into the little cove with lily pads. There were largemouth bass, bluegills, perch and crappy. Don't come after August 1 due to seeding which leaves many big suspended particles and impedes visibility.

RUSH LAKE   VAN BUREN COUNTY

Acreage: 118 acres   **page 27 of the DeLorme Atlas**

Location: Take I-94 west beyond Paw Paw, north on 687, west on 372, north on Rush Lake Road, and the public access site is on the right.

This lake is somewhat of a question mark, but I am including it as it did have potential, and I think I was just unlucky enough to hit it at a time of an algae bloom. It's uncrowded and the setting is exceptional. There's great fish habitat here and the vegetation is thick but clean. There are plenty of openings to snorkel and great lily pads both to the left and right of the entrance.   I saw largemouth bass and the usual panfish, though they did not seem plentiful.   This needs a revisit, but I cannot in all conscience eliminate it.

SCOTT LAKE   VAN BUREN COUNTY

Acreage: 203 acres   **page 27 of the DeLorme Atlas**

Location: Take I-94 west beyond Paw Paw, north on 673, east on 24th Street, and the public access site is on your right.

Scott Lake had all sorts of goodies in it, at least when I was there. I got some great video of a spotted gar cruising leisurely--he posed willingly for my camera, and there's no doubt with his needle nose, he is one of the more spectacular fish around. The clarity in this lake is good but not great--I still feel it's worthwhile. Sometimes clarity isn't everything. Let's just say the visibility is as good as it needs to be. I saw two spiny softshell turtles here--one as big and flat as a dinner plate. A brown bullhead posed nicely for my camera and ambled around in absolutely no hurry. Of course those fish reactions depend on your not making any sudden movements. There are great lilypads on either side, many housing big largemouth bass and bowfin. The usual panfish were also here, as well as big snails and big clams.

SHAFER LAKE   VAN BUREN COUNTY

Acreage: 81 acres   **page 27 of the DeLorme Atlas**

Location: Take I-94 west beyond Paw Paw, south on 681, east on 64th Avenue, and the public access site is on your left.

Visibility is good but not great here. Stay in the shallows in order to see well. This is a very clean lake that is not necessarily exciting but provides a very relaxing experience. Excellent for beginners. Lots of lily pads along the shore and lots of high and attractive pinkish watermilfoil and a good bit of elodea which the turtles love, and I did indeed see a painted turtle.

THREE LEGGED LAKE   VAN BUREN COUNTY

Acreage: 40 acres   **page 27 of the DeLorme Atlas**

Location: Take I-94 west into Paw Paw, go north on 40, west on 4th, south on 3850th, east on 6th. The public access site will be on your left.

Three Legged is in a gorgeous scenic setting, very rural, very tranquil, with no cottages, canoeists and fishermen only. It's primarily a muskie lake. The lake has great clarity and is very popular with divers.

THREE MILE LAKE   VAN BUREN COUNTY

Acreage: 176 acres   **page 27 of the Delorme Atlas**

Location: Take I-94 west through Paw Paw, heading south on 40th Street. Take a right on Paw Paw Road and another right on 41st Street which will dead end into the public access.

This is a very clear spring fed lake with wall to wall northern watermilfoil, loaded with lily pads--there are even lily pad islands. I found a great deal to see here including big bowfin, schools of big largemouth bass, big snapping turtles, the marbled shadow bass, rock bass, perch and bluegills. There were lots of snails and huge clams everywhere. Fortunately, there were no power boats--only pontoons. It's a very quiet lake, even on weekends. You can profitably go either left or right--most of the lake near the access is shallow.

BRUIN LAKE   WASHTENAW COUNTY

Acreage: 136 acres   **page 32 of the DeLorme Atlas**

Location: Take I-96 east out of Lansing, south on 52, east on North Territorial Road, north on Hadley Road, east on Kaiser Road, and the public access road will be on the right.

This is a State Campground in the Pinckney Recreation Area. Bruin is a scenic lake that gives you a wilderness feeling, even though there are a few cottages. The lake is surrounded by high hardwood trees. The hard sand bottom is littered with snails. The lake has great clarity and very little vegetation, just some scattered chara beds and broadleaf pondweed. There are some weedbeds off to the left. Go straight out about 40 feet to get enough depth to snorkel comfortably.

CEDAR LAKE   WASHTENAW COUNTY

Acreage: 73 acres   **page 32 of the DeLorme Atlas**

Location: Take I-96 east out of Lansing, south on 52 into Chelsea, west out of Chelsea on Cavanaugh Lake Road. The public access site is on the right.

This attractive lake in the Waterloo Recreation Area has subpar visibility at the entrance, but it's *great* as soon as you get past the entrance. A big largemouth bass shot out from shore just as I entered the water. Lots of black striped minnows. Nice vegetation--northern watermilfoil, broadleaf pondweed, chara and lilies. It was pouring rain all the time I was in the lake, but that did nothing to affect the experience. Definitely a lake I plan to return to.

CROOKED LAKE
(Dexter Township)

WASHTENAW COUNTY

Acreage: 58 acres

page 32 of the DeLorme Atlas

Location: Take I-96 east out of Lansing, south on 52, east on North Territorial Road, north on Town Hall Road, northwest on Silver Hill Road, and the public access site will be on the left.

A spring fed lake in the Pinckney Recreation Area. Drive in to Silver Lake, but instead of following the paved road to Silver Lake, take a left at the first dirt road and go 1.3 miles to Crooked Lake, a State Campground. There are no cottages here, just a scenic wilderness, a feast for the eye. There's a big fishing dock here, nothing primitive. The lake looks very dark, but surprise, you get in and are bowled over by the clarity. In fact the dark aspect just makes it look more striking and dramatic underwater and in no way impedes the visibility. The vegetation is very eyecatching. Go out to the dropoff and then snorkel all along the edges. I snorkeled mostly to the left but I plan to return and spend one or two entire days here exploring the entire lake--there's that much potential here and plenty of space to move around. The vegetation is arranged in a unique way that is hard to describe--you just have to experience it for yourself. The underwater scenery here is ever changing and endlessly fascinating. Vegetation consists of northern watermilfoil, broadleaf pondweed, curly pondweed, Brazilian elodea, coontail, beds of chara, and tons of lilies. Definitely a keeper. You must wear a skin here, as the water is unsafe for swimming.

CROOKED LAKE   **WASHTENAW COUNTY**
(Sylvan Township)

Acreage: 113 acres   **page 32 of the DeLorme Atlas**

Location: Take I-94 east of Jackson, north on Clear Lake Road, east on Green Road, cross Loveland Road and dead end into the public access.

This is an outstanding snorkeling lake in the Waterloo Recreation Area. Clarity is tops and the sights are plentiful. I even saw the dime-sized blue jellyfish undulating in and out, a real treat and never a guarantee, as any wind can cause their disappearance. Head out to the dropoff about 20 feet from shore. There were largemouth bass, perch, bluegills and black striped minnows, all set against northern watermilfoil, chara and broadleaf pondweed. A lake to come back to.

GREEN LAKE   **WASHTENAW COUNTY**

Acreage: 90.5 acres   **page 32 of the DeLorme Atlas**

Location: Take I-96 east out of Lansing, south on 52 and the public access will be on your right, just west of the town of Chelsea.

This lake is a tough call, as I have been in it when visibility was good, but the last time I was there, it was only fair, although fish and vegetation could be seen. So I'll let you be the judge. I didn't care for the entry by the boat launch as it was mucky. Next to the road on M-52 visibility was fine, and there were lots of bluegills, pumpkinseeds, and largemouth bass, as well as a variety of minnows and a small beach with a solid footing to walk in. This is not strictly speaking an access, but there is limited parking by the side of the road if it were for not too long. Also, at the State Campground, I went through an arch in the bushes and found a solid small beach with lily pads, attractive vegetation, bluegills and largemouth bass. It has possibilities and I plan to explore more.

HALF MOON LAKE   WASHTENAW COUNTY

Acreage: 236 acres   **page 32 of the DeLorme Atlas**

Location: Take I-96 east out of Lansing, south on 52, east on N. Territorial Road, north on Hankerd Road, and the public access site will be on your left.

This is a very clear lake BUT BUT BUT, on the two occasions I checked this out it was just mobbed with jet boats and skiers. I know there is potential here—maybe you will be luckier than I was.

MILL LAKE   WASHTENAW COUNTY

Acreage: 142 acres   **page 32 of the DeLorme Atlas**

Location: Take I-96 east out of Lansing, south on 52, west on Waterloo Road, south on Bush Road, take a right on McClure Road. Follow McClure Road to the west, and the public access site will be on your left.

This is an outstanding lake in the Waterloo Recreation Area. It's super clear with varied vegetation—broadleaf pondweed, curly pondweed, chara, lilies, northern watermilfoil and wild celery. It's a completely unspoiled wilderness lake with no cottages. It's not so easy to find a lake that has the drop-dead setting along with the water clarity, but this definitely fills the bill. There were big largemouth bass cruising around, as well as rock bass, perch, bluegills. The bottom is mostly gravel. It was great, even in the pouring rain.

PICKEREL LAKE   WASHTENAW COUNTY

Acreage: 19.9 acres   **page 32 of the DeLorme Atlas**

Location: Take I-96 east out of Lansing, south on 52, east on North Territorial Road, north on Hankerd Road, and the public access site will be on the right.

If a lake can be darling, this really is. Just small and intimate with a nice beach that attracts young lovers, as on the three occasions I was here, there always seemed to be couples enjoying the tranquility and serenity that this lake offers. There are no cottages here--just a little sunning area and a small fishing dock. The underwater foliage is extremely picturesque with a great variety of plant life--beautifully colored chara beds, striking coontail, pinkish northern watermilfoil, broadleaf pondweed, curly pondweed and lots of lilies, both to the left and right. The left side is especially scenic, but the great bowl shape really defines it--just snorkel along the ledge on both sides of the entrance--you can go all the way along the lake, and it just dazzles the eye. Boats are seldom on this lake due to its small size. Lots of largemouth bass, big pumpkinseeds, perch, bluegills and pickerel. This is a popular swimming lake, so bring your swim suit for an after-snorkel swim in an environment that will really enchant you.

SILVER LAKE   WASHTENAW COUNTY

Acreage: 15 acres   **page 32 of the DeLorme Atlas**

Location: Take I-96 east out of Lansing, south on 52, east on North Territorial Road, north on TownHall Road, angle to the left on Silver Hill Road, and the public access site will be on your right.

This spring fed lake in the Pinckney Recreation Area is a fine experience. Visibility is very good, and there's certainly plenty to see--it's very scenic and excellent for photography. There's lots of large and small bluegills, large red eared sunfish, largemouth bass, perch, crappies and great numbers of black striped minnows. For best results head for the very large weedbed about 25 feet to the right of the end of the wooden dock. There's wild celery, curly pondweed, chara, broadleaf pondweed, northern watermilfoil, and an abundance of lilies on both sides of the entrance. There is no boat launch here, but there is a big picnic and beach area, so non snorkelers can find plenty to do. There's badminton, volleyball and a well stocked concession stand, as well as a huge parking lot. This would be a great lake for groups, due to the large amount of room and size of habitat.

SOUTH LAKE   WASHTENAW COUNTY

Acreage: 197 acres   **page 32 of the DeLorme Atlas**

Location: Take I-96 east out of Lansing, south on 52, east on Boyce Road, south on Joslin Lake Road, and the public access site will be on your right.

This might not be everybody's cup of tea, but I loved it. The visiblity is excellent and there's loads of vegetation--maybe too much for some people--not everyone would like the thick grasses, but there were many big largemouth bass and bluegills swimming above them. This lake in the heart of the Pinckney Recreation Area, has no cottages, is totally uncommercial and surrounded by wilderness. Plant life consists of northern watermilfoil, curly pondweed, chara, and those very thick grasses. The lake is only about 5 feet deep for quite a distance out, but that is deep enough for a comfortable snorkel.

SUGAR LOAF LAKE   WASHTENAW COUNTY

Acreage: 180 acres   **page 32 of the DeLorme Atlas**

Location: Take I-96 east out of Lansing, south on 52, west on Waterloo Road, south on Clear Lake Road, east on Seymour Road, south on Loveland Road, and the public access site will be on your left.

This is a part of a State Campground in the Waterloo Recreation Area. It has a lovely wide paved entrance and a good swimming beach. There are a few cottages, and on the whole, it is a very pleasant experience. The background underwater consists of wild celery, broadleaf pondweed, curly pondweed, chara and elodea, housing all the usual panfish.

ABOUT THE AUTHOR

Nancy Washburne is a lifelong resident of Michigan and a graduate of the University of Michigan. She founded the four Washburne Travel Centers in the Lansing area and, besides traveling the U.S. extensively, she has made numerous trips to Europe and the Middle East, the Far East, the Caribbean, South America, the South Pacific, Siberia and Outer Mongolia, Around the World, the Arctic and Antarctica. As a certified scuba diver, her underwater experience includes dives at the Great Barrier Reef, the Red Sea, Truk Lagoon, the Solomon Islands, the new Hebrides, Bonaire, Cozumel, Isla Mujeres, Cancun, Acapulco, Ixtapa, Manzanillo, Hawaii, the Florida Keys and an underwater photography course in Grand Cayman.

When she and her teenage son decided to explore camping in Michigan, she discovered that there was little or no knowledge of Michigan's inland lakes from a snorkeling viewpoint. It was this lack of available information that spurred her to make an underwater survey of all of Michigan's public access lakes so that snorkeling could be developed in Michigan as a leisure activity. This book is the result of that survey.

She teaches in the School of Marketing and Supply Chain Management at Michigan State University and resides in East Lansing with her husband and son.